A Legacy of Wisdom

Wisdom and Encouragement from Women in the Lives of Adam, Abraham, Jacob, Moses, Samuel, David, Solomon, and from the Ministry of the Lord Jesus and the Apostle Paul

Clara Molina

WestBow Press books may be ordered through booksellers or by contacting:

WestBow Press
A Division of Thomas Nelson & Zondervan
1663 Liberty Drive
Bloomington, IN 47403
www.westbowpress.com
1 (866) 928-1240

ISBN: 978-1-4908-9992-3 (sc)
ISBN: 978-1-4908-9994-7 (hc)
ISBN: 978-1-4908-9993-0 (e)

Print information available on the last page.

WestBow Press rev. date: 01/28/2016

I dedicate this book to these generations of women:

My daughter Cristina and all my granddaughters,

My mother Fulgencia (Sinita), My grandmother Gregoria/Goya
My sisters Altagracia (Tati) and Paula,
My nieces Crystal, Carolina, and Stephanie

To my mother-in-law Adalgisa, To Anania, Jennifer,
Adelaide, Sarah Maritza (Mari), Gaelen,
and Nora

I also want to thank God for the following women
who influenced my walk with Him:

Altagracia Columba: A woman who loves me with
Jesus' unconditional love and friendship

Paula Hemphill: A woman of prayer who introduced
me to women's international missions

Paula López: A woman who taught me to be
persistent when reaching women for Christ

Olga Padrón: A woman who taught me to serve women unconditionally and who has a servant's heart

Lynette Petrie: A woman with a generous heart, my dear faithful long distance friend who loves the unborn

Paula Salinas: A woman with a generous heart who prays for and loves my children.

Betty Salazar: A woman who models to me daily that nothing is impossible for God

Edie Vega: A woman who has given her life to minister to women and who encouraged me to write this book

A profoundly heartfelt thank you to **Patty Hunt:** She was the first example I had of how a Christian woman, wife, and follower of Christ should live her life and I am eternally grateful.

A very special thank you goes to Lorrie A. SeGraves for taking the time to give this book a second look. May God bless her ministry!

Contents

Jacob

Moses

Samuel

King David

King Solomon

The Lord Jesus

Paul

Introduction

The purpose of *A Legacy of Wisdom* is to enrich the lives of Christian women by enabling them to gain spiritual wisdom from the examples of biblical women who touched the lives of *great biblical men of God as well as the Lord Jesus Christ.* The biblical women featured in this book are examples of faith and character. They were real women who left a legacy of wisdom on how the presence of God guided their everyday lives.

Understanding these women's partnership with God and the great men featured in this book will enhance your everyday life when you are dealing with decision making, joy, pain, and sorrow, your personal walk with God, family life, and ministry. Through the lives of these women, the Lord God provides us with valuable examples of good and bad decisions that produced good and bad consequences. Today's women can learn from these model women and apply the lessons learned to have a better relationship with Jesus Christ and live righteous lives.

Applying the wisdom learned from these godly women will help you to heal from the hurts and pains of your past and to experience spiritual restoration. This book will encourage discouraged women and challenge curious women through the persistent application of God's Word. As you read this book, you will see great examples of women making God-led adjustments to their everyday lives and experiencing His transforming power. You will also find constant reminders of God's promises to watch over us, "I will not fail you or forsake you" (Josh 1:5b); and Jesus' words, "I am with you always, even to the end of the age" (Matt 28:20a). Just like Jesus passed the baton to His disciples, God uses the women of the Bible to pass a baton of wisdom to other women who are determined to follow Christ. *A Legacy of Wisdom* features examples of those women who passed the baton of wisdom to other women so women of today can pass on these timeless truths to generations to come.

—Clara Molina

> "Wisdom is supreme—so get wisdom. And whatever else you get, get understanding. Cherish her, and she will exalt you; if you embrace her, she will honor you. She will place a garland of grace on your head; she will give you a crown of beauty" (Prov 4:7-9 HCSB)

Adam

"The man gave names to all the cattle, and to the birds of the sky, and to every beast of the field, but for Adam there was not found a helper suitable for him. So the LORD God caused a deep sleep to fall upon the man, and he slept; then He took one of his ribs and closed up the flesh at that place. The LORD God fashioned into a woman the rib which He had taken from the man, and brought her to the man" (Gen 2:20-22NASB).

Day 1

Eve
A Woman Created by God for Adam

Genesis 1:26–3, 1–4, 2 Corinthians 11:3, 1 Timothy 2:13–14

Adam named Eve "the mother of all the living."

Eve was the first woman that ever existed. She was the one and only sinless woman to walk the earth (until she sinned). She was never a baby, a girl, or a teenager. She went from a rib to a full-grown woman. The Lord created man from the ground, but with the woman, He started by using a part from the man He had already created. This action by the Lord made the woman a part of the man.

According to God's Word, one of the purposes of Eve's creation was to be the suitable helper Adam was longing for in the garden. After Adam had finished naming animals and having "me" time, he was ready to share his life but there was no one suitable for him to share it with! "The man gave names to all the cattle, and to the birds of the sky, and to every beast of the field, but for Adam there was not found a helper suitable for him (Gen 2:20). The Lord considered Adam's loneliness and decided to make him a "helper suitable for him". Even though Eve was part of God's future plans, He waited until Adam got lonely and needed her. Adam was able to really appreciate God's greatest gift to him, his mate. The Word of God tells us that, "So the Lord caused a deep sleep to fall upon the man, and he slept; then He took one of his ribs, and closed up the flesh at that place" (Gen 2:21). The Lord performed the first surgery ever recorded in the Bible to make the woman. "And the Lord God fashioned into a woman the rib which He had taken from the man, and brought her to the man" (Gen 2:22). Adam probably said, "Wow!" It is true that good things come to those who wait! After God created Eve, there were two in the garden created in God's image. They were created for each other and to honor God.

Eve was the one Adam needed to meet his needs of companionship because she was the other of his kind that made him complete. The Lord also made the woman in order to multiply His creation. She came to complement Adam, but not to take God's place in his heart because Adam's loneliness was not spiritual. After Adam named all the animals (Gen 2:20) and saw them reproduce and live with one of their kind, God provided Eve and Adam stopped seeking for one like him because God met his need.

When Adam saw Eve for the first time, he called her woman because "she was taken out of Man" (Gen 2:23). The Bible does not tell us if God healed his wound in such a way that Adam was able to notice it. Perhaps God told Adam about how He made Eve, but we'll never know. One thing is for sure: Adam knew she was a part of him. After the fall, Adam named his wife Eve and realized she was going to be the mother of all the living. Perhaps Adam remembered that God also created them to be fruitful and multiply (Gen 1:26–28). God's mercy did not allow Eve to bear children before they fell into sin, but Adam remembered that bearing children was part of Eve's purpose when he named her.

God the Father, Jesus the Son, and the Holy Spirit created the first man and first woman.

> Then God said, "Let Us make man in Our image, according to Our likeness; and let them rule over the fish of the sea and over the birds of the sky and over the cattle and over all the earth, and over every creeping thing that creeps on the earth." God created man in His own image,

> in the image of God He created him: male and female He created them (Gen 1:26–27).

A lot of people do not think about the fact that it took God in three persons to make humanity. One thing that touches me every time I read about the creation of the world is that God took time to make people because we are so special to Him. He did not say, "Let there be man" or "Let there be woman." Instead He labored to make man in His image and fashioned the woman also in His image. More special attention came when God "breathed into his nostrils the breath of life; and man became a living being" (Gen 2:7). Whereas dogs, cats, and even monkeys were commanded by God into existence, the man was the only creature created especially by God in His image.

Some might think it is unfair that the woman was originally created to be "a helper suitable" (Gen 2:18) for Adam. Women are part of God's purpose, and He will use women to do great things for His kingdom whether they are married or not. There are important women who left a legacy of service in Christian history like Lottie Moon, who was the first missionary to China, and Fanny Crosby, who wrote more than nine thousand hymns that are sung by Christians in churches all over the world! God does not love men more than women because He created both with the same love and in His image: we all have a soul that will live eternally and we are responsible, relational and rational. The fact that the woman was created under different circumstances does not indicate that God loves women less. He made women to be unique.

Search Your Heart, Thank God, and Pray

Is there anything that keeps you from thanking God for making you a woman? Read Psalms 139:13-14. God has a purpose for you as a woman and you should remain loyal to Him and give Him your heart (2 Chronicles 16:9a). Read Psalms 139:13-14 and James 1:5–6.

Day 2

Eve
The Sinner

Genesis 3:1–24

Instead of being known as God's beautiful creation, Eve, the woman, is mostly known for being the first woman who gave in to sin by disobeying God resulting in the sinful mess we find ourselves in today. God told Adam, "From any tree of the garden you may eat freely; *but* from the tree of the knowledge of good and evil you shall not eat, for in the day that you eat from it you shall surely die" (Gen 3:2). God was speaking of spiritual death here and Satan knew this. This tree, which was created and placed in the garden by God (Gen 2:8b), became the object Satan used to tempt Eve.

Eve was fully aware of God's command to not eat of that particular tree. If you read Genesis 3, you can see that Eve was arguing with the serpent because she was aware of God's command concerning the forbidden tree. Even though she knew the correct behavior, she decided to disobey God anyway by eating of the forbidden fruit. She had a perfect relationship with God, and she ruined it by allowing herself to be deceived. The temptation, in and of itself, was not a sin. Giving in to the temptation was a sin. Satan used tactics with Eve that he still uses today to tempt us into sin. Eve became prideful, and she listened to the serpent. She then looked at the fruit, tasted it, liked it, and finally passed it on to Adam. The guilt of Adam and Eve's sin of disobedience was passed on to the whole world, prompted Jesus to die on the cross and rise again to fix the problem.

Eve's temptation was ideal from Satan's point of view. She had the object that would cause her to sin right in front of her eyes, she was curious, she had free will, and all she needed was Satan's encouragement. God gave us free will to such an extent that we can decide where we want our souls to live for eternity. I think Eve probably wondered and asked herself, "*What is it that God doesn't want me to know?*" She failed to trust God, disobeyed, and when God asked her why, she said, "The serpent deceived me and I ate" (Gen 3:13a). She did not take responsibility for her sin but instead blamed someone else.

Adam also refused to take responsibility when he blamed God and Eve for his disobedience (Gen 3:12–13). Perhaps Adam thought that since Eve was living proof he was not going to die physically from eating the fruit, then, why not eat? God took notice of this because when He judged Adam, He started by reminding Adam that he listened to his wife: "Because you have listened to the voice of your wife, and have eaten from the tree" (Gen 3:17). This does not excuse Adam. He was the leader who also had a free will, and he exercised his freedom to make the wrong choice. I often wonder what would have happened if Adam had not eaten the fruit. What would have happened to Eve?

Now, three of the Lord's masterpieces were living in disobedience in His wonderfully created garden and Adam and Eve were in danger of eating from the tree of life and living forever in a state of spiritual separation from Him. The serpent was one of God's creatures as well. *God made the serpent with the special ability of being the craftiest beast of the field. Satan used his craftiness, and in the garden the serpent was the manifestation of Satan himself (2 Cor 11:3).* The Bible says, "The serpent was more crafty than any beast of the field which the Lord God had made" (Gen 3:1), and Satan knew that.

Satan knew Eve, Adam's wife, was the most cherished earthly gift Adam had. Sometimes Satan will use a loved one to cause us to fall into sin. Satan always attacks God's people's relationships, God's work, and God's Word. In this case we can see that Satan used God's relationship to His children. God's mercy is beyond measure because if Adam and Eve had eaten of the tree of life, you and I would have never had the opportunity to know God. We would have sinful men living in eternal spiritual death. But praise God for His love for us!

God had to clean house and take all sinners out of the garden in order to protect generations to come. He is the God of second chances! God still loved Adam and Eve with the same everlasting love He used to create them. God hates the sin but loves the sinner.

Today the consequences of Eve's sin can be exchanged for a reconciled relationship with God because of the love of Christ. The Bible tells us in Romans 3:23 that because of Adam and Eve's sin, we "all have sinned and fall short of the glory of God." But God in His infinite wisdom gave us Jesus! The Bible also tells us, "The wages of sin is death, but the free gift of God is eternal life in Christ Jesus our *Lord"* (Rom 6:23). In Romans 10:9 we are encouraged to accept Jesus as our Savior and overcome the effects of Adam and Eve's sin: "If you confess with your mouth Jesus as Lord, and believe in your heart that God raised Him from the dead, you will be saved." This is the perfect solution to the world's greatest problem.

Search Your Heart, Thank God, and Pray

Have you chosen a life of sin for yourself in disobedience to God? Are you blaming others for your sins? God does not excuse your sins because you blamed your sins on someone else. You need to take responsibility for your actions. Confess to the Lord any sin in your life and repent (say no to sin). Read 2 Corinthians 5:9-11. Remember that the greatest sin a person can commit is the sin of not believing (trusting) in Christ Jesus.

Day 3

Eve
The Mother and Her Sin, Part I

Genesis 3:16

The process of childbirth was the first thing that God addressed concerning Eve's discipline after her sin of disobedience. As we already know, Eve is "the mother of all the living," and she was the first woman to give birth to a child, thus fulfilling the command of God to all living things to "be fruitful and multiply'. This has obviously been accomplished because we are all here. When we look into Genesis 3:16, it is important to realize that God never used the word *curse* when He addressed Eve. He only cursed the serpent (Gen 3:14a), and because of Adam, He cursed the ground (Gen 3:17a). Adam and Eve were judged, and so was the serpent. God expressed disapproval with all three and pronounced judgment on them. They suffered the consequences for their sin, and their sin ultimately changed our lives forever.

To the woman He said, "I will greatly multiply your pain in childbirth, in pain you shall bring forth children." This was the first part of God's judgment of Eve. These words from God assured her of future physical pain on top of the spiritual death she had already experienced because of her sin. Eve brought sin into the world in two ways: first, by disobeying and eating the forbidden fruit, resulting in spiritual death, and second, by giving birth to a child who already had her and Adam's sinful nature. She started the chain reaction of children coming into the world in a sinful state. Every time she had a child, she would remember her sin.

I think that Eve's judgment is the worst of all the three that were judged. For me, after giving birth to two children, one with the aid of pain-relieving drugs and the other without drugs, I can testify that it was a very painful experience! The pain alone is hard enough. Eve had guilt on top of the pain as a consequence of the situation into which she had gotten herself. God intended for Eve to experience pain at childbirth to begin with because He said He was going to "multiply the pains of childbirth" (Gen 3:16); God just made the pains worse. God is merciful to mothers because He gives mothers comfort after childbirth. We remember it was painful but generally overlook the pain! Many of us decide to go through the same agony all over again
to get a replica of God's creation to call our own, and it is all worth it! A special miracle happens at childbirth. Childbirth pains are so great that even Jesus uses them to illustrate a point to His disciples. In John 16:21 He says, "Whenever a woman is in travail she has sorrow, because her hour has come; but when she gives birth to the child, she remembers the anguish no more, for joy that a child has been born into the world." Jesus was talking to them about His salvation of mankind and return, and He used the miracle of child birth to explain it to them. He would return to them, and they would be comforted even though He was leaving them temporarily. God allows us to focus on the baby instead of the pain, and in the same way, Jesus got the disciples to focus on His salvation of mankind and second coming instead of His departure.

Jesus was not the only one to use childbirth as an example of pain and suffering in the Bible. One of my favorite illustrations can be found in the book of Jeremiah. He is referring to the prophecies against Damascus when he says in 49:24, "Damascus has become helpless; she has turned away to flee, and panic has gripped her; distress and pangs have taken hold of her like a woman in childbirth." This is one of the best biblical descriptions of being in labor. What Eve had to face was not easy. But God forgave Eve just like He forgives you and me, and forgiveness allows us to let God restore our lives so we can have a new beginning.

Search Your Heart, Thank God, and Pray

Do you think giving birth is a curse? Well, the Bible calls them a gift (Psalm 127:3). Every child has a purpose and every conceived child deserves to live. Read Genesis chapters 1 through 3. Meditate on these chapters, and ask God to open your mind to teach you more about how and why He created you.

Day 4

Eve
The Mother and Her Sin, Part II

Genesis 4, 5:1–8

Eve did not have anybody to help her when she was in labor except for God and Adam. Adam and Eve probably had a very good idea of what was going to happen at childbirth because by the time she had a child, they most likely had seen animals reproducing and giving birth to their young. When Cain, her firstborn, came into the world, Eve said, "I have gotten a manchild with the help of the Lord" (Gen 4:1). She knew God was the ultimate giver of life, and He loved her so much that He didn't allow her to go through childbirth alone. How He helped her is not recorded, but we know she was grateful. Even though God as her Father disciplined her, He did not abandon her. The only woman born without sin became a sinner, and that sin was inherited by her newborn baby and the babies she had thereafter. Along with her sin, Eve also passed on the feeling of shame to her children (Gen. 3:9-12). After Adam and Eve sinned, they experienced shame for the first time. God in His mercy took care of it: "The Lord God made garments of skin for Adam and his wife, and clothed them" (Gen 3:21). He provided them with the animal skins to serve as their clothing.

God's love was so intense for this couple that He even kept a close eye on their children. He spoke to their children and accepted their sacrificial offerings. Cain's sinful nature was evident as his jealousy turned to rage and he killed his brother, Abel. God questioned Cain about Abel's death.

He knew what happened, but the Lord wanted to make sure Cain knew that He was watching him (Gen 4:6–16). Eve lost two children when Cain killed his brother because God sent Cain away from his family. Maybe this incident made Eve conscious of the effect of physical death. Perhaps she particularly understood God's pain when He lost Adam and Eve to sin.

As a mother, Eve probably did not have to worry about the common cold and other things we mothers worry about these days when it comes to children's health. She originally had a perfect body, and her children were healthier than any child born to any woman. However, sin was alive and well inside her children. Even though Eve had many children, including daughters, only three of her children are named in God's Word: Cain, Abel, and Seth. She was unique in that she was the one woman to experience many things first, including the pain of having one of her children kill the other. The third son Eve had was Seth, and Eve felt he was God's replacement for Abel. She said, "God has appointed me another offspring in place of Abel; for Cain killed him" (Gen. 5:25). This child is referred to in the Bible as Adam's "own likeness, according to his image" (Gen 5:3). This indicated that Seth physically resembled Adam. Noah was a descendant of the generation fathered by Seth (Gen 5:1–32).

Eve is one of the four women I call the four *jewels of creation*. God uniquely used four women to make the world we have today. He used Eve as the mother of all the living. Noah's wife was the mother of the new world after He destroyed the old. He used Sarah as the mother of the nation of His beloved people with whom He made His covenant. Finally, He used Mary to be the mother of His precious Son, Jesus, who died for us on the cross at Calvary to create a new people who would honor God. Mary's Son offers eternal life to all of humanity for all of those who receive Him as Lord and Savior—a new life in place of the old death that resulted from Adam and Eve's sin (2 Cor 5:15).

The result of Eve's sin shows us how sin affects other people, what is around us, and who is around us. David said in Psalm 51:5, "Behold I was brought forth in iniquity and in sin my mother conceived me." His mother, along with yours and mine, was born with Adam's and Eve's sin nature. God is just, and He does not leave sin unpunished. Jesus takes the punishment we deserve on the cross and serves as the healing agent to reconcile the broken relationship between God and humanity.

Search Your Heart, Thank God, and Pray

Have you experienced the loss of a child? If you have children, is your disobedience to God affecting their lives? If you have lost a child, that child cannot be replaced, but you can allow God to help you heal. Read Ps. 147:3.

Day 5

Eve
Wife of Adam

Genesis 2:21–25, 3:16

Eve brought upon herself spiritual death through her sin (a broken relationship with God). God disciplined her by increasing her labor pains along with maintaining her sexual desire and dependence on Adam.

First of all, she would desire her husband sexually. She would need to be with him in a physical way; Eve would be attracted to Adam. A woman's sexual desire for her husband is a longing or need to be part of that person with a feeling of belonging. It's as if there is a void in the relationship that only gets filled when we share ourselves with one another. Of course, the fact that God gave women a desire for their husbands was very wise; God intended for women to want their husbands sexually so we could be fruitful and multiply and enjoy the unity at the same time. God probably caused this desire so Eve would have a deep attraction to Adam and only Adam. Her desire for Adam would allow them to continue the permanent union God created when they became one flesh through the bond of marriage. Adam and Eve's sin did not impede God's plan of populating the earth because Eve's desire for Adam played a major part in reproduction. You may have noticed that God did not deal with Adam's sexual desire for Eve because Adam's desire was there from the beginning, but for some reason unknown to us, Eve's desire was refocused just for Adam.

Second of all, Eve had to submit to Adam's authority. God created a hierarchy within the covenant of marriage, but He did not change His love for each of them or make one better than the other. He simply gave them roles they had to follow, just as we have to follow them today. Eve had to follow Adam's lead because God said so: "He shall rule over you" (Gen 3:16b). He did not give us any explanation, and He does not have to give us one because He is God. Where was Adam's leadership when Eve ate of the fruit of the garden she was not supposed to eat? After their sin, Adam was going to lead his wife and family whether he wanted to or not. It was his God-given job.

The people who believe that God made the woman less than the man usually misunderstand this part of Genesis 3:16. God just rearranged Adam and Eve's relationship according to His perfect wisdom. God knew how important Eve was to Adam, and God did not command Adam to abuse or suppress Eve as if she were inferior to Adam. She was made from a part of him, so how could Adam hurt or belittle a part of himself! Paul said Ephesians 5:28, "So husbands ought also to love their wives as their own bodies. He who loves his own wife loves himself."

God also made it clear to Adam that his relationship to his wife was special when He took part of Adam to make her. Adam understood how precious Eve was because when God gave Eve to Adam, Adam said, "For this cause a man shall leave his father and his mother, and shall cleave to his wife; and they shall become one flesh" (Gen 2:24). Jesus backed up Adam's words when said, "But from the beginning of creation, God made them male and female. For this reason a man shall leave his father and mother, and the two shall become one flesh; so they are no longer two, but one flesh. What therefore God has joined together let no man separate" (Mark 10:6–9).

Paul put even more of an emphasis on Eve's submission and Adam's responsibility, applying this to all couples, when he said the following in Ephesians 5: "Wives, be subject to your own husbands, as to the Lord. For the husband is the head of the wife, as Christ also is the head of the church, He Himself being the Savior of the body" (Eph 5:22–23). Paul also wrote, "Husbands, love your wives, just as Christ also loved the church and gave

Himself up for her" (Eph 5:25). Jesus' love for the church is so great that He died for it. Eve submitted to Adam as God commanded her because she was secure in God's love for her. She knew from personal experience that she sinned not against Adam but against God, her Creator.

Among many things, Eve was the only woman to walk with God in person, to have a relationship with God in a sinless state. Eve was the first woman who ever lived who experienced life in both a sinless and sinful state; she was the first wife and the first mother, and she is mostly known as the first woman to sin. Her sin has affected women for generations, and will affect women who do not know Christ for generations to come. Her sin separated her spiritually from God but not from His love.

Search Your Heart, Thank God, and Pray

Do you resent God's order in the family? Do you have a problem submitting to a legitimate male authority figure (father, husband, or male boss)? Thank God for *not* making Eve's consequences more severe. Pray after you read Romans 8:28–29.

Abraham

"As for Me, behold, My covenant is with you, and you will be the father of multitude of nations. No longer shall your name be called Abram, but your name shall be Abraham; for I have made you the father of a multitude of nations" (Gen 17:4–5 NASB).

"Then God said to Abraham, "As for Sarai your wife, you shall not call her name Sarai, but Sarah shall be her name. I will bless her, and indeed I will give you a son by her. Then I will bless her, and she shall be a mother of nations; kings of peoples will come from her" (Genesis 17:15-–16 NASB).

Day 1

Sarah

The Wife of Abraham

Genesis 11:29–31,12:1–20, 16:1–16, 17:15–27,18:6–15, 21:1–12, 23:1–20, Galatians 4:21–31, 1 Peter 3:6, Hebrews 11:11

Sarah is one of the most well-known women in the Bible to Christians and Jews because she was the first wife of the patriarch Abraham. She was from Ur of the Chaldeans. Sarah and Abraham had the same father, Terah, but not the same mother, which made her Abraham's half-sister. Her name was Sarai until the Lord changed it to Sarah. She was so beautiful that her beauty was a threat to her husband's life. When a famine was in the land of the Negev where Abraham and Sarah were staying, Abraham decided to go to Egypt to meet his family's needs. When they were close to the city, Abraham said to his wife:

> See now, I know that you are a beautiful woman; and it will come about when the Egyptians see you, that they will say, This is his wife; and they will kill me, but they will let you live. Please say that you are my sister so that it may go well with me because of you, and that I may live on account of you. (Gen 12:11–13)

He spoke a half-truth because Sarah was also his half-sister. Sarah did as her husband asked her to do; she lied with her husband's blessings. Under those circumstances, what woman that loves her husband would not do what Sarah did? Egyptians had respect for marriage and in order for an Egyptian to take Sarah as a wife they would have had to have Abraham killed.

Sarah was taken into the pharaoh's house, and Abraham was treated very well because of Sarah. Abraham got "sheep and oxen and donkeys and male and female servants and female donkeys and camels" (Gen 12:16). Sarah was wise and obeyed her husband, but the Lord did not like Abraham's little arrangement, so He struck the house of Pharaoh with a bunch of plagues. Pharaoh was very angry to find out the truth concerning Sarah because the plagues affected him as well.

God showed His mercy toward Abraham by the protection He provided for Sarah. God was so merciful that He did not allow any men, including Pharaoh, to touch Sarah. If he had, in the eyes of God, Sarah would have turned into an adulterous woman (adultery became part of God's law in Ex 20:14). Pharaoh sent Abraham out of Egypt with everything he owned, including Sarah. Abraham and Sarah played the same game again at the house of Abimelech king of Gerar (Gen 20:1-18).

Again the Lord showed His mercy by keeping Sarah safe from Abimelech. God let king Abimelech know in a dream the truth about Sarah. He said, "Behold, you are a dead man because of the woman whom you have taken, for she is married" (Gen 20:3). God knew Abimelech's heart; He knew Abimelech was deceived by Abraham and Sarah and that he had practiced the custom of his day by taking Sarah into his harem. The Lord also said to Abimelech, "Now therefore, restore the man's wife, for he is a prophet, and he will pray for you, and you will live. But if you do not restore her, know that you shall surely die you and all who are yours" (Gen 20:7).

Abimelech obeyed God and gave Sarah back to Abraham. Abimelech also allowed Abraham to choose the land where he wanted to live and restored Sarah back to her status as the wife of Abraham. Abimelech said to Sarah,

"Behold, I have given your brother a thousand pieces of silver; behold, it is your vindication before all who are with you, and before all men you are cleared" (Gen 20:16). Abraham was so thankful that he prayed for the House of Abimelech so they could have children because God had closed all the wombs of the women in the household of Abimelech while Sarah was there.

Sarah was a very submissive wife to Abraham; she did what Abraham thought was right even when it was wrong. Having a submissive wife does not give a man the right to make his wife sin under the umbrella of submission to him. Sarah submitted to Abraham's leadership, and in turn the Lord blessed her. The Lord blessed Sarah because she was part of His plan in the life of Abraham to make him a great nation. Abraham acquired wisdom as he grew in the knowledge of God, and he never again placed his wife in harm's way.

The same way that God in His perfect wisdom had a plan for Sarah and Abraham, He also has a plan for each one of us just as He had for the nation of Israel. In Jeremiah 29:11, the Lord gives Israel a great promise: "For I know the plans that I have for you, declares the Lord, plans for welfare and not for calamity to give you a future and a hope." God rescued Sarah by fixing the situation Abraham got her into. He can solve any situation you might find yourself in as well.

Search Your Heart, Thank God, and Pray

What would you have done if you were Sarah? God does not accept sin, no matter how little or simple it may be or the sin's good intention. Abraham and Sarah did not have the Ten Commandments or Jesus, but we do. Read Exodus 20. Which of the Ten Commandments are you breaking? Is there a sin that keeps you from receiving God's blessings and wisdom? Read 1 John 1:9.

Day 2

Sarah
Wife of Abraham—the Doubting Barren

Beautiful Sarah had a big problem: she was barren, unable to give her husband Abraham a son. Sons were a blessing, and were very important to have in those days because there was a lot of emphasis on making sure that the family name would be carried on for generations to come. The Lord made a covenant with Abraham that He would make Abraham a great nation and give him a son that would carry his name (Gen 15:4–5, 17:1–21). A son for Abraham became more than just an expectation of a boy to carry the family name; it was now a promise from God to make him a big nation that would be fulfilled through Sarah.

When God was speaking to Abraham about this future son, Sarah, who was listening from the tent, laughed. She knew she was too old to have children. She said, "After I have become old, shall I have pleasure, my lord being old also?" (Gen 18:12). This is an important passage because it shows that Sarah considered having sexual relations with Abraham as pleasurable and also shows the respect Sarah had for Abraham, she called him *lord.* In 1 Peter 3:6, Peter noticed this little but important detail about Sarah toward her husband. Peter wrote about the relationship of husbands and wives, and he used Sarah to encourage women on the subject of submission; he also used the fact that Sarah called Abraham lord.

For Sarah, having a child as old as she was—ninety—was very funny. I think it would be very funny to me if I found out I was going to have sex at ninety! Can you imagine a woman today, all full of wrinkles, with chemically dependent hair, artificial parts, and sagging all over the place, getting pregnant! You would laugh too! I do not think Sarah doubted Gods' power; sex was probably not part of her life anymore, and it would have been funny to have sex with an old man who was full of wrinkles as well. Looking at it from a human point of view, having a child when the menstrual cycle had become dormant would cause me to think about a miracle. Sarah had God's promise of a nation to Abraham through her.

Sarah thought it was so funny that she even forgot God knows everything, so she denied to God that she had laughed. She lied because she was afraid and said, "I did not laugh" (Gen 18:15). But God said, "No, but you did laugh." God knows it all, so we might as well come clean and admit our sins. Sarah was not the only one to laugh and about the idea of child bearing at an old age. Abraham also laughed when the angel of the Lord told him that he would be back at the same time next year and they would have Isaac by then. "Abraham fell on his face and laughed, and said in his heart, 'Will a child be born to a man one hundred years old? And will Sarah, who is ninety years old, bear a child?'" (Gen 17:17). The promised son was born, and before he was born, God named him Isaac (Gen 17:19) which means "he laughs".

Sarah learned that nothing is impossible for God. Abraham became a father at the age of one hundred (Gen 21:5), which made Sarah about ninety! In spite of her unbelief, she received a blessing from God based on God's promise to Abraham. Every time Sarah or Abraham called on their son, they would remember the fact that they laughed when God told them they would have a child even though they were so old. Sarah and Abraham learned to trust God and wait on His promise while growing in faith. In Hebrews 11:11, Sarah is mentioned as a woman of faith. "By faith even Sarah herself received ability to conceive, even beyond the proper time of life, since she considered Him who had promised" (Heb 11:11). She had to have faith because God almighty told her that she would have a son (Gen 17:21).

Sarah had to face the fact that no matter what we think or do, God's still in control of our lives. She probably had to step back and look at God's resume of promises kept. God is a God who keeps promises. Sarah's old age had nothing to do with God's ability to achieve His purpose in her life. He is sovereign. She learned to trust God and have faith. She would not be a biblical example of faith in the Bible unless she had learned what it meant to have faith.

Isaac was conceived after Abraham's circumcision and his covenant with God (Gen 17:1–27), and the thought of being parents made Sarah and Abraham laugh at God's plan for their life as future parents (Gen 17:17, 18:12,15). Maybe Sarah didn't tell her friends about her anticipated parenthood, but she probably took steps to prepare for the great event. If she did tell her friends, they probably thought Abraham and Sarah were crazy. Perhaps Sarah became the talk of the town! God displayed His power through her by having her give birth and breast-feed a child at the age of ninety!

Search Your Heart, Thank God, and Pray

Are you trying to have a child? Remember that nothing is impossible for God. If you are married, do you consider your sexual life as pleasurable like Sarah did? Thank God for the life He has given you. Whether you are a mother, single, or married, God still loves you, and He can still give you the desire of your heart. Pray for contentment if you are late in age without the child you desired. Read Philippians 4:11, 2 Corinthians 12:9, Hebrews 13:5.

Day 3

Sarah
Wife of Abraham—the Mistress and Her Authority

Before Isaac was born, God had apparently taken too long for Sarah, and she got tired of waiting for God's promised child to Abraham. She took matters into her own hands. She knew of Abraham's need to have a son. Abraham had lost all hope of becoming a father to the point that he started to assume that Eliezer, his right-hand man, would be his heir (Gen 15:2). Possibly due to a combination of personal embarrassment, discouragement because of her barrenness, and her desire to please her husband, Sarah decided to give Hagar, her Egyptian maid, to Abraham for him to have a child with her (Gen16:2). Sarah allowed her emotions to cloud her judgment, and she strayed from God's will to produce a child for Abraham. She attempted to make it happen her way instead of trusting God to fulfill His promise in His way and in His timing. Sarah's decision to have Abraham have a child with her maid, Hagar, created all kinds of problems for her family and created a lot of stress for Abraham.

It became very difficult for Sarah to live with Hagar, Ishmael, Isaac (the son Sarah has later on with Abraham), and Abraham in the same household. Sarah didn't want anyone to share her son's inheritance. She wanted Hagar and Ishmael to go away, so she looked for a way to get rid of them. She started by being cruel to Hagar. Then she began watching Ishmael and found him mocking Isaac. This led her to complain to Abraham about Ishmael because she had enough!

She told Abraham "Drive out this maid and her son, for the son of this maid shall not be an heir with my son Isaac" (Gen 21:10). Abraham complied with his wife's request because God told him to comply with her request. Abraham loved Ishmael. He did not want to send him away because even before Isaac was born, Abraham had asked God to bless him through Ishmael. The Lord answered his request by saying, "No, but Sarah your wife shall bear you a son, and you shall call his name Isaac; and I will establish My covenant with him for an everlasting covenant for his descendants after him" (Gen 17:19). When Sarah told Abraham to send Hagar and Ishmael away, God said to Abraham, "Do not be distressed because of the lad and your maid; whatever Sarah tells you, listen to her, for through Isaac your descendants shall be named. And of the son of the maid I will make a nation also because he is your descendant" (Gen 21:12–13). God was telling Abraham not to worry because He was still in charge, and He would take care of Ishmael.

Sarah was a good mother to Isaac. She raised him to be a man of God and a faithful husband. In the process of bringing up her son, Sarah learned that the consequences of our decisions affect other people. When God said to Abraham, "For I will make you the father of a multitude of nations," He didn't call on Sarah to help by bringing Hagar to the rescue! He already had a role for Sarah to play within His plans.

At times, the Lord allows things to happen in our lives so we can learn to trust in Him. Sarah died at the age of 127 (Gen 23:1), and Abraham had to buy a place to bury her because even though he was very rich, he lived in tents and was living in a foreign land (Gen 23:2–20). The place was called Machpelah in the land of Canaan, and Abraham put his wife Sarah's dead body there in a cave. This later on became the burial site for Abraham (Gen 25:9), Jacob (Gen 50:13), Leah, Rebekah, and Sarah's precious son Isaac (Gen 49:29-32).

The lives of Sarah and Hagar are unforgettable and an inspiration to all of us. Paul was differentiating between living under the law and living under grace to the Galatians and he referred to Sarah's and Hagar's feud; Paul called Isaac the son of the free woman and the son of promise. He referred to Ishmael as the son of a bondwoman and he recognized Sarah as the "mother of nations" whom the Lord blessed (Gal 4:22-31). Be wise. We can learn lessons from Sarah's life and one of them is not to use others to suit our purposes and then afterward get rid of them as if nothing had ever happened. Also, we do not need to help God direct our lives. He is all powerful and all knowing. He knows what is best for us. When the consequences of our decision are put in God's hands, we need to abandon ourselves in His will.

Search Your Heart, Thank God, and Pray

Is there someone in your life you always like to manipulate? A wise woman waits on God and does not get tired of waiting on God. Think about a time when you took matters into your own hands instead of waiting on God. Identify an area or areas in your life that you have not submitted to Him and give it to God. Read Psalm 27:14, 130:5, and pray for wisdom according to James 1:5.

Day 4

Hagar
Abraham's Concubine and Servant of Sarah

Genesis 12:1–20, 16:1–16, 21:9–21, 25:12–18, Galatians 4:22–31

As you recall, Sarah and Abraham had lied to the pharaoh of Egypt about Sarah's identity. When the pharaoh found out he had been lied to, he was very upset and sent Abraham, with all he had, out of Egypt. There is a possibility that Hagar became Sarah's property when Sarah was part Pharaoh's household in Egypt. As part of Pharaoh's household, Sarah had to have a maid, and this is when I think Sarah got Hagar. Hagar could have been one of the gifts Pharaoh gave to Sarah, which became part of what was sent out when the pharaoh got rid of Abraham and all his belongings (Gen 12). Perhaps Hagar was a purchased or a gift from Abraham to Sarah; Abraham was a rich man (Gen 12:4-5). Regardless of how Hagar became part of Abraham's household, she turned out to be an Egyptian immigrant slave/maid, owned by a Jewish family (another culture), who had to move in order to follow the one she served, Sarah (Gen 16:6).

When Sarah was sent away from the house of Pharaoh and was already far from Egypt, her desire for a child became stronger. She decided to use Hagar by giving her to Abraham for him to conceive a child through her. Sarah said to Abram, "Now behold, the Lord has prevented me from bearing children. Please go in to my maid; perhaps I shall obtain children through her" (Gen 16:2). Notice Sarah's selfish statement, she said, "I shall obtain children ..." Perhaps that was the reason Abraham listened to his wife. It is possible that he was also discouraged about waiting for the promised child who had not yet come. Because of Sarah's childless state, he gave into Sarah's request and took Hagar as his concubine. Hagar became Abraham's temporary concubine under Sarah's supervision. Hagar had no rights as wife of Abraham, and the child she was going to have really belonged to Sarah according to the custom of the day.

This relationship created a lot of problems between the two women. Hagar changed her attitude toward Sarah because now she had the things that were really important to Sarah: her husband and his child! Sarah expressed her frustration when she said to Abraham, "May the wrong done me be upon you. ... I gave my maid into your arms; but when she saw that she had conceived, I was despised in her sight. May the Lord judge between you and me" (Gen 16:5). Sarah tried to make Abraham responsible, but Abraham refused to take sides. He reminded Sarah that Hagar was her maid; whatever was going on between the two of them was really Sarah's business. So Sarah decided to treat Hagar badly (Gen 16:6). Hagar couldn't handle it and ran away from the household.

The Lord was merciful with Hagar and did a beautiful thing for her: He gave her the privilege to speak face to face with the angel of the Lord. The angel made sure Hagar understood that she really had no place to go because she was a slave. He said to her, "Return to your mistress, and submit yourself to her authority" (Gen 16:9). Regardless of what was happening in her life at the moment, Hagar was called to change her attitude and be submissive. The angel of the Lord told her she was carrying a baby boy in her womb and gave her a promise that God would make him a great nation. He said, "I will greatly multiply your descendants so that they shall be too many to count" (Gen 16:10). This gave Hagar comfort to know that it was going to be well with her son. God even blessed her by choosing a name for her son. God named him Ishmael, which means, "God hears." His name would always remind Hagar that God would always hear her cry. The angel also told her a little bit of the child's future, he said to her, "And he will live to the east of all his brothers" (Gen

16:12b). God was already telling Hagar that her son would not be around Abraham's promised son Isaac. Hagar obeyed the angel and went back to the only home she had, Sarah's.

The beauty of Hagar's life is that she was nobody and God made her somebody. She didn't have anything that belonged to her. In fact, she didn't even own herself! *But God* took notice of her. Hagar actually gave a name to God! She called Him, "Thou art a God who sees." Hagar was amazed at the presence of God, and to explain how she felt, she said, "Have I even remained alive here after seeing Him?" (Gen 16:13a). She knew she was in the presence of God. She recognized her worthlessness in the eyes of men and realized her importance in the eyes of God. She submitted to God's authority and to her earthly authority, Sarah.

Search Your Heart, Thank God, and Pray

Do you think God notices you? Do you think you are important to God? Look at Hagar's life, thank God for making you unique, and pray for God's peace in your life. He sees your problems in the same way He saw Hagar's because He is our Father. Read Matthew 10:29-31.

Day 5

Hagar
The Mother of Abraham's First Son

Hagar had to live with the consequences of Sarah's decision to use her to bear a child for Abraham. Hagar became a woman who knew where she belonged, even though it probably was not her favorite place to be. She knew God was with her and that nothing escaped His eyes. *God took the time to speak with her—a slave.* This was a very rare occasion in the Bible for a woman. God didn't address any other woman in the Bible in the way He did Hagar in her time of need.

Hagar gave birth to Abraham's son Ishmael when Abraham was eighty-six years old. The fact that Abraham named Hagar's son Ishmael indicates that Hagar, or perhaps Sarah, had told Abraham about Hagar's experience with God. After Ishmael was a teenager (Gen 17:25), Sarah had already given birth to Isaac, and according to Sarah, Ishmael became a threat to her son. She caught Ishmael making fun of Isaac. Consequently, Sarah requested that Abraham send Hagar and Ishmael away. The Lord told Abraham to do as Sarah requested (Gen 21:12). He did so even though it hurt him because he loved his son Ishmael. God gave Abraham a great promise that He would make Ishmael a great nation. The Bible tells us that trusting God, Abraham "took bread and a skin of water and gave them to Hagar, putting them on her shoulder, and gave her the boy, and sent them away" (Gen 21:14). Here we see Abraham's faith in God. He sent his dearly loved son, the apple of his eyes, away solely on the basis of his trust and obedience to God. Paul wrote about Abraham in Romans 4:20: "Yet, with respect to the promise of God, he did not waver in unbelief, but grew strong in faith, giving glory to God."

Hagar did not have a place to go, so she went into the wilderness of Beersheba with her son. Now the provisions Hagar had taken were all gone, and the boy was dying. She remembered she was only a cry away from Him who promised He would be with her and bless her. She cried out to God, "Do not let me see the boy die" (Gen 21:16), and the Lord once again heard her. "And God heard the lad crying and the angel of God called to Hagar from heaven, and said to her, 'What is the matter with you, Hagar? Do not fear, for God has heard the voice of the lad where he is'" (Gen 21:17). God provided water and encouragement to Hagar. "And God was with the lad, and he grew; and he lived in the wilderness, and became an archer" (Gen 21:20). Hagar got an Egyptian woman to marry her son. Hagar's son became "the father of twelve princes [tribes]" (Gen 17:20). He became the great nation that God promised Hagar and Abraham that he would become. Ishmael died at the age of 137, but before he died, he was able to bury his father, Abraham. After Abraham died, "his sons Isaac and Ishmael buried him in the cave of Machpelah" (Gen 25:9) in the same place Abraham's wife, Sarah, was buried.

Hagar was a woman who called upon the Lord because she knew He would deliver. Regardless of how she became part of the blessing of making Abraham a great nation, God used her to teach us to always depend on Him, even when things are not going the way we want them to go. God became very real to this Egyptian girl, and He is real to us today, especially when we put our trust in Him. Sarah, Abraham, and Hagar tried to live their own lives—sometimes apart from God's will—and ended up impacting the world. Nevertheless, God in His holiness, love, and wisdom had mercy on all three of them. He kept His word to Abraham, He still used Sarah, and He blessed Hagar. Even though we can't feel His presence at all times, He will never leave us or forsake us. Hagar faced the world alone with her child; she is the first single mother named in the Bible, and she trusted the Lord in the middle of a big crisis.

Search Your Heart, Thank God, and Pray

Have you put your trust in God while you are going through a very difficult time in your life? Has someone used you for personal gain and hurt you in the process? Read Psalm 139:1–5. Think of a time when you had doubts in your heart of God's ability to supply all your needs. Examine Hagar's life, and pray that the Lord will make Himself real in your life.

Day 6

Hagar
Abraham's Concubine—Mother of Ishmael and Single Mother

So far we have seen Hagar as the slave and a victim of circumstances. We have seen her as the concubine of Abraham and the mother of a nation through her son Ishmael. But on this day, I want you to see her as a single mother. Hagar had to accept herself and really understand the people God had placed in her life before she was prepared to face the task God had planned for her as a single mother. If you remember, in Genesis 16:1–16, Sarah decided to give Hagar to Abraham so she could bear children on her behalf since Sarah was not capable of doing so herself. When we read the story of Hagar, it is obvious that Sarah wanted her to have a short-term relationship with Abraham, just to procreate; Hagar's only job was to be Abraham's concubine until she got pregnant with his child. Hagar started to think she outranked Sarah, her mistress, and started to act like it as well (Gen 16:4). Hagar's presumed new station in life had gone to her head! Sarah retaliated. As a result, Hagar decided to run away. Here is where Hagar got her first taste of being a single mother. She found herself alone with an unborn child, no father, and no place to go. The following are some of the things she learned:

First, Hagar forgot that she was dealing with the wife of the man God had chosen to build His nation. One should never mess around with God's chosen people! The angel of the Lord appeared to her when she ran away from Sarah. He taught her how to be obedient (Gen 16:9) and submit to her mistress's authority. Hagar was a servant. "A servant yields his will completely to the one he serves. He serves his master with complete disregard for his own interests. His time and strength, his all, belong to his master. He owns nothing apart from the one he serves."[1] The child Hagar was carrying belonged to Sarah, her owner, and was a gift for Abraham! *Hagar could not run away with what was not hers!* The angel of the Lord found her at Shur, which was "somewhere on the road from Beersheba to Egypt" some believe that this indicates that Hagar had decided to go home (Gen 16:7). Egypt, however, was no longer her home. Her home was going to be wherever Sarah lived. It is heartbreaking to read what happened to Hagar, but God loved Hagar. The Bible says, "For those whom the Lord loves He disciplines" (Heb 12:6), and Hagar needed to be disciplined.

Second, Hagar had to deal with the fact that she did not really know who God was. A person cannot respect, obey, or pray to God when he or she does not know who God is. *She found out who God was when God loved her enough to guide her, and show her that she was not abandoned and was important to Him.* Through the first appearance of the angel of the Lord, she learned that **God is all knowing**. He told her that she was pregnant; He told her that she was going to have a boy and even gave the child a name (Gen 16:11–12). When the angel of the Lord appeared to her again, it was because she called upon Him! She knew **He was trustworthy**. She had no food, no water, and no place to go. When Hagar cried for her son in desperation, God answered her. *For the time being, God became her all.* She realized at this point that with God, she had all she needed. The angel of the Lord gave her hope with the following promise: "Arise, lift up the lad, and hold him by the hand; for I will make a great nation of him" (Gen 21:18).

Third, Hagar needed to know that God could provide for her and she should depend on Him. The first time He made His presence known to her, He protected her from her own bad judgment by making her go back to where there was protection and provision for her and her unborn son. Later on when she was in trouble again, God provided water for her out of nowhere! "God opened her eyes and she saw a well of water; and she went and filled the skin with water and gave the lad a drink." (Gen 21:19) God opened her eyes to the water and to the great love He had for her.

There are no records in the Bible that Hagar ever married or had other children. In Hagar's life of freedom, Ishmael became the testimony of the promise God made to her. I believe Hagar was called by God to be a single mother and was able to accomplish God's will in her single life as a mother by the faith she developed in God and the lessons she learned through the experiences He allowed her to have. Hagar learned obedience and discipline. She learned who God really is and to trust, depend on, and obey Him. She was used by Sarah and abandoned by Abraham, but God loved and rescued her. There is no better companion for a single mother than almighty God Himself.

Search Your Heart, Thank God, and Pray

Have you ever experienced God's discipline? Is almighty God first in your life? Trusting God is crucial for all believers. Thank Him for a lesson learned, and pray that He will give you wisdom to see when He is directing your life and allow Him to lead you. Read Proverbs 3:5, Read Hebrews 11:1.

1 Millie Stemm, *Be Still and Know* (Grand Rapids: 1978), Reading for May 15.

2 Ibid, reading for May 7

Day 7
Keturah

Abraham's Second Wife—Single Mother of Five

Genesis 25:1–6, 1 Chronicle 1:32–33

"Now Abraham took another wife, whose name was Keturah" (Gen 25:1). Abraham was ten years older than Sarah. He died at 175, and Sarah died at 127 (Gen 23). Abraham had forty-eight more years to live with Keturah. It is not fully clear when Abraham started his relationship with Keturah because she is listed as his concubine in the book of Chronicles and as his wife in Genesis. The Bible does not even tell us how old she was when she became involved with Abraham. Regardless of her status in the house of Abraham, she gave him six sons. Their names were Zimran, Jokshan, Medan, Midian, Ishbak, and Shuah (Gen 25:3–4). Many of these names have been identified with various Arab tribes, fulfilling God's promise to Abraham that he would be the father of many nations."[1] Keturah's children also ended up away from Abraham's son Isaac. They became the ancestors of the Arab people, and "The best known tribe bearing the name of Keturah's children were the Midianites. We come upon the first as camel-riding merchants traveling from Gideon to Egypt with gum, and myrrh. These same Midianites sold Joseph to the Ishmaelites for twenty shekels of silver." [2]

> "Now Abraham gave all he had to Isaac; but to the sons of his concubines, Abraham gave gifts while he was still living, and sent them away from his son Isaac eastward, to the land of the east" (Gen 25:5–6).

He had to send Hagar away from Isaac, so he did the same with Keturah's sons even though Isaac was already grown. The sons of Keturah are not mentioned as participants in Abraham's burial (Gen 25:9) and are not mentioned as great men of God either. Notice that in the above verses it says "*concubines*"; which assures us that there were, at least, two other women in Abraham's life beside Sarah (wife), Hagar (concubine by Sarah's orders), and Keturah, who became his wife/concubine (1 Chron 1:32–33).

Only God knows Keturah's purpose for being in Abraham's life and for us it is a matter of opinion. Some people say that she was only married to him for companionship. Others feel she was a very personal nurse for Abraham, who was old. She was a very personal nurse because she gave him six children! Why would someone so quiet be mentioned in God's Word? *We don't need to be great in the world's eyes, to be great in God's eyes.* We don't know if it was God who chose Keturah for Abraham or if Abraham went out of God's will and chose her for himself. My old pastor once said that God had to renew Abraham's body to produce a strong seed so he would be able to get Sarah pregnant with Isaac at one hundred years old. That new virility lasted for a long time, and Keturah was the woman with whom Abraham chose to release his newly regenerated sexual abilities. Regardless of how Keturah got into the life of the patriarch, she was one of the big contributors to Abraham's fatherhood.

Keturah's faith is never discussed in the Bible, so we can assume she believed in the true God of Abraham, but according to Abraham's relationship with God, she probably honored God with her life. After reading about Keturah, I found faith and encouragement in her. And as I learned and researched Keturah, one thing came to mind: we do not need to be number one in someone's life to make a difference in his or her life.

Keturah did not struggle to be number one in Abraham's life. There is nothing documented in the Bible or history that shows Keturah's desire to be important! She did not present an argument to Abraham to have her children inherent Isaac's property. Her children did not rebel against Abraham's decision. She obeyed Abraham and went away with her children, and she trusted her family would be all right.

Was she a doormat? I don't think so! The silence about her lifestyle can be a symbol of humility, obedience, and trust. *She became the second single mother on Abraham's behalf.* Because of her biblical silence, Keturah is not well known. Many people who have never read the Bible in its entirety do not even know she exists because Keturah existed in Abraham's shadow. When God promised Abraham a great nation based on Isaac's generations, no one ever imagined God would also create two more nations using a slave, Hagar, and an unknown, such as Keturah.

Search Your Heart, Thank God, and Pray

Keturah's purpose in the life of Abraham is only known by God. Are you willing to serve God and be an unknown in the process? Read Philippians 2:3–4.

1 *The Ryrie Study Bible* (Chicago: The Moody Institute of Chicago, 1978), 45

2 Edith Deen, *All the Women of the Bible* (New York: HarperCollins, 1983), 276.

Day 8

Milcah
Abraham's Niece and Great-Grandmother of Isaac

Genesis 11:29, 22:20–23, 24:15, 24, 47

Milcah was the wife of Abraham's brother Nahor, who was her uncle, and the daughter of Abraham's other brother, Haran. She was married to her uncle, and she was probably a very young bride. In those days, girls were married very young. She was also the sister of Abraham's famous nephew Lot (Gen 11:26–29). Milcah gave eight children to Nahor, and their names were Uz, Buz, Kemuel, Chesed, Hazo, Pildash, Jidlaph, and Bethuel (Gen 22:20–24). Milcah had to share the love of her husband with another woman named Reumash (Gen 22:23), a concubine of Nahor. Reumash had four children with Nahor, Tebah, Hagan, Tahash, and a girl Macaah. These children of Reumash did not become part of God's plan for Abraham's great family, but Milcah's did. Milcah was the great-grandmother of Abraham's great nation (Gen 24:15). Isaac, Abraham and Sarah's son, married Milcah's granddaughter Rebekah. Bethuel was one of Milcah's sons who became the father of Rebekah. This event keeps all in the family; the promised generation has Abraham's blood from both sides!

Many times we are called by God to do things and we do not know why and probably will never know why. Who was going to tell Milcah that by her getting married to her uncle, she was going to have Bethuel, who would be the father of the mother of Isaac's wife, the promised son from God to Abraham! I'm very sure that by the time Jacob, Milcah's great-grandson, fathered the twelve tribes of Israel; her name still was part of his life. Today it takes about three generations for a person to be forgotten in a family. The names of families were important and not forgotten; the contribution to the building of a family was valued from generation to generation. When we give birth to a child, we can never know what this child is going to be when he or she grows up. We can only pray for God's direction in his or her life. It took three generations for God to build the promised family He told Abraham he was going to have with his wife Sarah, and Milcah was part of it. This can serve as encouragement for us because God has the perfect time for everything! It took many generations for the Lord to break the chain of unbelief in Christ in my family.

There are no indications of how Milcah's life really was, what she looked like, or what her true beliefs were, but the one thing we can be sure about is that God used her. God made Milcah part of the Bible because she is one of the pieces that helped put together the puzzle of God's plan for His people and His promise to Abraham. **You might be the piece of the puzzle God wants to use to enrich your friends and family to have a life with Christ. Like Milcah, you and I are important parts of the puzzle that is going to accomplish God's plan in someone's life.** Impact eternity, and be bold! Share Jesus with your friends and family members, and see them also grow in a relationship with Jesus. *Jesus is the essential aspect of the plan of salvation.*

Search Your Heart, Thank, and Pray

Are you aware that God can use anybody to enrich His kingdom? He can use you as well. Thank God for His Son, and pray that He would use you for His glory. Read Galatians 3:20.

Day 9

Rebekah
Abraham's Daughter-in-law and Wife of Isaac

Genesis 22:23, 24:1–67, 25:19–34, 26:7–11, 27, 49:31

Rebekah was the daughter of Bethuel, the son of Milcah and Abraham's brother Nahor, and the sister of Laban the Aramean. She was chosen by Eliezer under Abraham's command to be Isaac's bride. She was to marry her cousin. Eliezer was Abraham's oldest servant, and Abraham made him swear that he would find a wife for Isaac from Abraham's family because Isaac could not marry a Canaanite woman (Gen 24:1–7). The Canaanites worshiped pagan gods, and since Isaac was the son of promise to Abraham, he had to marry a woman who did not worship idols but someone who knew the real God. Eliezer asked the Lord to let him know who the wife of Isaac would be by her action of willingly giving him and his camels water to drink:

> Now may it be that the girl to whom I say, "Please let down your jar so that I may drink," and who answers, "Drink and I will water your camels also," may she be the one whom You have appointed for Your servant Isaac; and by this I will know that You have shown lovingkindness to may master. (Gen 24:14)

I heard someone once say, "Can you imagine what would have happened if Rebekah had said, 'I don't do camels'"? She would have missed out on the blessing of being used by God!

God made it very clear to Eliezer that Rebekah was the one Isaac had to marry (Gen 24:15–27), so Rebekah, a beautiful woman and a virgin, consented to marry Sarah's son. Rebekah came into Isaac's life when he needed her the most. Isaac's mother, Sarah, had died, and he missed her. Rebekah served as a wife and as comfort for his great loss (Gen 24:67). Isaac was a godly man and a faithful husband to Rebekah. There are no records of Isaac having another wife, concubine, or anybody else's children except Rebekah's. He lived very much protected under Sarah's umbrella, and when he got married, he lived under Rebekah's.

Rebekah seemed to be a very strong willed woman because her parents actually allowed her to make the decision of when to go and marry Isaac (Gen 24:55-59). In those days, women did not make those kinds of choices. She gave water to 10 camels, and camels drink a lot of water! (Gen 24:10-27). She also walked around without her veil (Gen 24:64-67), but placed it back when she first saw Isaac at a distance in order to meet protocol and not allow her husband to see her face before the wedding night. It is also interesting to notice that Rebekah didn't have a big fiesta for her wedding (at least is not mention in the Bible) and her feelings towards Isaac are never described. Rebekah was found, she was asked, she agreed, she traveled to her destination, and she became part of Isaac's life.

Rebekah had a problem. She could not have children, and "Isaac prayed to the Lord on behalf of his wife, because she was barren; and the Lord answered him and Rebekah his wife conceived" (Gen 25:21). They lived a twenty-year romance before they had children, which gave them more than enough time to enjoy each other and get to know one another. It looks like Rebekah did a better job in the "getting to know you" part because she learned to lie to her husband and that created problems for her family!

By the time Rebekah gave birth to her children, Isaac was sixty years old (Gen 25:19). Rebekah turned out to be the mother of the famous twins

Jacob and Esau. She is one of the only two women named in the Bible who had twins (the other was Tamar in Gen 38). When she was pregnant, there was a struggle inside of her. She had to go to the Lord and inquire from Him why this was happening to her and the Lord answered her directly and said: "Two nations are in your womb; and two peoples shall be separated from your body; and one people shall be stronger than the other; And the oldest shall serve the younger" (Gen 25:22–26). While these two boys grew up, they knew there were differences between them. "Now Isaac loved Esau, because he had a taste for game" (Gen 25:28). He was a skilled hunter, a man who worked hard in the fields, "But Rebekah loved Jacob" (Gen 25:28).

Rebekah, like I said before, was a beautiful woman whose beauty was a threat for Isaac's life. Her beauty caused Isaac to lie about his and Rebekah's relationship to the house of Abimelech, king of the Philistines, by saying that she was his sister. (This happened after Rebekah was the mother of twins!) If you recall, Isaac's father, Abraham, also said the same lie and got caught, and Isaac got caught as well. Abraham told a half-truth, but Isaac lied altogether because Rebekah was not his sister! "And it came about, when he had been there a long time" living in Gerar and still lying about Rebekah's real identity, "that Abimelech king of the Philistines looked out through a window, and saw, and behold, Isaac was caressing his wife Rebekah" (Gen 26:8). Then Abimelech called Isaac and said to him, "One of the people might easily have lain with your wife and you would have brought guilt upon us" (Gen 26:10). The king gave out orders that said, "He, who touches this man or his wife, shall surely be put to death" (Gen 26:11). God's love and mercy were with Rebekah. God rescued her just as He did with Sarah. No one touched her. God is the loving God of individuals.

Search Your Heart, Thank God, and Pray

Have you been rescued by God when you made a wrong decision? Read Romans 3:23-24. Sin is a way of life for many, but it does not have to be for you. Repent from a sin that has kept you away from God. Thank God for a time when you followed His lead.

Day 10

Rebekah
Abraham's Daughter-in-law and the Mother of Isaac's Sons

Rebekah had one big weakness, and that was her son Jacob. Because of Rebekah's love for her son Jacob, she became a deceitful wife to Isaac. She allowed her feelings for her son get in between her relationship with her husband. Ever since God told her of her son's destinies, she decided to make Jacob her favorite (Gen 25:23, 28). Isaac made Esau his favorite, but he did not allow that to affect his relationship with Rebekah. Rebekah helped her son Jacob acquire Esau's blessing from his father, Isaac, by deceit (Gen 27:1–30). Jacob already had managed to buy Esau's birthright for a meal (Gen 25:27–30), and now Rebekah helped Jacob pretend that he was Esau so Jacob would acquire all the blessings from his father, Isaac, who was old and blind. She took advantage that Isaac had asked Esau to go and hunt and cook a delicious meal for him by asking Jacob to bring her all the ingredients she needed to make the meal for Isaac so Jacob could go and present it to his father, pretending he was Esau (Gen 27:6–18). She even dressed Jacob to feel like Esau! Jacob was disturbed about the deception concerning the preparation of the meal because he did not want to be cursed by his father, but Rebekah told him, "Your curse be on me, my son; only obey my voice, and go get them for me" (Gen 27:13).

Rebekah's actions caused a lot of problems between the two brothers. They became enemies. Esau threatened to kill Jacob as soon as Isaac died

(Gen 27:41). Rebekah was very crafty, and she handled this situation very carefully because knew she had to save the lives of both of her sons. She knew that Esau said, "The days of mourning for my father are near; then I will kill my brother Jacob" (Gen 27:41b). If Esau killed his brother, then the nearest relative had to come and kill Esau because the death of Jacob had to be avenged. Rebekah immediately came up with a plan to have Isaac send Jacob away to her brother Laban's house, but she made Isaac believe (deception again) that the purpose for her request was that she did not want Jacob to marry a woman from Canaan (Gen 27:42–46, 28:1–7). Isaac listened to Rebekah, and Jacob was sent away, as she planned. She told Jacob that she wanted to send him away "until your brother's anger against you subsides, and he forgets what you did to him. Then I shall send and get you from there. Why should I be bereaved of you both in one day?"(Gen 27:45). Rebekah's plan worked, but it took Jacob twenty years to leave the house of her brother Laban (Gen 31:31–38, 41). She paid for her deception because she never saw her son Jacob again.

Rebekah's husband loved her, but her favoritism for Jacob caused her castle to crumble because favoritism is a deadly sword in a family. We have to show our love to our children the same way regardless of their personality, gifts, physical appearance, or God's direction in their lives. After twenty years of marriage, God heard Isaac's prayers and allowed Rebekah to get pregnant. And God took the time to tell her personally that she was having twins and their fate (Gen 25:22–27). Motherhood changed Rebekah; she was overcome by a twisted ruling passion to make Jacob what God promised he would be—the ruler over his brother Esau. God did not need her help to do it. Eventually these two brothers found healing for their broken relationship (Gen 32:1–23, 33:1–16), but Rebekah was no longer around to see it because she was dead. Rebekah's sons buried their father Isaac together (Gen 35:29).

Rebekah died and was buried in the same tomb as Abraham, Sarah, and Isaac (Gen 49:31, 25:9–10, 50:13). A mother can love her children, but she can also harm them when her mind is not guided totally by God.

Search Your Heart, Thank God, and Pray

If you have children, do you have a favorite? Which one? Why? A mother should love all her children and keep her family together. Read Psalm 127:3 and 1 John 4:7–8. Thank God for your children, and pray for them. Allow the Lord to build your house according to His will, not yours (Ps. 127:1).

Day 11

Lot's Wife
The Wife of Abraham's Nephew Lot

Genesis 19:15–26, Luke 17:32

She was the wife of Abraham's nephew Lot. For me, Lot's wife is one of the biggest examples of curiosity and disobedience, with immediate results. God decided to destroy Sodom, where Lot and his family lived, and its sister city Gomorrah. It was a land of perversion full of sin and ungodliness. God had to destroy them because their sins called for such treatment. Not even Abraham was able to help save the people of these cities because he couldn't even find ten righteous people there for God to stop his wrath against them (Gen 18:20–33).

God gave Lot's family a chance to escape the destruction of Sodom because of His compassion (Gen 19:16) and because of His love for Abraham (Gen 19:29, 18:23–32). He did it by sending two angels to save them (Gen 19:1). The angels had to practically force Lot, his wife, and their two daughters out of the city, showing us the mercy of God at work. He saved those who didn't deserve it. The Bible says Lot "hesitated"—procrastination at its best! Leaving his home and everything he had was not part of Lot's plan. So Lot could escape death in Sodom, "The men seized his hand and the hand of his wife and the hands of his two daughters, for the compassion of the Lord was upon him: and they brought him out, and put him outside the city" (Gen 19:16).

The two angels said to Lot, once he and his family were out of harm's way, "Escape for your life! ***Do not look behind you,*** and do not stay in the valley; escape to the mountains, lest you be swept away" (Gen 19:17). Lot did not want to go to the mountains. Instead he requested to go to another city close to him called Zoar. God allowed Lot to go to the city he requested and even waited for Lot to get there (Gen 19:21–22). After the destruction of Sodom, Lot changed his mind because of fear and went to the mountains (Gen 19:20–22, 30).

Lot is an interesting character; he even had the nerve to interfere with God's destruction of Sodom. After he lived there and knew the sinful lifestyle its citizens lived, the angel had force him out and wait for him to be safe as he escaped to the mountains. The angel told him, "Hurry, escape there, for I cannot do anything until you arrive there" (Gen 19:22), and during all these episodes, Lot's wife's thoughts were not expressed. It is obvious that she followed her husband and the men of God because she made it outside the city! What was in her heart? My grandfather used to say, "Curiosity killed the cat," but was she curious? Was she attached to something she was leaving behind? All the Bible says is, "But his wife, from behind him, looked back; and she became a pillar of salt" (Gen 19:26). She disobeyed the command from the angels, and she had no time to repent! She is an example of disobedience with instant consequences.

In Luke 17:20–37, Jesus was answering questions from the Pharisees about His second coming, and He used Lot's wife as an example. Just like in the days of Noah and the days of Lot, some people will not be ready for God's wrath, and Lot's wife was not ready. Jesus reminded us of her disobedience and lack of readiness to welcome the new changes God had planned for her when He said, "Remember Lot's wife" (Luke 17:32). Don't look back at what you are leaving behind.

As I wrote this book, I was doing a survey in which every woman who filled out the survey was asked to indicate who her favorite woman of the

Bible was. ***One lady wrote that Lot's wife was her favorite biblical woman!*** She was the only one who chose Lot's wife. She wrote, "Because she encourages me. She couldn't let go of her stuff, and because of that she lost her family and her life. Am I that way? Do I have a hold on things in my life that I can't let go of for God?"

Reading this woman's answer, I appreciated her honesty, and at the same time, it challenged me as well to look into my heart and see if there is anything I feel I cannot let go of in order to honor God. What about you? Lot's wife was not ready to move on with her life, was not ready to let go, and will always be remembered as the woman who did not obeyed God's command. After Eve, Lot's wife is the second woman mentioned in the Bible who sinned intentionally by not following a command given by God.

Search Your Heart, Thank God, and Pray

Has God shown you a sin in your life that you are not able to overcome or let go? Are you hanging on to your past, or are you allowing God to direct you toward a new goal? Are you holding on to something that does not allow you to serve God or allow you to move on with your life? Read 1 John 1:9, Job 1:21. Confess any disobedience, commit to be obedient, and pray to the Lord for strength.

Day 12

The Daughters of Lot
Abraham's Nieces

Genesis 19:8, 14–15, 30–38

These two girls were residents of the city of Sodom, but they were not destroyed because the Lord God had mercy on them and their father, Lot. God allowed them to escape the destruction of Sodom and Gomorrah by personally sending angels to get them out of the city, along with their parents, before destroying those cities. We can see by their behavior later on that their bodies were saved from the cities but not their hearts. They kept the sinful ways they learned from their community in their hearts. The best description of these girls comes from Herbert Locker. He describes them as "shameless as they are nameless."[1] They were definitely the bad side of Abraham's family! Lot was not any different when he displayed his greed! Abraham and Lot had acquired a lot of livestock and possessions, and they began to have problems among their herdsmen and between the two of them (Gen 13). "Because Abraham was older and God had promised the land to him, he was entitled to first choice of the land. But he waived his rights, letting Lot choose first. Then he took what was left."[2] "So Lot chose for himself all the valley of the Jordan; and Lot journeyed eastward. Thus they separated from each other" (Gen 13:11). Charles Ryrie wrote, "The valley of the Jordan . . . well watered. Irrigation systems were in use long before Lot's time. Lot's greed to inhabit the Jordan valley with its vegetation exposed him to the wickedness of Sodom and Gomorrah."[3] Lot

Lived in Sodom with his family, and his family suffered the consequences of Lot's sin of greed.

When the two angels came to the house of Lot to save the family from the destruction of the city, the homosexuals outside the house in the town wanted to have relations with the two angels. Lot said to them, "Behold I have two daughters who have not had relations with man; please let me bring them out to you, and do to them whatever you like; only do nothing to these men, inasmuch as they have come under the shelter of my roof" (Gen 19:8). I understand that protecting his guest was an important custom of hospitality, but he could have thought of something else, like money or animals from his flock. It didn't have to be his virgin daughters! Fortunately, the angry crowd of homosexuals outside turned down Lot's offer.

It's ironic that just like Lot decided to give his daughters to immorality to save his guest, his daughters decided to commit immorality with him. After the destruction of Sodom and Gomorrah, these girls were left without future husbands because their husbands-to-be were killed at Sodom. They decided to continue the family line on their own terms. The oldest said to the youngest, "Our father is old, and there is not a man on earth to come in to us after the manner of the earth. Come, let us lie with him, that we may preserve our family through our father" (Gen 19:31–32). These girls got their father so drunk that he didn't know what happened. Each of them took turns with him, one per night. The Bible says Lot "did not know when she lay down or when she arose" (Gen 19:33-38).

They both got pregnant with their father's child. Lot's oldest daughter gave birth to a son named Moab, who was the father of the Moabites who lived east of the Dead Sea and were idolaters. The youngest also gave birth to a son who was named Ben-ammi, who "is the father of the sons of Ammon" (Gen 19:38). In God's mercy, interestingly enough, we find that Ruth, the Moabite, was the mother Obed who is part of the lineage of David (Ruth 4:22).

The daughters of Lot proved to be ungodly by their actions. After all they were exposed to a very sinful lifestyle by their parents. In Matthew 12:33 Jesus said, "Either make the tree good, and its fruit good; or make the tree bad, and its fruit bad; for the tree is known by its fruit." And Proverbs 22:6 says, "Train up a child in the way he should go, even when he is old he will not depart from it." Lot's daughters did not receive proper training, and the fruit does not fall far from the tree. These two women's mistakes can encourage us to make sure that we teach our children in the way they should go, to walk with God and to hold on to the promises so when they get older, they will not depart from them.

Search Your Heart, Thank God, and Pray

Are biblical values practiced in your life or family when it comes to what you read, see, think, say, or do? Are you getting godly nourishment so you can have and give godly fruit? Read Joshua 1:8–9. If you are following God's command to teach your children, thank Him for giving you that wisdom. If not, pray that the Holy Spirit would give you discernment to guide yourself and your family.

1 Herbert Lockyer, All *the Women of the Bible (*Grand Rapids: Zondervan Publishing House, 1995), 176

2 Millie Stemm, *Be Still and Know* (Grand Rapids: 1978), Reading for May 21

3 *The Ryrie Study Bible* (Chicago: The Moody Institute of Chicago, 1978), 26.

Jacob

"Isaac prayed to the LORD on behalf of his wife, because she was barren; and the LORD answered him and Rebekah his wife conceived ... When the days to be delivered were fulfilled, behold, there were twins in her womb. Now the first came forth red, all over like a hairy garment; and they named him Esau. Afterward his brother came forth with his hand holding on to Esau's heel, so his name was called Jacob; and Isaac was sixty seven years old when she gave birth to them"
(Gen. 25:21, 24-26 NASB).

Day 1

Leah
Jacob's First Wife and Cousin

Genesis 29; 30; 33; 1–2, 7, 46:18, 49:31, Ruth 4:11

Leah was Jacob's cousin and also his first wife. She was the daughter of Rebekah's brother Laban. Rebekah was Jacob's mother and Leah's aunt. All in the family! When Isaac sent Jacob away to his brother in-law's house, Laban, because of his wife Rebekah's request (to save Jacob from the wrath of his brother Esau), Jacob ended up in a love triangle between two sisters, Leah and Rachel. Jacob did not choose Leah to be his wife, but she was married to Jacob first because her father deceived Jacob (Gen 29:21–28). Jacob had asked for Rachel and Laban promised Jacob he could marry Rachel after serving him for seven years. However, when it was time for Laban to keep his word, Laban prepared and gave a feast for Rachel's wedding but placed Leah in Jacob's tent for the wedding night instead of Rachel. In the morning Jacob was a very disappointed man. Next to him was Leah, not Rachel. What a way to get married! Laban's argument was, "It was not the practice in our place, to marry off the younger before the first" (Gen 29:26). He asked Jacob to work another seven years for Rachel.

Leah was an unwanted purchase for Jacob, and he never loved her as he loved Rachel. She was not a beautiful woman; the Bible described her as having "weak" (Gen 29:17) eyes, while her sister is described as beautiful of face and figure. Leah spent her life longing for the love of Jacob. She was aware of the fact that her husband's love was her sister's, but she was consoled by having children.

Genesis 29:31 tells us, "Now the LORD saw that Leah was unloved, and He opened her womb, but Rachel was barren." She felt that the Lord loved her and was rewarding the lack of love from Jacob by allowing her to give birth to Jacob's sons. Leah was the mother of Rueben, Simeon, Levi, Judah, Issachar, and Zebulun. Even though Jacob had other daughters, Leah gave birth to the only one named in the Bible, Dinah.

Leah's hope for Jacob's love never ended. Even when she gave birth to her last boy, which was boy number six, she still said, "God has endowed me with a good gift; now my husband will dwell with me, because I have borne him six sons" (Gen 30:20). She went from desiring his love to just wanting him to live with her and have him near. She saw her children as blessings from God, but they did not help her to win her husband's love. She turned out to be the biggest contributor to the twelve tribes of Israel because of her six sons and the two she got through her maid with Jacob. Leah decided to give Jacob her maid to have more children so she could compete with her sister, Rachel. The fact that Leah had so many children with Jacob implies that there was something about her that he liked because I don't think he went to her tent and got her pregnant seven times, and maybe more, out of duty!

Leah learned to rely on God because she felt He answered her prayers every time she had a child. Every one of her boys was named after something that had to do with God. She was always grateful to God for every child she was blessed to birth into the world. She always had hope! I admire her for that. Her hope did not end even though God did not give her what she wanted the most—Jacob's love. After her sister Rachel died, she became the main wife but not Jacob's main love. She had to watch him suffer for the love he lost. Leah contribution to Jacob's life and the house of Israel can be traced all the way to David because of her son Judah and by the line of priest through Aaron and her son Levi.

Leah was honest (Gen 30:16), and God always heard her and blessed her (Gen 29:31, 30:17). Her bones were gathered with Jacob's because Leah was the one who was buried in the same place as he was, but even there she was not alone with him. Jacob remembered on his deathbed that he wanted to be buried where "they buried Abraham and his wife Sarah, there they buried Isaac and his wife Rebekah, and there I buried Leah" (Gen 49:31). Jacob did love Leah because Genesis 29:30 says that Jacob loved "Rachel <u>more</u> than Leah." It is moving that he showed a longing for Leah when he was dying, though it was a little too late for Leah to enjoy it!

Search Your Heart, Thank God, and Pray

What has God not given you that you are grateful to Him for not giving to you? Have you lost hope of God's answer to your prayers? God knows why He allows things to happen in your life. He always answers prayer, whether you like the answer or not. Pray that He would give you what is best for you according to the counsel of His own will. Read Proverbs 3:5.

Day 2

Rachel
Jacob's Second Wife and Cousin

Genesis 29–31, 33:1–2, 7, 35:16–20, 46:19, 22, 25, 48:7; Ruth 4:11; 1 Samuel 10:2; Jeremiah 31:15; Matt 2:18

Rachel was the second wife and cousin of Jacob. She was the daughter of Laban, who was Jacob's mother's brother. She was the sister of Leah, who was Jacob's first wife. Jacob, her husband, had a tremendous love for her. Rachel was beautiful in face and body (Gen 29:17) and was a shepherd girl. Jacob worked fourteen years to have her as his wife (Gen 29:18). He loved her so much that he was willing to work for free in the household of her father-in-law to make her his wife.

Rachel was barren. She could not have children, and it was very difficult for her to know that even though her husband loved her more than Leah (Gen 29:18, 30–31), she could not give him a child. It was very hard for Rachel to see her sister, Leah, give birth while she was not able to give a child to the man who loved her so much. She got jealous! "Now when Rachel saw that she bore no children, she became jealous of her sister; and she said to Jacob, 'Give me children or else I die'" (Gen 30:1). Jacob reminded her that he was not God and he could not solve her problem. So Rachel gave Jacob her maid, Bilhah, to have children for her, and she did (Gen 30:3). This did not make Rachel complete because she wanted to be the one to give birth, but it calmed her desire. She gave thanks to the Lord for giving her a child through her maid. "Then God remembered Rachel, "…and

God gave heed to her and opened her womb. So she conceived and bore a son and said, 'God has taken away my reproach" (Gen 30:22). And she named him Joseph, saying, "May the lord give me another son" (Gen 30: 23–24). The Lord gave her another son, but when she gave birth to him, "she suffered severe labor" (Gen 35:16) and "she named him Ben-oni; but his father called him Benjamin" (Gen 35:18). Ben-oni meant, "Son of my sorrow" while Benjamin meant "son of fortune"[1]. It is interesting to see that Rachel felt blessed by having Joseph, her first child, but she did not feel blessed after giving birth to Benjamin because she knew she was going to die. Jacob honored Rachel by loving her sons. Jacob's favorite son among all his sons was Joseph, who turned out to be the most famous of all his sons, and the one with the most love, trust, and respect for God. God used Joseph to save the people of Israel from dying of hunger. (You can read Joseph's story in Gen 37–50.)

Some people argue that Rachel first got pregnant with Joseph because she consumed an herb called *mandrakes*, but it was God (Gen 30:22) who decided Rachel was going to finally have a child. The story in Genesis says that one day Rueben, who was Leah's oldest son "went and found mandrakes in the field, and brought them to his mother Leah. Then Rachel said to Leah, 'please give me some of your son's mandrakes.' But she said to her, 'Is it a small matter for you to take my husband? And would you take my son's mandrakes also?'" (Gen 30:14–15). The two sisters agreed to exchange the mandrakes for Jacob for the night! Rachel got the mandrakes and Leah got Jacob for the night. Mandrake is an herb of the nightshades (Solanaceae), very common in Syria and Palestine, as throughout the Mediterranean region. It is considered to be an aphrodisiac to enhance or intensify sexual desires and promote conception." [2]

Rachel's life was miserable because she was consumed with the longing for a child. She tried to give children to her husband by giving him her maid, by taking a special kind of herb, and by complaining to him about her situation. But it was not until God decided she was going to have children that she started having them. The Lord knew she was going to die, but He answered Jacob's prayers, because Joseph needed to be born. God allowed Rachel to become a mother, which was her biggest longing.

Search Your Heart, Thank God, and Pray

Have you ever wanted to have something so bad that it consumed your life? God healed Rachel by blessing her with children. What will it take for you to feel blessed by God? Read Philippians 4:19.

1 Allen C. Myers, The *Eerdmans Bible Dictionary (*Grand Rapids: WM. B. Eerdmans Publishing Co, 1987), 137

2 Ibid, 685

Day 3

Rachel Jacob's Second Wife—the Idolater

Jacob served twenty years in the house of Laban his uncle. Fourteen of them were to pay for Rachel and Leah and six for his flocks, but Jacob decided it was time to move on with his family. The possessions acquired by both men were too many to be kept together (Gen 30:25–36). Laban cheated Jacob too many times. He changed Jacob's wages ten times over those twenty years, and he tricked Jacob into marrying both of his daughters. Jacob did not like what was going on in his father-in-law an uncle's house! God told Jacob to "return to the land of your fathers and to your relatives, and I will be with you" (Gen 31:3). Jacob called his wives and told them what he had in mind, and they agreed to follow him, so they left without telling Laban (Gen 31:20–23).

Rachel committed a great sin during this time: "When Laban had gone to shear his flock, then Rachel stole the household idols that were her father's" (Gen 31:19). Why she did this is not really known because God's Word doesn't say why. When Jacob fled from the household of Laban, Rachel took these idols with her, and her husband was completely unaware of it. When Laban found out Jacob had left, he followed after him because he couldn't understand why Jacob had deceived him by leaving without allowing him to say good-bye to his daughters and family. Besides, there was another question: "Why did you steal my gods?" (Gen 31:30b). Jacob did not know what his wife Rachel had done.

God was merciful. He spoke to Laban in a dream and told him, "Be careful that you do not speak to Jacob either good or bad" (Gen 31:24).

But Laban still wanted his gods. Jacob was so sure no one in his family had Laban's idols that he told Laban, "The one with whom you find your gods shall not live; in the presence of your kinsmen point out what is yours among my belongings and take it for yourself" (Gen 31:32). Little did Jacob know that his beloved Rachel had them! She was very smart because she "had taken the household idols and put them in the camel's saddle, and she sat on them" (Gen 31:34). Her father never found the idols because when Laban approached her while she was sitting on the camel, she said to him, "Let not my lord be angry that I cannot rise before you, for the manner of women is upon me" (Gen 31:35). She lied and told him she was menstruating and that was the reason why she was not properly standing up in presence of her father like she was supposed to according to their tradition. A woman was considered unclean while she was menstruating, so her father couldn't look under the saddle to find the idols. Since Laban couldn't find proof of wrongdoing by Jacob, he was humbled for accusing Jacob of something he had not done. Before Rachel's death, it is recorded in Genesis 35:2–5 that Jacob gathered all the pagan gods that came out of Mesopotamia and "hid them under the oak, which was near Schechem."

Laban and Jacob had a good relationship after they separated, and they made a covenant of peace between them. Jacob promised he would not bring another woman into Laban's daughters' household for a wife. Even though Jacob had Leah, after Rachel died, his love for his beloved Rachel did not end. His love came out in a focus toward her two sons, Joseph and Benjamin. God heard the voice of Rachel begging her husband for a child: "Give me children or I will die." It is ironic that the Lord gave her children and she died right after giving birth to her last son.

God blessed Rachel by giving her a husband, who loved her unconditionally, by giving her the children she desired, and by saving her life by not allowing her father Laban to find the idols she took from him. Rachel's' love for God is not displayed in the Bible, but God's love for her is demonstrated in His Word.

Search Your Heart, Thank God, and Pray

What will it take for you to feel God's love for you? Have you ever shared something that belongs to you that you did want to share? What happened? If you lied to a loved one, confess to him/her and God. Allow the Lord to heal your heart. Read Colossians 19:9-10, and John 8:44.

Day 4

Bilhah
Jacob's Concubine

Genesis 29:29, 30:1–7, 35:22, 25, 37:2, 46:25; 1 Chronicles 4:29, 7:13

Bilhah was a maid given to Rachel, Jacob's second wife, by her father Laban (Gen 29:29). She became a concubine of Jacob under Rachel's command (Gen 30:1–7). Rachel used Bilhah to give Jacob children since she was barren. Bilhah gave Jacob two sons who became part of the twelve tribes of Israel. When Bilhah's first son was born, Rachel said, "God has vindicated me, and has indeed heard my voice and has giving me a son' Therefore she named him Dan which means "Justice" (Gen 30:6). Dan became the head of the Danites, from which tribe came Samson (Judges 13:2, 4:13–25). This tribe brought idolatry into Israel (Lev 24:11, Judges 18, 1 Kings 12:28–29), and this was probably the reason why Dan's tribe was not mention in Revelation 7:4–8 as part of the Jews the Lord decided to redeem during the tribulation period.

Bilhah's second son was Naphtali, also named by Rachel, because she said, "With mighty wrestlings I have wrestled with my sister, and I have indeed prevailed" (Gen 30:7–8). Naphtali means "wrestling." This son was also one of the twelve tribes of Israel. His father Jacob said to him when he was blessing all of his children, "Naphtali is a doe let loose, he gives beautiful words" (Gen 49:21). Moses also blessed him through his tribe. When Moses was dividing the land among the tribes, he said, "O Naphtali, satisfied with favor, and full of the blessing of the Lord, take possession of the sea and the south" (Deut 33:23). Naphtali received the fertile land west and south of the Lake of Galilee.

Bilhah was a victim of Rachel's desire, just like Hagar was of Sarah's. Rachel used Bilhah to achieve something she could not do herself: give birth. Here also Jacob is to be blamed. He got angry with Rachel (Gen 30:2), and instead of continuing in prayer to the Lord to open Rachel's womb, he accepted the maid to keep his wife happy. Jacob did not follow after his father Isaac, who prayed for his wife, Rebekah, who was also barren, but instead he followed his grandfather Abraham's example, who took Hagar at Sarah's request (see Hagar). God blessed Jacob and Bilhah with another son which gave Rachel another son to brag about. By Rachel giving Jacob her maid Bilhah, a competition started between the two sisters to see how many children each could give Jacob (Gen 30:9). Then Leah gave her maid to Jacob for her to have more children to call her own!

Bilhah was part of a great sin committed against Jacob; she had sexual relations with Jacob's firstborn son, Reuben, a son of Leah. "And it came about while Israel (Jacob) was dwelling in that land, that Reuben went and lay with Bilhah his father's' concubine; and Israel [Jacob] heard of it" (Gen 35:22). Jacob did not forget this event, and he remembered really well when it was time to give blessings to his sons. *Jacob punished Reuben for his sexual sin by giving his firstborn blessing to Joseph.* Reuben lost his blessing and Jacob said to him at the time of blessing, "Uncontrolled as water you shall not have preeminence, because you went up to your father's bed; then you defiled it" (Gen 49:4). As you read the Old Testament you will find that the tribe of Reuben did not produce prophets, heroes, or any character that are well known today.

Bilhah was used twice, once by Rachel and once by Leah's son Reuben. The first time she did not have a choice because she was a slave owned by Rachel, and she had to do what she was told. The second time she was used by Reuben when he lay with her (Gen 35:22). It is not clear if Bilhah had a sexual relationship with Reuben willingly; the Bible does not go into specifics. She was the mother of two of Reuben's brothers! Bilhah was slave, a mother of many, a concubine to Jacob, and also a woman who is remembered by her sin.

Her character is not discussed in the Bible, and neither is where she comes from, but her life left a mark in the life of Israel the man and the nation.

Search Your Heart, Thank God, and Pray

Are you using someone for self-satisfaction or to gain importance? Are you a victim of incest? When you are a victim of incest or any other type of abuse, part of your healing will include forgiving the one who offended you (Read Luke 11:4, Ephesians 4:32). Reuben paid for his sexual sin with Bilhah and if you have ever fallen into an immoral relationship, pray, confess and allow God to cleanse you by confessing to Him and changing your life.

Day 5
Zilpah
Jacob's Second Concubine

Genesis 29:24, 30:9–13, 35:26, 37:2, 46:18

Zilpah became the second concubine of Jacob by orders of his first wife, Leah (Gen 30:9). Leah's father, Laban, gave Zilpah to Leah to be her maid (Gen 29:24). Leah stopped giving birth for a while, so she gave Zilpah to Jacob so she could have more children to call them her own (Gen 30:9–13). Zilpah was supposed to have the children Leah was no longer having. As you recall from previous reading about Leah and Rachel, there was a competition between them to give sons to Jacob. It was not necessary for Leah to give her maid to Jacob because she already had children. Soon after she gave her maid to Jacob, she started having children again; she had two more sons and a daughter (Gen 30:17–21). Again Jacob did what he was told. There was not one complaint out of Jacob's mouth about the subject! Now he had two wives and two concubines. It was a good thing that Laban made Jacob promise not to take another woman into his household (Gen 31:50), besides God only planned to give him twelve tribes!

Zilpah had two sons who are credited to Leah. When the first was born Leah, said, "How fortunate" (Gen 30:11), and she named him Gad which means "luck" or "fortune." Leah was pleased to have one more son to add to her name for Jacob. You may remember that the more children Leah had, the more she thought Jacob was going to love her. Gad was the father of the Gadites. This tribe was big: "At the time the first census was made in the wilderness it numbered 45,650" (Num 1:24–25), and these were only the men. Jacob's blessing to Gad resembles what the Gadites tribe became: warriors. Jacob said, "As for Gad raiders shall raid him, but he shall raid at their heels" (Gen 49:19). In 1 Chronicles 5:18, this tribe is included and described as one of the tribes "of valiant men, men who bore shield and sword and shot with bow, and were skillful in battle."

Then Zilpah had another son, and Leah said, "Happy am I! For women will call me happy," and she named him Asher (Gen 30:13), which means "happy." Here you can see that other people were also involved in the competition among the two sisters because Leah was concerned about what the other women around her would say because another son had been born to her. Once again we see someone being used to accomplish another person's goals or desires. Jacob recognized Zilpah's sons as he did the others by blessing them before he died (Gen 49:20).

It is important to notice that Jacob, like his mother, Rebekah, created jealousy among his own children (and that included Zilpah's sons) by loving Rachel's son Joseph more and making it obvious to the other children (Gen 37:3–4). Jacob expressed this love also in Genesis 33:1–7 when he met his brother Esau. He was scared because he had offended Esau in the past by taking away his birthright (Gen 27). When Jacob met Esau, he placed himself first in line, and then divided all of his wives and his children and in order of importance in case any danger should arise. "He put the maids and their children in front, and Leah and her children next, and Rachel and Joseph last" (Gen 33:2). After he made sure everything was all right with his brother Esau, he made all the children in order of importance to bow down to Esau (Gen 33:4).

Zilpah was not a troublemaker and is not famous; she was a slave who God gave a place in the life of His people. She is not remembered for a great sin, but she is remembered as one of the women who made possible the twelve tribes of Israel. She is always going to be under the shadow of Jacob and Leah because both used her, **but God blessed her**. He gave her children even though they were not legally hers but her mistress's, and He made her part of His plan to make Abraham a great nation!

Search Your Heart, Thank God, and Pray

Joseph was loved more than his brothers. Was there a favorite child in your family? Was it you? If it wasn't you, is it still bothering you? If you have children, are you creating jealousy among your children? If you are hurt because of favoritism when you were growing up, remember that Jesus died for you because you are His favorite among many favorites. Zilpah was not famous but God used her. Are you God's behind the scenes kingdom worker? Read Matthew 5:16, Job 5:2.

Day 6

Dinah
Jacob's Daughter

Genesis 30:21, 34:1–41, 46:15.

Dinah is the only daughter of Jacob recorded in the Bible by name (Gen 30:19–21), but he had other daughters (Gen 37:35, 46: 7, 15). We do not know, specifically, who was the mother of Jacob's other daughters. We only know that it was not Rachel because she only gave birth to two sons and then she died. Dinah was Leah's daughter. It must have been refreshing for Jacob to get a daughter after he had so many boys!

The way Dinah's birth is recorded in Genesis 30:21, it appears as if she was the first daughter Jacob fathered and that is probably why she is named in the Bible. The other reason she is probably named in the Bible could be the great tragedy that took place in her life. Jacob had taken his family to the city of Shechem (Gen 33:18–20), a city in Canaan, and Dinah decided to go out for a walk, "to visit the daughters of the land" (Gen 34:1). The prince of the land spotted her. "And when Shechem [named as the city], the son of Hamor the Hivite, the prince of the land, saw her, he took her and lay with her by force" (Gen 34:2). Sadly, this is the first case of individual rape recorded in the Bible.

Jacob found out what happened to his little girl, and since her brothers were working hard in the fields, "Jacob kept silent until they came in" (Gen 34:5). When Dinah's brothers found out, they "...were grieved, and were very angry…" (Gen 34:7) because it was a disgrace what had happened to their sister.

Even though Shechem raped her, "He was deeply attracted to Dinah the daughter of Jacob, and he loved the girl and spoke tenderly to her" (Gen 34:3). The prince asked his father, "Get me this young girl for a wife" (Gen 34:4). Shechem went about getting Dinah the wrong way. What a way to ask someone out! He raped her, and then he asked for her hand in marriage! Shechem's father, Hamor, went over, accompanied by his son, to ask Jacob to allow Dinah to marry his son. He said, "The soul of my son Shechem longs for your daughter; please give her to him in marriage" (Gen 34:8). At this point Shechem got desperate and said to Jacob and his sons, "If I find favor in your sight, then I will give whatever you say to me" (Gen 34:11). Dinah was under Shechem's skin! The man was in love, even though he did everything backwards and wrong!

Dinah's brothers told Hamor and Shechem that the only way Dinah could become a wife into that family was if all the men in their household were circumcised! It would have been "a disgrace" for Jacob's family to have Dinah married to an uncircumcised man! (Gen 17:14). The desire of Shechem for Dinah was so strong that he agreed. "The young man did not delay to do the thing, because he was delighted with Jacob's daughter" (Gen 34:19). Shechem and Hamor convinced all their men to get together with Jacob's family. They could marry each other's women and share livestock and become one people. Their men followed and agreed to be circumcised.

Jacob's sons had other ideas in mind, which they did not share with Jacob. After Shechem's men were all circumcised, "It came about the third day, when they were in pain, that two of Jacob's sons, Simeon and Levi, Dinah's brothers, each took his sword and came upon the city unawares, and killed every male" (Gen 34:25), including Hamor and Shechem. And they rescue their sister Dinah from Shechem's house. Jacob was angry when he found out what had happened, but the brothers answered, "Should he treat our sister as a harlot?" (Gen 34:31). Dinah went out to do something very common to many of us—to see what was out there. Edith Deen said,

"Like most girls in a large family of brothers, she longed for the company of other girls and went out to visit the daughters of the land." [1] The lust of one man, Shechem, ruined Dinah's outing and her life, made a path for two of her brothers to become murderers, and caused the death of many.

What happened to Dinah happens to many women today, but many keep the secret to themselves, and most of these Dinahs end up grieving, feeling unworthy, and living a dysfunctional life because of it. Dinah received justice (not the way it should have been done) and healing by knowing that Shechem would not hurt her again or anyone else. Women who are sexually abused need to seek help from someone who can help them, like a counselor, the police, their pastor, or a close friend. The most important thing for a victim of sexual abuse and rape to understand is that it is not their fault. This is called false guilt and false guilt can destroy a person.

If you were are a victim of rape or sexual abuse remember that God loves you, and that what happened to you, is not your fault. Because of sin, someone decided to violate you. That does not mean that you are not worthy of God's love and God's presence in your life. God will take care of the abuser but you need to take care of you with help and counseling. Also remember God's words, "Never take your own revenge, beloved, but leave room for the wrath *of God*, for it is written, "Vengeance is Mine, I will repay," says the Lord" (Romans 12:19).

Search Your Heart, Thank God, and Pray

Is there a Shechem in your life? If you have been raped, have you faced this fact and asked for help? Read Isaiah 41:10, Philippians 4:13, and seek help. Past experiences can ruin your life. Seek a Christian counselor who will help you healing and help you to forgive the one who hurt you.

1 Edith Deen, *All the Women of the Bible* (New York: HarperCollins, 1983), 38.

Day 7

Tamar #1 The Wife of Jacob's Grandson's Er, Onan, and Harlot to Judah

Genesis 38:6–30; Ruth 4:12; 1 Chronicles 2:4; Matthew 1:3

There are three Tamars in the Bible. This is Tamar #1, who was Jacob's granddaughter, the wife of Er (Gen 38:6-–0). Tamar #2 was the daughter of King David (2 Sam 13:11), and Tamar #3 was the daughter of David's son Absalom (2 Sam 14:27). There was also a town named Tamar near the Dead Sea (1 King 9:18).

Tamar #1 was the wife of Er, Judah's (son of Jacob) firstborn. Er "was evil in the sight of the Lord, so the Lord took his life …" (Gen 38:6). The Bible does not tell us what Er did to offend God, but whatever it was had to be very bad because God took care of it right away. This event made Tamar an instant widow. Following the custom of the day, Judah talked to his son Onan and said, "Go into your brother's wife, and perform your duty as a brother-in-law to her, and raise up offspring for your brother" (Gen 38:8).

This was a Hebrew law that was carried out on those days, but Onan didn't like this arrangement! "And Onan knew that the offspring would not be his; so it came about that when he went into his brother's wife, he wasted his seed on the ground, in order not to give offspring to his brother" (Gen 38:9). Well the Lord did not like Onan's attitude either! "What he did was displeasing in the sight of the Lord; so He took his life also" (Gen 38:10). Tamar became a widow, again!

Well, Judah was not about to lose another son! Judah told Tamar to go to her father's house until Shelah, the son next in line, would be old enough to marry her.

But Judah did not keep his promise to Tamar. Tamar was left with the duty of having children for the wicked Er (her first husband). She decided to take matters into her own hands. When Judah's wife died and his mourning time was over, Judah decided to go to visit "his sheepshearers at Timnah he and his friend Hirah" (Gen 38:12). When Tamar found out he was "going to Timnah to shear his sheep" (Gen 38:13), she set up a trap for Judah because he did not keep his word of giving her his youngest son to marry.

"She removed her widow's garments and covered herself with a veil, and wrapped herself, and sat in the gateway of Enaim, which is on the road to Timnah" (Gen 38:14). Judah thought Tamar was a prostitute, and he in turn invited her to have sex with him and offered her payment (Gen 38:15–17). He offered her a "kid from the flock." By Judah offering Tamar a livestock, a young goat, demonstrated that he had wealth. This was a way for Judah to impress the woman he thought to be a prostitute! Tamar had to protect herself because she knew she was not a prostitute; she needed to have proof of her encounter with Judah, so she asked Judah for a temporary payment until he delivered the kid. She asked him to give her "your seal and your cord, and your staff that is in your hand." He agreed, she accepted it, they had sex, and she got pregnant (Gen 38:18). Judah sent his payment to Tamar with a friend, but when Judah's friend came back to pay Tamar with the animal and get Judah's belongings back, Tamar was gone! His friends asked at the gates where the temple prostitute went, and the people said, "There has been no temple prostitute here" (Gen, 38:21). Judah's personal identifications were gone!

Three months went by, and Tamar was found to be pregnant (Gen 38:24) from an unknown man, and she was accused of being a harlot. Judah was informed of it and said, "Bring her out and let her be burned" (Gen 38:24). Little did he know what he was about to burn! When she was being accused of harlotry, she took Judah's seal, cord, and staff, sent them to Judah, and said, "I'm with child by the man to whom these things belong" (Gen 38:25). Surprise! Judah was humbled because he knew that he did not keep his word to Tamar and did not give her his youngest son to marry her. He said, "She is more righteous than I, inasmuch as I did not give her to my son Shelah" (Gen. 38:26). Judah did not have sexual relations with Tamar again, but because of his previous encounter, which involved prostitution, he became the father and grandfather of his son's Er children. What a way to keep the law! God used Judah's moment of weakness and lust and Tamar's determination to do her duty of having children for undeserving Er to accomplish His purpose. Tamar had twin sons named Perez and Zerah (Gen 38:27–30). Perez is named as part of the genealogy of Christ (Matt 1:3). Tamar and Judah became ancestors in the geology of David because Boaz was a descendant of Tamar's son Perez, and Boaz was the father of Jesse, who became the father of King David (Ruth 4:18–22).

Search Your Heart, Thank God, and Pray

Do you keep your promises? Have you forgiven someone who did not keep a promised made? Read Ephesians 4:32. God always has a reason for allowing things to happen to us because He has a purpose for you (Jeremiah 29:11). God always keeps His promises.

Day 8

Asenath
The Wife of Jacob's Son Joseph

Genesis 41:45–52; 46:20

Asenath was the wife of Joseph, the beloved son of Jacob; she was the wife of one of the godliest men who ever walked on the face of the Earth. She was a gift to Joseph from the pharaoh of Egypt (Gen 41:45). The Pharaoh wanted to honor Joseph so much that he decided to marry Joseph into a family of an Egyptian priest, whose god was the sun. Asenath was the daughter of Potiphera, priest of On. No doubt Asenath was a beautiful woman, and in her arms Joseph was able to quench the pain from the treason of his brothers, who sold him into slavery because they were jealous of Jacob's love for him (Gen 37:1–36). Asenath gave Joseph two sons. The first was Manasseh, who was a big blessing for Joseph because when this son was born, he said, "God has made me forget all my trouble and all my father's household" (Gen 41:51). The second son was named Ephraim. Joseph said, "God has made me fruitful in the land of my affliction" (Gen 41:52).

The pharaoh of Egypt had a very disturbing dream, and no one could tell what it was and what it meant. Joseph was the only man capable of interpreting the pharaoh's complicated dreams (Gen 41:1–43). Joseph told the pharaoh that there was going to be a great famine in the land that would last seven years. He advised the pharaoh to "appoint overseers in charge of the land" (Gen 41:34) for them to save enough food for the seven years of famine. Pharaoh was a smart man, and he said to Joseph "Since God has informed you of all this, there is no one so discerning and wise as you are" (Gen 41:39). So the pharaoh made Joseph second in command, and in the land of Egypt, only Pharaoh was more important than Joseph. Joseph got Pharaoh's ring as a symbol of authority and was dressed like a pharaoh. Joseph's name was even changed to an Egyptian name: "Pharaoh named Joseph Zaphenath-paneah; and he gave him Asenath, the daughter of Potiphera priest of On, as his wife. And Joseph went forth over the land of Egypt" (Gen 41:45).

When the Lord decided to bless Joseph for being a faithful man, He supplied for all his needs. God gave him a new home in the house of the pharaoh of Egypt and a wife to release his controlled passion and find comfort. He gave him people to rule, enough food for him and all of Egypt, and worldwide recognition. Joseph had the honor to save the house of Jacob, his father, from famine (Gen 42–47).

It is very interesting to see how God used the land of Egypt throughout Scripture. He used Egypt to supply for Abraham and Sarah during a famine (Gen 12:10). Abraham's first son, Ishmael, came from an Egyptian woman, Hagar (Gen 16). The daughter of pharaoh saved Moses from the Nile and raised him as Egyptian (Ex 2:5–11), and later on the same Moses saved God's people from bondage from the Egyptians (Ex 2–14). The Lord used Egypt to give Joseph a new life and to preserve His own people from dying of starvation (Gen 42–47). The first wife of the great Solomon was the daughter of the pharaoh of Egypt, at that time. Solomon made an alliance with this pharaoh of Egypt (1 Kings 3:1). Even our Lord Jesus was touched by this land because when He was a child and His life was in danger due to the anger of Herod, God ordered Joseph to take his family to Egypt to keep Him safe (Matt 2:13–16).

Asenath was created for God's purpose, and part of that purpose was to be Joseph's wife. I am sure her heart had to be changed when she saw that Joseph's words to the pharaoh came to pass and when she lived with him and saw his way of life. She was the wife of a man who was committed to purity and to honor God. Joseph was blessed with Asenath as well because she never tried to separate him from God. She accepted Joseph for who he was, not for who she probably wanted him to be, an Egyptian.

Search Your Heart, Thank God, and Pray

Like Joseph, can people see God by the life you live? Do you accept your mate the way he is? Have you ever been overwhelmed by God's provision in your life? Read Philippians 2:1-11

Day 9

Potiphar's Wife the Greatest Threat to Jacob's Son Joseph

Genesis 39:1–23

Potiphar's wife committed the biggest sexual harassment case recorded in biblical history, but she made a mistake; she harassed a man of God. When we look at this episode very carefully, we can see she lost the case. After Joseph was sold into slavery by his brothers, Potiphar, an Egyptian officer of Pharaoh, "bought him from the Ishmaelite ... And the Lord blessed Joseph, so he became a successful man" (Gen 39:1–2). Potiphar knew there was something special about Joseph because everything he did prospered. This was the Lord blessing Joseph. Potiphar put Joseph in charge of everything he owned, and the Lord showed His power by using Joseph.

Potiphar's wife knew what Joseph meant to her husband, but she was interested in Joseph anyway. "Joseph was handsome in form and appearance" (Gen 39:6). She longed to have him, so she ordered him, saying, "...Lie with me..." (Gen 39:7). Joseph said no, and he reminded her of the trust her husband had put in him. How he could in return offend him by taking his wife? Joseph said, "There is no one greater in this house than I, and he has withheld nothing from me except you, because you are his wife. How then could I do this great evil, and sin against God" (Gen

39:9). Even though she insisted, Joseph was not concerned with her desires. He was concerned with pleasing God. Even though Potiphar's wife did not respect her marriage, Joseph did. Joseph knew what his priority was, and he was able to discern God's will in his life. He knew committing adultery was against God's will. **Even though it had not been written yet, Joseph was living one of the Ten Commandments**, "You shall not commit adultery" (Ex 20:14). Joseph wanted to honor his employer and the one who lead him to his employer, God. Potiphar's wife did not give up, and one day she tried to force herself onto Joseph, but Joseph got out in time (Gen 39:10–12). Unfortunately, Joseph left part of his garment in her hand because she was pulling on his clothes, trying to convince him to have sex with her. She sexually harassed Joseph daily (Gen 39:10). Joseph had to face a daily battle, but Joseph did not give in.

This evil woman then made up a story that Joseph tried to force himself on her. (She wished!) There were no human witnesses in the house to defend Joseph because her behavior only happened in the presence of God, Joseph, and Satan. She said to Potiphar, "The Hebrew slave, whom you brought to us, came to me to make sport of me; and it happened as I raised my voice and screamed, that he left his garment beside me and fled outside" (Gen 39:17–18). She was a deceiving woman. She needed to take revenge on Joseph for not doing what she wanted. Joseph was put in jail in "the place where the king's prisoners were confined" (Gen 39:19). In jail Potiphar's wife could not have him, she could not see him, and Joseph was safe from her! Joseph was an itch she would never scratch!

Like always, God was with Joseph. God blessed Joseph and he always ended up in charge of places and situations. In jail, he was put in charge of all the prisoners (Gen 39:21–23). He was even responsible for the actions of the prisoners. This incident with Potiphar's wife allowed Joseph to find his way to the house of Pharaoh, where he became next in command to Pharaoh (Gen 41:38–49).

There are a lot of Potiphar's wives out there, and we need to pray for our husbands, pastors, brothers, cousins, and leaders of our nation to be strong in their walk with the Lord so when the Potiphar's wives of the world appear, they can become Josephs! Keeping one's life pure is and will be a daily battle. Joseph was a living example of the word of God that tells us, ". . . let marriage be held in honor among all, and let the marriage bed be undefiled; for fornicators and adulterers God will judge" (Heb 13:4). Joseph focused on his trust and faith in God, ". . . not at the things which are seen, but at the things which are not seen; for the things which are seen are temporal, but the things which are not seen are eternal" (2 Cor 4:18). He knew God would take care of him. Joseph honored those who where around him and he was faithful to God, to his friendship to Potiphar, and his unworthy wife. Joseph was a man of God, a faithful friend, a man of integrity who was able to battle with sin, Potiphar's wife, and a man whose obedience allowed God to show him a wonderful life.

Search Your Heart, Thank God, and Pray

Have you ever committed adultery? Are you equipped with God's Word like Joseph was to battle the temptations of adultery? Read Joshua 1:8–9 and 1 John 1:9. If the sin of adultery has been an issue in your life, the best thing to do is to confess it to God first because He is more offended than your mate, and then confess it to your mate. Read 2 Corinthians 4:18. Confession is actually good for the soul!

Day 10

Deborah
The Nurse of Jacob's Mother Rebekah

Genesis 35:8, 24:59

There are two Deborahs in the Bible: Deborah the judge and prophetess (Judges 4:4), and this Deborah, who was Rebekah's nurse, who was Isaac's wife and Jacob's mother. When Rebekah decided to go and be Isaac's wife, she was sent away with Abraham's servant, his men, and her personal nurse (Gen 24:59). Her father, Nahor, gave Deborah to Rebekah. In those days, nurses were given to children to be breastfed, as it happened to Moses (Ex 2:7). But it was also a custom of those days to give a female slave to the bride, and they were also called nurses. In *Manners and Customs of the Bible,* by James M. Freedman, a nurse is described as follows: "In an Eastern family the nurse is a very important personage. She is esteemed almost as a parent; and accompanying the bride to her new home. She becomes the adviser, the assistant, and the friend of the bride. To the nurse, as to a mother, the bride will confide her greatest secrets."

Rebekah was very young when she went out to marry Isaac; someone had to take care of her. Deborah's age is not mentioned anywhere in the Bible, but we know she was with Rebekah from the time Rebekah was sent to be Isaac's wife. She was the woman to help and guide Rebekah after her sons were born. Remember that Rebekah had her twins, Jacob and Esau, after she had been married to Isaac for twenty years, which means Deborah, was like a granny/nanny to Jacob. Deborah's death is recorded before Jacob's wife Rachel had her second and last child, Benjamin (Gen 35:8, Gen 35:16–17).

Deborah was around for many years. She was a faithful maid and an important person in the household because of where she was buried. "She was buried below Bethel under the oak tree" (Gen 35:8). The place she was buried was named *Allon-bacuth,* which means "oak of weeping." Edith Deen wrote in her book *All of the Woman of the Bible,* "Humble though Deborah's role was, her place in the life of Jacob's family is not to be underestimated, for not only is her name recorded but she was buried in a place of holy association." [2] The oak tree where she was buried is believed to be the same tree mentioned in 1 Samuel 10:3 where Samuel gave instruction to Saul to go to be the first king of Israel (1 Sam 17–24).

There is no record of Deborah having a family of her own or doing anything wrong. She lived to nurture Rebekah's life and the lives of Rebekah's sons, Jacob and Esau. We all have had a person who aids us when we need it, hears us when we need to talk, or gives us advice when we need it. It could be a neighbor, our mother or sister, or just a special faithful friend. When we have the support of one of these people, it makes a world of difference in our lives. Deborah was called to serve Rebekah all her life. We are also called to serve one way or another; Jesus was our first example of service and the One who encourages us to serve (John 12:26).

Search Your Heart, Thank God, and Pray

Is there someone you are serving right now who doesn't appreciate you? Do you have a person like Deborah who you can trust with your personal life and thoughts? Read John 12:26. Pray for joy when you serve, especially if the person you are serving does not deserve it or is not someone you want to serve. (For more encouragement on service, read the day based on "Mary, a Woman in Rome.")

1 M. James Freeman, Manners *and Customs of the Bible (*New Kensington: Whitaker House, 1996), 31

2 Deen, *All the Women of the Bible* (New York: HarperCollins, 1983), 260.

Day 11

Judith, Basemath I, Basemath II Wives of Jacob's Brother Esau

Genesis 26:34–35, 28:9, 36:2–19

Judith (also known as Oholibamah) and Basemath #1 (also known as Adah) were wives of Esau, Jacob and Rebekah's other son. Like Jacob, Esau practiced polygamy. "And when Esau was forty years old he married Judith the daughter of Beeri the Hittite, and Basemath the daughter of Elon the Hittite; and they brought grief to Isaac and Rebekah" (Gen 26:34–35). These were heathen women who proved that Esau was not walking with the real God—the God of his father—and that God was not in control of his life. Having these wives pushed Esau away from God and his parents. Esau married these women before he sold his birthright to Jacob for food.

Rebekah remembered the fact that Esau's wives were making her life miserable, and she used it to convince Isaac to send Jacob to her brother Laban's house. "I am tired of living because of the daughters of Heth; if Jacob takes a wife from the daughters of Heth, like these, from the daughters of the land, what good will my life be to me?" (Gen 27:46). Jacob had stolen Esau's blessing from his father already, and he was even blessed to go in his journey. "Now Esau saw that Isaac blessed Jacob and sent him away to Paddan-aram, to take to himself a wife from there, and that when he blessed him he said 'You hall not take a wife from the daughters of Canaan' (Gen 28:-13). Esau finally got the picture that the Canaanite women he had would not be accepted by Isaac.

Esau kept his other wives and tried to fix the mess he was already in by marrying another wife. This time he married Basemath II, one of the daughters of Ishmael (Gen 36:3), Abraham's other son. Ishmael was Isaac's half-brother, the son of Hagar the maid. Basemath gave Esau five sons. Esau also had a lot of children, but Esau's wives and children are not remembered for doing anything great. His roots did not flourish like his brother Jacob's. Esau's family became so big in the land of Canaan and he had so many possessions that he separated himself by taking his family and moving it away from Jacob's family (Gen 36:6–8).

Esau was also known as Edom: "So Esau lived in the hill country of Seir; Esau is Edom" (Gen 36:8). Edom was a name given to Esau before he sold his birthrights (Gen 25:30) because the food he wanted to eat was red and also because he was described as red and hairy (Gen 25:25). God promised Abraham a great nation through his son Isaac, and Esau's sons are part of it because Esau is one of the sons of Isaac. When God told Rebekah she had two nations in her womb (Gen 25:23), she could not have imagined how different her sons would be. Esau's famous brother, Jacob, is the father of the twelve tribes of Israel, but Esau also had a big, but not famous, nation (Gen 36:9–19) and all are descendants of Abraham. Esau's sin was always before him, and there are no signs of repentance on his part. When God spoke to the nation of Israel in Malachi 1:3 because of their idolatry, He said, "Yet I have loved Jacob; but I have hated Esau, and made his mountains a desolation and appointed his inheritance for the jackals of the wilderness."

In Hebrews 12:15–17, the author is writing about the direction of our lives, and he uses Esau as an example of what should not be done in the eyes of God:

> See to it that no one comes short of the grace of God; that no root of bitterness springing up causes trouble, and by it many be defiled; that there be no immoral or godless person like Esau, who sold his own birthrights for a single meal. For you know that even afterwards, when he desired

> to inherit the blessing, he was rejected, for he found no place for repentance though he sought for it with tears.

Esau married the wrong women. He made the wrong choice for his future because he "despised his birthright," and then he had to live with the consequences. He lived a life of bitterness, and even when he tried to fix his mistakes, it did not work. The women in his life did not make history for their goodness or obedience to God, and neither did Esau. Esau, along with his wives, are considered to be godless, and that is not a legacy anyone wants to carry for a lifetime into eternity.

Search Your Heart, Thank God, and Pray

Living a life of bitterness and not repenting from a life of sin was Esau's doom. Is your life full of bitterness? Read Ephesians 5:5. We all make mistakes in our lives, but today we have hope for a better life in Jesus. Esau could not come to Jesus, but we can.

Moses

"Now a man from the house of Levi went and married a daughter of Levi. The woman conceived and bore a son; and when she saw that he was beautiful, she hid him for three months. But when she could hide him no longer, she got him a wicker basket and covered it over with tar and pitch. Then she put the child into it and set it among the reeds by the bank of the Nile. His sister stood at a distance to find out what would happen to him. (Exodus 2:1–4)"

The child grew, and she [Jochebed] brought him to Pharaoh's daughter and he became her son. And she named him Moses, and said, "Because I drew him out of the water." (Exodus 2:10a)

Day 1

Jochebed
The Mother of Moses

Exodus 2:1–10, 6:20, Numbers 26:59, Hebrews 11:23

Jochebed was the wife of Amram, a man from the household of Levi. She was the sister of Amram's father, so she was Amram's aunt and wife at the same time. She was the mother of three very famous people in the Bible: Aaron, Miriam, and Moses. She is mostly known for putting her youngest son, Moses, in a basket to save his life from the hands of the pharaoh of Egypt. After Moses was born, she hid him for three months, because "she saw that he was beautiful" (Ex 2:2).

The pharaoh had ordered the midwives to kill every male child born to the Hebrew women, saying, "When you are helping the Hebrew women to give birth and see them upon the birth stool, if it is a son, then you shall put him to death; but if it is a daughter, then she shall live" (Ex 1:16). The midwives didn't listen to him. Jochebed knew that if someone found Moses in her house, he would be killed, so she decided to trust God and give Moses up by putting him in a basket in the Nile River in order to save his life. God's eyes were focused on him.

When Jochebed put Moses in the Nile River, his sister Miriam followed him to see where he would end up. He ended up as part of the household that originally wanted to kill him, Pharaoh's daughter's household. When Pharaoh's daughter saw the basket, she asked to see what was in it. It was the crying baby Moses. This baby was beautiful, and again Moses was saved because of his beauty. Moses had to have had some kind of extra-special divine beauty that created a feeling of protection in his mother and in Pharaoh's daughter as well, which ultimately saved his life. Even Hebrews 11:23 says, "By faith Moses, when he was born, was hidden for three months by his parents, because they saw he was a beautiful child; and they were not afraid of king's edict." In Acts 7:20 he is described as "lovely in the sight of God."

Jochebed's daughter Miriam followed that basket with her little brother in it. After Moses was picked up at the Nile, he was taken to Pharaoh's daughter's house. Miriam was smart enough to talk to Pharaoh's daughter and offer a nurse for the baby. And of course, the Lord reserved the job of nurse for Jochebed. Jochebed was not only taking care of her own son and nursing him, but she was also getting paid for her services as the same time. After Moses was weaned, Jochebed gave him back to God by leaving him in a household that would *not* train him to be a godly man, but would show him the suffering of God's people to whom later on he became the great deliver. It does not say how long Jochebed influenced the life of Moses, but I believe she was the one who taught him God's Word and commands while he was a boy. She had time to bond with her son and also to secretly show Moses the way he should go. The prayers of this woman I'm sure were numerous and consistent.

Jochebed has inspired many to trust the Almighty God. Here is a woman who loved her child and who had to make a sacrifice, learn to separate her feelings, emotions, and trust God to save the life of her child. Jochebed kept her secret, of being Moses' mother, until the Lord decided that Moses should know who she really was and who he really was. She gives us a lesson on letting go by challenging us to give our children to God from the heart. Jochebed's children were all used by God for His kingdom and glory. She was a woman of faith and, courage, and the legacy she left through her children will live forever.

Search Your Heart, Thank God, and Pray

Are you working on leaving godly children behind after you die? Read Deuteronomy 6:4–7. The key to a legacy of godly children is teaching them God's Word and the love of Jesus. Pray for your children, grandchildren, nieces, and nephews, and if you do not have children, pray for the children in your family church, and neighborhood. Our chidden are our future, if you do not pray for your children, who will?

Day 2

The Daughter of Pharaoh the Woman Who Saved Moses' Life

Exodus 2:5–10

The daughter of Pharaoh was the woman who saved Moses' life from the hands of her own father. Her name is never mentioned, but God used her for His glory and to benefit His people. Moses' mother trusted God to save her son from the wrath of Pharaoh by putting Moses in a basket on the Nile River and Pharaoh's daughter took him and made him a member of the royal Egyptian household. It's ironic that Pharaoh tried to get rid of him and ended up taking care of him. The Bible says, "The daughter of Pharaoh came to bathe at the Nile, with her maidens walking alongside the Nile; and she saw the basket among the reeds and sent her maid, and she brought it to her" (Ex 2:5). It was a great step of faith by Jochebed because Pharaoh's daughter could have ordered the baby killed! However, the Bible says, "When she opened it, she saw the child, and behold, the boy was crying. And she had pity" (Ex 2:6). She knew that the child was Hebrew when she saw him, but she decided to keep and adopt him anyway.

Pharaoh's daughter named the baby she found Moses because she drew him out of the water (Ex 2:10). It is noteworthy to notice that *water* played such an important role in Moses' life. For instance, he was placed in the waters of the Nile and was saved from death. He received his name which also was tied to water (Ex 2:10). The first plague with which the Lord struck the Egyptians was turning the waters of the Nile into blood, the same river from which Moses was rescued. God used Moses to open the Red Sea to have his people walk to freedom (Ex 14:1–22). After God delivered them from Egypt (Ex 15:22–27), God used Moses to provide water for the people when they complained that the water was bitter in the wilderness of Shur. God used Moses to provide water for the people when there was no water to be found in Rephidim (Ex 17:1–7). Water also played a part in Moses' great sin, causing him to lose the privilege of crossing over into the Promised Land (Num. 20:1–13):

> Then Moses and Aaron came in from the presence of the assembly to the doorway of the tent of meeting, and fell on their faces. Then the glory of the Lord appeared to them; and the Lord spoke to Moses saying, "Take the rod; and you and your brother Aaron assemble the congregation and *speak* to the rock before their eyes, that it may yield its water.

But Moses did not obey God's command. Instead, he "lifted up his hand and *struck* the rock twice with his rod; and water came forth abundantly." The Lord does not accept any form of sin, and He had to discipline Moses for his sin of disobedience. God did not allow Moses to enter the promised land but the Lord, in His love for Moses, allowed him to at least see the land from a distance (Deut 34:1–12). He allowed Moses to go to a place where he could see it all! God said to him, "This is the land which I swore to Abraham, Isaac, and Jacob, saying, I will give it to your descendants; I have let you see it with your eyes, but you shall not go over there." Water also played a prominent role in our Lord Jesus' ministry. He walked on water, He turned water into wine, and He tells us "unless one is born of water and the Spirit, he cannot enter into the Kingdom of God" (John 3:5). He also gives us the water of life because He is our well of living water.

The daughter of Pharaoh had the privilege of naming Moses with a very symbolic name and she also had the privilege of bringing up the man who knew God personally. "The Lord used to speak to Moses face to face, just as a man speaks to his friend" (Ex 33:11a). Her personal life was not exposed in the Bible; the only thing we know is that she made a difference in the life of God's people by saving Moses, and she was a vessel used by God to achieve His purpose. **Moses, a Hebrew child, was given into Pharaohs' house by his mother, and was adopted by the enemy.** The daughter of Pharaoh adopted Moses into her heart, her life, her household, her beliefs and customs, only to later lose him to the heritage he had when he was born.

Search Your Heart, Thank God, and Pray

Like Pharaoh's daughter had compassion on the Hebrew baby Moses, do you have enough compassion to share Jesus with those who do not know Him so they might be saved? There are a lot of homeless children in the world. Have you ever thought of adopting a child? Read John 14:6. If you do not have a burden for the lost, ask the Lord to grant you that love. It was that love that cost Jesus His life.

Day 3

Miriam
Moses' Sister and Prophetess

Exodus 2:6–7, 15:20–21, Numbers 12:1–15, 20:1, 26:59,
Deuteronomy 24:9, 1 Chronicles 6:3, Micah 6:4

Miriam was the daughter of Jochebed and Amram and the sister of Moses and Aaron. She was the little girl who followed her brother Moses while he was in the waters of the Nile River. She was clever and she talked Pharaoh's daughter into getting a nurse for Moses and facilitated Jochebed being able to breastfeed and take care of her own son, Moses, until he was weaned. When Pharaoh's daughter decided to keep Moses, Miriam's suggestion to her was, "Shall I go and call a nurse for you from the Hebrew women, that she may nurse the child for you?" (Ex 2:7). Pharaoh's daughter did not even think about it twice and said yes. "So the girl went and called the child's mother. 'Take this child away and nurse him for me' said Pharaoh's daughter, 'and I shall give you your wages'" (Ex 2:9). By Miriam acting as the big sister that she was, and by the grace of God Moses' life was saved. Moses' mother's trust in God, the compassion of a princess, and the smarts of a sister, (and later in his life his wife, Ex 4:24–26) protected Moses so that he was able to carry on God's plan for his life. There were women all around Moses' life!

There are no records in the Bible of whether Miriam ever got married or had children. From what we know, she was a single woman dedicated to

God. She was a prophetess (Ex 15:20) who led the women into songs and dancing to celebrate the defeat of Egypt and their Pharaoh by God's power. She was part of the leadership team that was taking the people of God to the Promised Land. Her life was not a bed of roses! Miriam got jealous of Moses' relationship with God (Num 12:1–16). She started gossip among the people about Moses because he had married a Cushite woman. God did not like the attitude of Miriam and her brother Aaron toward Moses, so He summoned them. He ordered the three of them to come out of the tent of meeting and He "came down in a pillar of cloud and stood at the doorway of the tent." He made these two understand how special Moses was to Him. He spoke to prophets through visions and dreams, but to Moses He spoke "face to face" even allowing Moses to see His form (Num 12:8). God was so righteously angry that he struck Miriam with leprosy, which might indicate that she was the one who started the gossip toward Moses. Moses and Aaron begged the Lord not to let their sister stay a leper. The Lord had mercy on her, but she had to stay leprous for seven days. Everyone knew what she did because lepers had to be separated from everybody else, and they couldn't continue their journey until she was free from her disease (Num 12:15).

I think that because God made Miriam sick, she understood how much she hurt God with her lack of respect toward her brother and her lack of reverence toward God's choice of a wife for Moses. God showed her and everyone around Miriam that He is determined to make people understand the importance of obeying His laws. Later on, Moses was able to use his sister's experience to encourage God's people to obey the Levitical priests' teachings. He said, "Remember what the Lord your God did to Miriam on the way as you came out of Egypt" (Deut 24:9).

Some sins stay between God and the sinner, but Miriam's sin was known by all, and everyone saw the results. She sinned, she received judgment, she repented, and the Lord forgave her, but she still had to face the consequences of her sin. Miriam died in the wilderness, and never saw the Promised Land, and she was buried in the wilderness in a place called Kadesh. God uses everyone who loves Him and follows Him. You probably have a person in your life who you think God uses more than you. The danger comes when you desire that person's life, but that is not the one God has intended for you to have. Miriam was jealous of her brother's relationship with God even though God used her as well (Num 12:2). He is the God of all, the God of mercy and He will use you according to the abilities and gifts he bestowed upon you. He took Miriam's life very personally, the same way He takes yours and all of us who love and serve Him. Miriam was able to experience God's love, mercy, guidance, judgment, and wrath. He showed her that He is the great "I Am."

Search Your Heart, Thank God, and Pray

Would you like to have someone else's Christian life? Why? Your walk with God will be unique because He made you unique. Read Jeremiah 29:11. Thank God for loving everyone, and pray for contentment.

Day 4

Zipporah Moses' Wife

Exodus 2:16–22, 4:18–26, 18:1–6

Zipporah was a shepherd girl, a woman of another faith who became the wife of one of the greatest men of the Bible, Moses. Even though she married a biblical giant, she never became a very famous woman. She was a Midianite from a tribe that derived from one of Keturah's son, Midian (Gen 25: 1-3). Her father Jethro, who was priest in Midian, and he gave her to Moses after Moses decided he was going to stay and live by Jethro. Jethro had seven daughters, and Zipporah was one of them. She was the woman God put in Moses life' after he became a fugitive and lost his identity and fame in Egypt. She was the part of the peace God gave Moses in a new land while He prepared Moses' heart for the work He had for him to do. Zipporah was the refuge Moses needed to forget his suffering in the desert. She gave Moses two sons, Gershom and Eliezer.

Zipporah was a brave woman who saved Moses' life from the wrath of God. God was angry with Moses and was ready to take Moses' life because he did not perform the command of circumcision on his son (Ex 4:24–26), so Zipporah did it herself. She shows us that a woman can do anything when the ones she loves are in danger. She was part of another culture and another belief system, but the simple thought of losing the one she loved made her go into action because she knew the God of Moses was for real. God was not kidding and she knew God would keep His word.

Maybe Moses did not obey God's command because of her background, or maybe he had forgotten where he came from and what he believed to be true. After all, Moses was born from a godly woman but raised by a pagan woman. Perhaps he allowed his upbringing to affect his judgment. Some of the things we are raised to believe stick with us for the rest of our lives, and Zipporah and Moses were no different than you and me.

She "took a flint and cut off her son's foreskin and threw it at Moses' feet, and she said, "You are indeed a bridegroom of blood to me." Because of her actions, the Lord let Moses live because the Lord "sought to put him to death" (Ex 4:24). Moses was now reconciled to God. No matter what our position in God's eyes may be, we still have to obey Him in everything. There are no jobs big enough in God's kingdom for Him to accept disobedience. Regardless of whether she followed the God of Israel, or not, she allowed Moses to accomplish his purpose in God's plan.

Moses' wife endured separation from Moses when he went to save God's people from the hands of the pharaoh of Egypt. We do not know exactly why they separated; the Bible doesn't say why. She started the journey to Egypt with Moses, but somehow she did not finish it (Ex 4:20–21). Perhaps Moses wanted to keep her safe and sent her home to protect her; after all he was a fugitive! Maybe part of her unbelief was too much for Moses and he decided to send her back to her father until God's work was done; or maybe she simply decided to leave and not be part of the adventure God had put before Moses. Regardless of the reasons, Moses and his wife came back together. "And Jethro, Moses' father-in-law, took Moses' wife Zipporah, after he had sent her away, and her two sons" (Ex 18:2) and brought them to Moses. Exodus 18:7 tells us that Jethro went to "the wilderness" where Moses "was camped, at the mount of God. And he sent word to Moses, 'I, your father-in-law Jethro, am coming to you with your wife and her two sons with her'" (Ex 18:6).

It is interesting to note that Jethro gave Moses his wife back after he recognized the Moses' God was the true God, and Zipporah did not complain! Perhaps she recognized the God of Moses as the true God! The Bible explains that after this reunion, Jethro made sure Moses knew that he recognized Moses' God as the true God and validated His words, "The Lord is greater than all the gods" (Ex 18:11). Jethro knew what God did by using Moses to save His people, and he believed. Jethro even became an adviser to Moses, giving him wisdom on how to handle his new responsibility as the leader of God's people (Ex 18:14–27).

Zipporah was the woman who filled the loneliness in Moses' heart when he needed it. She was the only woman Moses married and the only one to give him children. There is no evidence she left a biblical legacy for her children, but there is also no evidence that she did the opposite. The one thing we know is that her children were not the ones Moses trusted with God's people; it was Joshua.

Search Your Heart, Thank God, and Pray

Like Zipporah, are you brave enough to stand tough and follow God's commands even if you don't understand why? Are you willing to miss the blessing of seeing God work, like Zipporah did by not being around during God's great rescue of His people? Do you do God's will with a bad attitude? Read 2 Timothy 1:7.

Day 5

Elisheba
Moses' Sister-in-law

Exodus 6:23

Elisheba was the wife of Aaron, Moses' brother. She was the daughter of Amminadab, who is part of the genealogy of King David (Ruth 4:19–20, 1 Chron 2:10), and the sister of Nahshon, who was the leader of the army of the sons of Judah (Num 2:3, 1:7). Elisheba had the honor of being the mother of the first order of priests in the Bible (Lev 9). Her son's names were Nadab, Abihu, Eleazar, and Ithamar, and they had the honor to minister in the holy temple of God. There are no biblical records that she had daughters.

Even though God chose Elisheba's sons for His service at the holy tent, two of her sons, Nadab and Abihu, decided to disobey God:

> Now Nadab and Abihu, the sons of Aaron, took their respective fire pans, and after putting fire in them, placed incense on it and offered strange fire before the Lord, which He had not commanded them. And the fire came out from the presence of the Lord and consumed them, and they died before the Lord. (Lev. 10:1–3)

They played with God's holiness, and God was offended. They paid with their lives. Moses comforted his brother Aaron by telling him what the

Lord had to say about the whole episode. The Lord said, "By those who come near Me I will be treated as Holy, and before all the people I will be honored" (Lev 10:3). The blessing also is shown by God because in His mercy, He did not allow these two to have children before they were killed (1 Chron 24:2). There were no sons to mourn them, not even Aaron and his sons were allowed to mourn.

I can imagine Elisheba's heart; not only did she lose two sons, but it was publically known to be a result of disobedience. These two sons were under the influence of some kind of alcohol. After this incident, the Lord spoke to Aaron, saying, "Do not drink wine or strong drink you nor your sons with you, when you come into the tent of meetings, so that you may not die-it is a perpetual statute throughout your generations" (Lev 10:9). Elisheba, as well as Aaron and his sons, learned of the seriousness of God. She knew the Lord God is a God of order who does not allow disobedience and requires respect from everybody for everything.

Elisheba left a legacy to God's people with her other two sons who were obedient to God. There are many other men named Eleazar in the Bible, but Elisheba's son Eleazar is well known today because he became leader of the Leviticus priests, "And Eleazar the son of Aaron the priest was the chief of the leaders of Levi, and had the oversight of those who perform the duties of the sanctuary" (Num 3:32).

Elisheba was probably very proud of the sons she had left because they did what was right before the Lord, after she suffered the embarrassment of the death of the first two. It is very unusual for God to kill two sons at the same time for the same crime. When God decided to take Aaron home and he died, it was Eleazar who God choose to replace Aaron (Num 20:25–29). In Numbers 25:1–13 a priest, one of Eleazar's grandsons, Phinehas, saved the nation of Israel from God's wrath:

> Phinehas the son of Eleazar, the son of Aaron the priest, has turned away my wrath from the sons of Israel in that he was jealous with My jealousy among them, so that I did not destroy the sons of Israel in My jealousy. Therefore say,

> 'Behold, I give him My covenant of peace …" (Numbers 25:11-13, you need to read chapter 25).

The Lord also honored Phinehas by including him in Psalm 106:30–31.

Her other son, Ithamar, was chosen by Moses to number the items needed for the making of the tabernacle (Ex 38:21). In 1 Chronicles 24:1–31, God allows us to see that these two sons of Elisheba became great and multiplied the Levitical lineage of priests. In these verses, we find the divisions of the descendants of Aaron through his two sons, Eleazar and Ithamar, where two descendants, one of the sons of Eleazar (Zadok) and one of the sons of Ithamar (Ahimelech), were mentioned in the service of King David (1 Chronicles 24:3).

She lived surrounded by great men of God, starting with her father and ending with her husband, Aaron, and two of her sons. Her life, character and personality, will forever be a mystery because God decided to keep it that way. The only thing we know is that she left a legacy of males who served God, who were disciplined by God, and used by God for His glory. We know today who she was because the Lord honored her by making her part of His Word by at least giving us her name.

Search Your Heart, Thank God, and Pray

Do you think Elisheba resented the fact that her two boys were dead by the hands of God? If you ever thought that God would forgive you for anything, you're right! In the name of Jesus He can! Elisheba's sons did not have Jesus. We do! Accept Him as Lord and confess any sin that keeps you captive. Read Romans 6:23.

Day 6

Cozbi
Idolater Executed by Phinehas—Witnessed by Moses

Numbers 25:15 (also read Num. 25:1–18, 31:1–20)

Cozbi was a Midianites, the daughter of Zur, the head of a family who worshipped the god Baal. She was the daughter of the leader of Media, which made her a princess (Num 25:15). She became an example to the other idol worshipers because she was killed by "Phinehas the son of Eleazar, the son of Aaron the priest" (Num 25:7). The idol worshipers of Baal of Peor decided to have a worship party for their god where they would make sacrifices and bow to worship before Baal. The Lord God became very angry because His people "joined themselves to Baal of Peor" (Num 25:3). And the Lord said to Moses, "Take all the leaders of the people and execute them in broad daylight before the Lord, so that the fierce anger of the Lord may turn away from Israel" (Num 25:4). Moses ordered the Israelites who didn't follow after Baal to do as the Lord said. God despises sin because He is *holy*! Cozbi was among the idolaters who needed to be destroyed.

The real sons of Israel who followed after God were gathered together before the tent of meeting, crying, and "one of the sons of Israel brought in a relative a Midianite woman, in the sight of Moses and all the congregation of the sons of Israel" (Num 25:6). Phinehas hated sin with a passion:

> When Phinehas the son of Eleazar, the son of Aaron the priest, saw it, he arose from the congregation, and took a spear in his hand; and he went after the man of Israel into the tent, and pierced both of them through, the man of Israel and the woman, through the body. So the plague on the sons of Israel was checked. After those who died by the plague were 24,000 (Num 25:7–9).

Because of this action, the Lord did not destroy the people of Israel!

> Then the Lord spoke to Moses saying, Phinehas the son of Eleazar, the son of Aaron the priest, has turned away My wrath from the sons of Israel, in that he was jealous with My jealousy among them, so that I did not destroy the sons of Israel in My jealousy. Therefore say, Behold, I give him My covenant of peace; and it shall be for him and his descendants after him, a covenant of a perpetual priesthood, because he was jealous for his God, and made atonement for the sons of Israel (Num 25:10–13).

The man killed by Phinehas was Zimri the son of Salu, a leader of a father's household among the Simeonites (v 14).

The death of Cozbi and her companion had a purpose in God's plan. God hates idolatry and sin. He ordered to have all the false idol worshipers killed, but the Lord saw something very special in the motive of Phinehas' reason to kill. Phinehas was feeling the same feeling of hatred toward the sin being committed before his eyes as God did, and because of it he helped save the lives of those who continued to follow God. The courage of Phinehas to serve the Lord with faith, love, and devotion was recorded in Psalm 106:30–31: "But Phinehas stood up and intervened, and the plague was checked. This was credited to him as righteousness for endless generations to come" (NIV). What a way to be remembered! Cozbi stands as a symbol of sin and dedication to evil. She was part of multitude of sinners—twenty-four thousand. The legacy in her case is only her name and her sin.

Search Your Heart, Thank God, and Pray

Sin can be a joint effort. Do you know of anyone who is pulling you into sinning? Ask the Lord to give you wisdom to figure out who or what is leading you into sin. Read Malachi 4:1–3.

Samuel

The Lord said to Samuel, "Behold,
I am about to do a thing in
Israel at which both ears of everyone
who hears it will tingle"
(1 Samuel 3:1-11--NASB).

Day 1

Hannah
Wife of Elkanah and Samuel's Mother

1 Samuel 1:1–28, 2:1–10, 19–21

Hannah was one of the two wives of Elkanah, and out of his two wives, he loved Hannah the most. He made his preference very clear between his two wives. Every year the faithful Elkanah would take his family to the house of the Lord to bring his offerings and sacrifices, and the Word of God says, "When the day came that Elkanah sacrificed, he would give portions to Peninnah his wife and to all her sons and her daughters; but to Hannah he would give a double portion, for he loved Hannah, but the Lord had closed her womb" (1 Sam 1:4–5). By Elkanah giving Hannah more he broke the law (Deut 21:15–16). The unloved woman and her children were supposed to receive more.

Hannah's heart was sorrowful because she was barren, and Elkanah's other wife, who mocked Hannah for it, made the situation worse. Hannah was so controlled by her desire to have a son that she would cry to the Lord, and sometimes she would not even eat. Her loving husband was so sorry to see the one he loved hurt that he asked her, "Hannah, why do you weep and why do you not eat and why is your heart sad? Am I not better to you than ten sons?" (1 Sam 1:8). He loved her so much that he tried to be her all in all to make her happy, but Hannah's desire for a child was too strong for him to fulfill.

Hannah resolved to stop crying and feeling sorry for herself. She picked herself up ate and drank, and went to the temple to pray to God, ". . . and she greatly distressed, prayed to the Lord and wept bitterly" (1 Sam 1:10). I can imagine the pain of Elkanah, seeing his wife in so much pain and not being able to do a thing about it. And Hannah became so desperate for a child that she made a vow to God. She said, "O Lord of hosts, if Thou wilt indeed look on the affliction of Thy maidservant and remember me, and not forget Thy maidservant, but wilt give Thy maidservant a son, then I will give him to the Lord all the days of his life, and a razor shall never come on his head" (1 Sam 1:11). Her uncontrollable need to be a mother was such that she offered her son to the Lord by making a vow. Vows were serious business. According to *Manners and Customs of the Bible:* [1]

> Vows usually involved free-will offerings to be given to God as recognition of his goodness, either subsequent to the reception of blessings desired, or in anticipation of them. There was no law compelling any one to make vows, but, when once made, they came within the limit of the law, and their fulfillment became obligatory.

The son Hannah's heart was longing for was going to be dedicated to serve God, and according to the Nazarite laws, it would be for his whole life (Num 6:1–5).

When Hannah prayed for a child she prayed with so much effort that Eli, the priest who was observing her, thought she was drunk. He said to her, "How long will you make yourself drunk? Put away your wine from you" (1 Sam 1:14). Hannah made sure to explain to Eli that he was wrong. She said, "No, my lord, I am a woman oppressed in spirit; I have drunk neither wine nor strong drink, but I have poured out my soul before the Lord" (1 Sam 1:15).

I love the way she described her prayer! She poured her heart out to God in prayer! She continued her conversation with Eli to make sure that he could understand that she was a not a "worthless woman." She knew somehow that the Lord was going to answer her prayer. She knew Eli would not forget her; she knew that later on she was going to come back with her baby to offer him to God's service. After she was done with Eli, he said to her, "Go in peace, and may the God of Israel grant your petition that you have asked of Him" (1 Sam 1:17). She did not tell Eli what her request to the Lord was, yet Eli asked the Lord to grant her the request she was so desperately putting before Him. After Eli finished talking to her, Hannah "went her way and ate, and her face was no longer sad" (1 Sam 1:18b).

Hannah arose early in the morning and worshipped before the Lord and "Elkanah had relations with Hannah his wife, and the Lord remembered her" (1 Sam 1:19). Hannah went out and worshipped the Lord before the Lord answered her prayer. She finally got her act together; she realized that only God could provide the desires of her heart. Hannah was blessed by calling on the name of the Lord, and this is the reason most people know her today. Her prayers blessed the world with a man of God, Samuel. If I could write on Hannah's tombstone, I would write, "She prayed to the One she trusted."

Search Your Heart, Thank God, and Pray

Have you ever poured out your heart to God in prayer the way Hannah did? I know a godly, faithful, woman in her early sixties who prayed for a child for years, and the Lord said no to her. If you did not know that she did not have children and you asked her, "How many children do you have?" She always answered, "I was not blessed." What would you do if you prayed to the Lord for a child and He said no to you? Read Romans 14:7–8 and Psalm 100.

1 M. James Freeman, Manners *and Customs of the Bible (*New Kensington: Whitaker House, 1996), 451

Day 2

Hannah
The Mother of Samuel and a Woman of Prayer

1 Samuel 1:1–28, 2:1–10, 19–21

Hannah was the happiest woman alive when the Lord honored her by allowing her to get pregnant. Her humility in prayer was beautiful, and her desire to be a mother was pure. There is no other woman in the Bible who prayed for a child like Hannah, and there is no other woman who was barren who relinquished her child to God like Hannah. Sarah received Isaac as a promise to Abraham (Gen 15:1–21, 17:4–5, 18:1–12). Rebekah was blessed by God with Jacob so the Lord could glorify Himself with the twelve tribes of Israel (Gen 25:21). After much pain and jealousy (Gen 30:1), God blessed Rachel (Gen 30:22) with Joseph, but she lost her life after giving birth to Benjamin. Righteous Elizabeth was blessed with John the Baptist after the Lord answered Zacharias's prayers (Luke 1:29–30). But Hannah humbled herself, prayed, was specific in her prayer (1 Sam 1:11), promised her unborn child to God, and kept her word. There were no guarantees that Hannah would have another child, but she gave her **only** child to God nevertheless. Hannah was blessed with a son and "she named him Samuel, saying, 'Because I have asked him of the Lord'" (1 Sam 1:20).

After Hannah's son was born, her husband Elkanah went with his family to offer to the Lord his yearly sacrifice, but Hannah stayed behind because she wanted to bring Samuel to the house of God and leave him there like she promised God. She decided to wean him first and then give him to God so that God could enjoy Samuel's service for the rest of Samuel's life. She kept her vow, just like the Word of God said she should (Eccles 5:4–5). When Samuel was weaned (1 Sam 1:22), Hannah took him up with a sacrifice offering to the house of the Lord and she said to Eli:

> Oh, my lord! As your soul lives, my lord, I am the woman who stood here beside you, praying to the Lord. For this boy I prayed, and the Lord has given me my petition, which I asked of Him. So I have dedicated him to the Lord; as long as he lives he is dedicated to the Lord (1 Sam 1:26–28).

She gave God her most valuable possession, the desire of her heart, her child. She promised the child to God, and she kept her word. Hannah, the prayer warrior, prayed one of the most beautiful prayers of thanksgiving to the Lord ever written (1 Sam 2:1–10). She exalted God for who He is and the things He can do. Hannah beautifully expressed God's sovereignty and holiness. She knew that God is knowledgeable, has all power, and is the judge of all the living. He also answers prayer!

Hannah gave her son to the service of God, but she did not forget him. The Word of God says, "And his mother would make him a little robe and bring it to him from year to year when she would come up with her husband to offer the yearly sacrifice" (1 Sam 2:19). Because of Hannah and Elkanah's dedication to the Lord, God blessed them. Eli prayed for Hannah before (1 Sam 1:17), but now he was more specific because Hannah revealed the reason for her previous prayer. Eli saw this couple's love for the Lord, and he blessed them with another prayer by saying, "May the Lord give you children from this woman in the place of the one she dedicated to the Lord" (1 Sam 2:20).

They went home and *"**The Lord visited Hannah**; and she conceived and gave birth to three sons and two daughters. And the boy Samuel grew before the Lord"* (1 Sam 2:21). I love this verse because it says that the Lord *visited*

Hannah. I believe that every time God answers our prayers, it is as if *He personally* ***visits us*** *because God is a God of individuals.* We are special to Him. He appreciated Hannah's love, faith, and dedication to Him. I can close my eyes and imagine God visiting me, and because of Jesus, He can visit me every day! What an honor …

Hannah's life challenged my prayer life, and so did one of my former Sunday school teachers, Bryan Moses. He was one of the greatest men of God I ever met. He emphasized in class the importance of our walk with God through prayer. He asked us to compare our prayer lives to the functions of a VHS (or DVD player today). He said, "When I gave thought to my prayer time, I asked myself, am I in 'rewind' where I can see God's mercy through previously answered prayer? Or, have I lost hope in prayer by putting myself on 'stop' by not praying at all? Have I stopped to thank Him for what He has already done? Am I in 'fast-forward' mode, praying so fast that I can miss God's blessing in my life? Do I take Him for granted? Have I put my prayer life on 'still,' or on "hold" until it is convenient? Or, am I continually on 'play,' where I'm praying regardless of my circumstances? Have I 'paused' to see the needs of others when I pray so I can pray for them? Am I in 'record' where I can save God's work in my life as a constant reminder of His love for me and be thankful?" Wow! What a way to see prayer. This simple illustration changed my prayer life forever.

Hannah is one of my favorite women in the Bible because of her godly legacy; she was prayerful, thankful, faithful, committed, unselfish, and loyal to God, and He blessed her for it! God had a plan for Hannah's child. Her beloved son, Samuel, became a prophet of almighty God (1 Sam 3:1-21).

Search Your Heart, Thank God, and Pray

Comparing you prayer life to a DVD player, and ask yourself, "What mode am I in today?" Hannah's legacy is a hard act to follow but so possible. Read Matthew 6:5–15. How should you pray according to these verses? Ask the Lord to give you a heart for prayer.

Day 3

Peninnah
Second Wife of Elkanah and Samuel's Step-Mother

1 Samuel 1:7

Peninnah was one of the wives of Elkanah. She was the main cause of pain and cruelty to Elkanah's other wife, Hannah. The only thing we know about Peninnah is the fact that she lived in the same town as her husband. Peninnah is in the hall of fame of the verbally abusive people in the Bible. I believe that Elkanah took Peninnah as a wife because Hannah was not able to give him any children. Polygamy was allowed in the case of a childless first marriage (Deut 21:15–17), which would make Peninnah the second wife. This practice of having more than one woman as a wife having the same sexual rights toward the main male figure in a household is a recipe for disaster that can create a lot of misery to all involved. One of the biggest examples of this kind of grief is what happened to Abraham when he took Hagar. Another is Jacob, when he had four women in the same household.

Peninnah had the privilege of giving birth to children, but instead of being grateful to the Lord for giving her this capability, she used her blessing to hurt Hannah. She knew Hannah was the love of Elkanah's life, and she saw the pain that Elkanah experienced because his favorite wife was not happy because she wanted a child. He did not care that Hannah did not have any children because he loved her anyway. But Peninnah, in her jealousy, was watching this unconditional love she was not getting. Her anger gave her more power to hurt Hannah. Peninnah "would provoke her bitterly to irritate her, because the Lord had closed her womb. And it happened year after year, as often as she went up to the house of the Lord, she would provoke her; so she wept and would not eat" (1 Sam 1:6-7). It is interesting to know that the house of the Lord is where Peninnah harassed Hannah and is where the Lord finally answered Hannah's prayer for a child.

Can you imagine living with a woman like Peninnah every day? When we are fully aware of our shortcomings, we do not need someone constantly reminding us of them. Peninnah's jealousy and the unloving way she treated Hannah made her husband love Hannah even more.

Hannah made a vow to God that if He gave her a son, she would give him to God to serve God for the rest of his life. There are no indications that Peninnah knew of Hannah's vow. *I can imagine her face when she found out that the woman she had been verbally abusing for years because she did not have children would give up her child after finally being blessed.* If she knew about the vow, Peninnah was probably waiting with anticipation for Hannah to give up her only son so she could have preeminence as the mother of the children of Elkanah. Little did she know that God would bless Hannah beyond her dreams and give her more children (1 Sam 2:21).

Why did God place Peninnah in Hannah's life? We will never know! There is one thing I know, and that is the truth of Romans 8:28: "And we know that God causes *all* things to work together for *good* to those who love God, to those who are called according to His purpose." This is a promise for those who love God. Hannah and Elkanah both loved God. Peninnah was called to aggravate the life of Hannah so that Hannah could learn to depend on God's mercy. God became real to Hannah in a very especial way. God called Hannah to be the Samuel's mother, but He did not give Samuel to Hannah until Hannah was broken. I am not saying that God will always allow us to suffer to prepare us to serve Him, but He needs to be first in our lives in order for us to serve Him as He deserves.

Search Your Heart, Thank God, and Pray

Do you have a person who makes your life miserable and causes you pain? Read 1 Peter 5:6–7. As in Hannah's case, sometimes we are going to hurt because of someone else's sinful way of life, but God is still on the throne. We serve the same God Hannah served and He will take care of us just like He took care of her.

King David

Then Naomi took the child and laid him in her lap, and became his nurse. The neighbor women gave him a name, saying, "A son has been born to Naomi!" so they named him Obed. He is the father of Jesse, the father of David. (Ruth 4:16-17--NASB)

Day 1

Rahab
Wife of Salmon, Mother of Boaz, and King David's Great-Great-Great-Grandmother

Joshua 2:1–22, 6:17–25, Matthew 1:5, Hebrews 11:31, James 2:25

Rahab was a prostitute who lived in the city of Jericho. Her biggest claim to fame is that she was the harlot who helped hide the spies Joshua sent into the land of Jericho to study the people and the land that God had given to them.

Joshua, the successor of Moses, sent his men out as spies to see the land. They "went and came into the house of a harlot whose name was Rahab and lodged there" (Josh 2:1b). Rahab sold her body for profit and sex for hire with no discrimination to any man. Her house was a perfect place to hide since men were common visitors in her household. The authorities of the day knew Joshua's men were hiding at her house, but when Rahab was asked about them, she told a partial lie to the king's men who came looking for them. She admitted their presence in her house, but she said, "Yes, the men came to me, but I did not know where they were from. And it came about when it was time to close the gate, at dark, that the men went out; I do not know where the men went. Pursue them quickly, for you will overtake them" (Josh 2:4–5). Rahab had hidden them on the rooftop of her house, and now the pursuers left and the gates were closed behind them (Josh 2:6).

She helped them escape. "She let them down by a rope through the window, for her house was on the city wall" (Josh 2:15), but not before she made them give her a promise. She first acknowledged that she knew about the God Joshua and his men served. A woman in her profession would find out everything that was going on in the town, and it was obvious Rahab knew the men she was hiding. Rahab said to them:

> I know that the Lord has given you the land, and that the terror of you has fallen on us, and that all the inhabitants of the land have melted away before you. For we have heard how the Lord dried up the water of the Red Sea before you when you came out of Egypt ... And when we hear it, our hearts melted and no courage remained in any man any longer because of you; for the Lord your God, He is God in heaven above and on earth beneath (Josh 2:9–11).

Based on the fact that she helped them and that she knew all of these things about God, she said:

> Now therefore, please swear to me by the Lord, since I have dealt kindly with you that you also will deal kindly with my father's household, and give me a pledge of truth, and spare my father and my mother and my brothers and my sisters with all who belong to them. And deliver our lives from death (Josh 2:12–13).

She received the promise, and it was kept (Josh 2:14–21, 6:17–25).

Rahab lied to the authorities because she had faith that the God who was with Joshua would protect and save her family from being killed, and for that she is remembered in the great chapter of faith in Hebrews 11:31: "By faith Rahab the harlot did not perish along with those who were disobedient, after she had welcomed the spies in peace." She is also remembered by James (James 2:25) for the same act, but he adds more to it. He wrote "And in the same way was not Rahab the harlot also justified by works, when she received the messengers and sent them out by another way?" *In other words, Rahab's saving faith is seen in her deeds.*

There was no Savior in the days of Joshua. Rahab was declared righteous after her kindness to these men. This is really important to know because Rahab is part of the Messianic genealogy of our Lord Jesus, as recorded in Matthew 1:1–17: "And to Salmon was born Boaz by Rahab; and to Boaz was Obed by Ruth; and to Obed Jesse: and to Jesse was born David the king." Somewhere along the way, Rahab left her life of prostitution and became a wife and mother. Rahab became a righteous woman and the wife of Salmon (Matt 1:5), the sinner who saved her whole family (Josh 6:17); the helper God gave Joshua's men (Josh 2:1–14); the mother in-law of the great Ruth, a woman commended for her faith (Heb 11:31); and eventually a relative of Jesus (Matt 1:1-16). Jesus came to save that which was lost, and having Rahab, a former prostitute, in His genealogy via Joseph, his stepfather, is a great example of God's mercy for sinners.

Search Your Heart, Thank God, and Pray

Do you believe that God can make something out of anybody? Read John 10:14–16 and Psalm 51. If you know someone who is living a life of sexual sin, ask the Lord to give you the conviction to share the gospel with that person. Jesus came to die for everyone, including all the Rahab's of the world.

Day 2

Naomi Wife of Elimelech, King David's Legal Great-Great-Great-Grandmother

Ruth 1–4

Naomi is one of the most famous women of the Bible. The reason for her fame is that her son, Mahlon, married a very special woman: Ruth. The Lord used Ruth to bless Naomi. Naomi was the wife of Elimelech, a man from Bethlehem who lived in Judah. She had two sons named Mahlon and Chilion. Naomi had to be the best mother-in-law anybody could ever have. She was unselfish, godly, brave, and deeply loved by her two daughters-in-law.

There was a famine in the land of Bethlehem, so Elimelech decided to move his family to the land of Moab to provide for them. Shortly after the move, "Elimelech, Naomi's husband, died, and she was left with her two sons." The Bible does not tell us how old he was or how old Naomi was, but it does state that after Elimelech died; his two sons took Moabite women as wives: Orpah and Ruth (Ruth 1:3-4). It is possible that Elimelech did not allow the boys to have mixed marriages. The new family lived in Moab for ten years, and then Naomi's sons died as well (Ruth 1:5). Naomi experienced even more sorrow. Life had become very tough for Naomi. Not only did she have to deal with her losses but with her daughters-in-law as well. They were three widows without a male provider in their household! How was Naomi going to provide for them?

Naomi decided to go back to Bethlehem because she heard that the Lord had blessed the land with food. Naomi knew her daughters-in-law were good wives to her sons, and in a very unselfish manner, she said to them, "Go return each of you to her mother's house. May the Lord deal kindly with you as you have dealt with the dead and with me" (Ruth 1:8). The women all cried together, and then Naomi got a little more specific with them. She did not want them to sacrifice the rest of their lives knowing that she had nothing to offer to them. She said:

> Return, my daughters. Why should you go with me? Have I yet sons in my womb, that they may be your husbands? Return my daughters! Go, for I am too old to have a husband. If I said I have hope, if I should even have a husband tonight and also bear sons, would you therefore wait until they were grown? Would you therefore refrain from marrying? No, my daughters; for it is harder for me than for you, for the hand of the Lord has gone forth against me (Ruth 1:11–13).

Orpah felt the same feelings of hopelessness as Naomi and decided to go back to her house. But Naomi did not stay alone because Ruth did not abandon her. Naomi tried to convince Ruth to leave like Orpah, but Ruth did not. Rather, she made Naomi a great promise. Ruth said:

> Do not urge me to leave you or turn back from following you; for where you go, I will go, and where you lodge, I will lodge. Your people shall be my people, and your God, my God. Where you die, I will die, and there I will be buried. Thus may the Lord do to me, and worse, if anything but death parts you and me (Ruth 1:16–17).

These verses contain one of the most beautiful expressions of commitment written in God's word. I liked them so much that I used them as part of my marriage vows. I love these two verses because they show Ruth's determination to accept whatever the Lord had for Naomi's future as her own, for better or for worse.

Naomi's godly example to Ruth had to be very powerful and special indeed. Her life was honored by the commitment of Ruth to follow her and her God. Naomi blamed God for causing her grief, but He also caused joy for her through Ruth. Naomi had no daughter, but the Lord provided one for her in Ruth.

Search Your Heart, Thank God, and Pray

Are you a mother-in-law? Do you accept the mate the Lord provided for your son or daughter? Naomi accepted the wives chosen by her sons, and God blessed her for it (Phil 4:6–7). Pray for acceptance and the peace of God and thank Him for anyone who loves you unconditionally.

Day 3

Naomi
Wife of Elimelech- King David's Legal Great-great-great-grandmother

Ruth 1–4

Elimelech's decision to take his family to the land of Moab changed the life of his family. It was a good move for Naomi's future because in Moab is where she found Ruth, and the Lord used Ruth to bless her with a beautiful new beginning. Now Naomi had Ruth as a companion, someone she could rely on and go through life with. Naomi and Ruth decided to go back together to Bethlehem, and there we can see that Naomi accepted the fact that God allowed her to lose her husband and sons. When she entered the city, the women looked at Naomi and questioned, "Is this Naomi?" (Ruth 1:19). Naomi was so hurt with sorrow and bitterness that she told the women:

> Do not call me Naomi; call me Mara, for the Almighty has dealt very bitterly with me. I went out full, but the Lord has brought me back empty. Why do you call me Naomi, since the Lord has witnessed against me and the almighty has afflicted me? (Ruth 1:20–21).

Naomi was so unhappy that she wanted her name to resemble her pain. She called herself Mara, which means bitter. Ruth showed a lot of respect for Naomi. Ruth knew Naomi was in charge of their lives. Even when Ruth knew she had to do something to keep her and Naomi alive, she asked Naomi's permission. She said to Naomi, "Please let me go to the field and glean among the ears of grain after one in whose sight I may find favor" (Ruth 2:2). Naomi said to her, "Go, my daughter." Naomi's leadership helped Ruth provide for both of them. There was a law passed in those days commanded by God that said to the owners of fields, "When you reap the harvest of your land, moreover, you shall not reap to the very corners of your fields, nor gather the gleaning of your harvest; you are to leave them for the needy and alien. I am the Lord your God" (Lev 23:22). This is the law that allowed Ruth to support Naomi. Even though Elimelech was dead, his shadow still helped Naomi because the field Ruth ended up gleaning belonged to Boaz, a relative of Elimelech a "man of great wealth" (Ruth 2:1).

God allows things to happen in our lives to bless us, His creation, with His provision and mercy. When I lived in Miami, at around five o'clock every morning when I got up and turned the light on in my bathroom, a gecko always came to the window. I called him my lizard friend. The lizard stayed motionless until the bugs, attracted to the light, would come to the windows, and then he would catch them and eat them. This was the way the Lord fed my lizard friend in the morning. I know that if I changed the time I got up, the Lord was still going to provide for the lizard regardless of my morning schedule to get up and turn the light so that the lizard could eat. I started to feel responsible for the lizard! Well, the lizard decided to invite another gecko friend to the feast, and then I had two lizard friends! These two geckos remind me of Ruth and Naomi because one came to eat and then provided for the other one. These geckos also remind me of the fact that God can provide for me every day, just like He provided for those geckos. I should never take the Lord's provision for granted. My family moved so my husband could go to seminary, and the geckoes were a constant reminder to me to wait for God's daily provision for our family. God was in charge of providing for the geckoes I left in Miami, not me. In the same way, He provides for me and provided for Ruth and Naomi.

God blessed Naomi through Ruth. As Ruth gleaned in the field of Boaz, the Lord used him to be the redeemer for both of these women. A great story developed between Ruth and Boaz as Naomi counseled Ruth on how to get Boaz to marry her. Naomi wanted to make sure Ruth was taken care of and she knew Boaz was the chance Ruth had to get married. The story ends up in a marriage between Ruth and Boaz, with a great new future for Ruth.

Naomi's love for Ruth was demonstrated when she helped Ruth get married. Solomon said, referring to God, that "He has made everything appropriate in its time" (Eccles 3:11a), and this is what happened to Naomi; God blessed her in His time. The new God-given happiness Naomi found probably did not make her forget her husband and sons, but Ruth's love was sufficient for her. Ruth loved her so much that Naomi's friends said she was "better than seven sons" (Ruth 4:15). Seven sons were considered a treasure and a blessing from God in those days. Read the next two days to find out how Naomi became the legal great-great-grandmother of King David.

Search Your Heart, Thank God, and Pray

Can you see the hands of God in your everyday life? Read Philippians 4:19. God never abandons His children. Stop and thank Him for always providing for you what you need, not necessarily what you want.

Day 4

Ruth
Wife of Boaz—King David's Great-Grandmother

Ruth 1–4, Matthew 1:5

Besides the mother of the Lord Jesus, Ruth, is the most respected and adored woman of the Bible. Her story has touched the lives of millions of Christian women all over the world. Even her name has been used for generations. There are millions of women in the world named Ruth! Her dedication to love and to stand by her mother-in-law, Naomi, has been the talk of many for hundreds of years, and God continues to touch the lives of women today through her example.

Ruth was a Moabite woman who married one of Naomi's sons, Mahlon (Ruth 4:10). The Moabites were descendants of Moab, the son of the oldest daughter of Lot by an incestuous relationship (Gen 19:37). The Moabites lived East of the Dead Sea, and even though the Moabites where a product of sin (Genesis 19:30-38), the Lord gave them their own land (Num 21:13, Deut 2:9). It is good to note that in His mercy, The Lord did not give children to Ruth or Orpah while they were married to Naomi's sons. Clearly, it would have been harder for Ruth to start a new life with Naomi if she already had children. As we all know, Ruth was the faithful daughter-in-law who very unselfishly gave up her life to follow her mother-in-law, Naomi, and was blessed by God for doing so. She followed, obeyed, and honored Naomi as well as provided food for her. Ruth's actions toward Naomi were well known in the town to the point of reaching Boaz's ears. Boaz was the man God used to protect and provide for Ruth. He saw her sitting, waiting for a chance to go into the field to glean, and he asked his servant in charge of the reapers, "Whose young woman is this?" And the servant answered, "She is the young Moabite woman who returned with Naomi from the land of Moab" (Ruth 2:5–6). Ruth humbled herself and went to see if she could reap from the leftover grain in the field left behind on purpose for people like her. The servant also said that Ruth asked him for permission, "'Please let me glean and gather after the reapers among the sheaves.' Thus she came and has remained from the morning until now; she has been sitting in the house for a little while" (Ruth 2:5–7).

Boaz went and asked her not to go to another field to glean; he wanted her to glean in his field. He asked her to stay close to his maid and said:

> "I command the servants not to touch you" and told her to go and get water to drink from his servants. Ruth fell on her face, bowing to the ground and said to him "Why have I found favor in your sight that you should take notice of me, since I am a foreigner" (Ruth 2:10).

And he said:

> "All that you have done for your mother-in-law after the death of your husband has been fully reported to me. May the Lord reward your work, and your wages be full from the Lord, the God of Israel, under whose wings you have come to seek refuge." (Ruth 2:12).

Ruth started her journey with a heart that was compassionate, determined, humbled, loving, and faithful. She is an example of the fact that actions speak louder than words. That's what impressed Boaz! That is what still touches the lives of women today who read her story!

Search Your Heart, Thank God, and Pray

Do you express your love with actions and not just words? Do you know that what you do says more than what you say you are going to do? Pray that the Lord will help you to show your love to other people with actions, especially to "those of the household of the faith." Confess the lack of effort on your part to show love and compassion to others. Read John 12:26.

Day 5

Ruth
Wife of Boaz—King David's Great-Grandmother and Her Request of Redemption from Boaz

After Ruth received assurance of protection and provision from Boaz, she thanked him for both. There is no indication of Ruth's physical appearance in the Bible. The only thing we can assume is that she was young, beautiful, and that there was something special about her, perhaps the spirit of God in her, allowing Boaz to notice her. Boaz went beyond the call of duty with her. He asked her to come and eat with him at mealtime. "Come here, that you may eat of the bread and dip your piece of the bread in the vinegar" (Ruth 2:14). He became a servant to her for a minute. The Bible says, "He served her roasted grain, and she ate and was satisfied and had some left" (Ruth 2:14a). Later on she brought what she had left over to Naomi so she could also eat. These actions by Boaz remind me of Jesus' love for us, how He became a servant by giving His life for us so we could have eternal life. Boaz provided security and food to Ruth, and our Lord provided for us eternal security and became to us the Bread of Life.

Boaz commanded his servants to purposely leave bundles of wheat behind so she could glean them. Boaz's was very kind and his kindness went beyond his obligation (Ruth 2:16). When Ruth got home to Naomi, she saw that Ruth had brought home enough food to feed the two of them for "five days." When she found out who was responsible for such provision, she said, "May he be blessed of the Lord who has not withdrawn his kindness to the living and to the dead" (Ruth 2:20a). Naomi realized that God was also being kind to her dead husband Elimelech. Naomi said to Ruth, "The man is our relative, he is one of our closest relatives" (Ruth 2:20). Naomi took this seriously. She said to Ruth, "My daughter, shall I not seek security for you that it may be well with you?" (Ruth 3:1). Naomi said to Ruth:

Wash yourself therefore, and anoint yourself and put on your best clothes, and go down to the threshing floor; but do not make yourself known to the man until he has finished eating and drinking. And it shall be when he lies down, that you shall notice the place where he lies, and you shall go and uncover his feet and lie down; then he will tell you what you shall do (Ruth 3:3–4).

Ruth followed Naomi's advice and did as she was told. Boaz woke up in middle of the night, and there was a woman sleeping by his feet: Ruth. He said to her:

May you be blessed of the Lord, my daughter. You have shown your last kindness to be better than the first by not going after young men, whether poor or rich. And now, my daughter, do not fear. I will do for you whatever you ask, for all my people in the city know that you are a woman of excellence (Ruth 3:11).

What a beautiful compliment Boaz gave. He described Ruth as a woman of excellence. Boaz told her, "It is true that I am a close relative; however, there is a relative closer than I" (Ruth 3:12). He told her to wait until morning and go home and that he would redeem her if the other relative would not. He kept her visit to himself. Boaz was actually the second in line to marry Ruth because of the law that said she had to be redeemed by the nearest relative to her husband (Deut 25:5–10).

Ruth resolved in her heart to honor Naomi in her life, and a part of that was waiting for Boaz to redeem her. To me, Ruth reflected a truth my husband shared with me: "We can never just put ourselves in neutral and just be. **We are always becoming**. The question is what have we resolved to become, and are **we in fact becoming that which we have resolved?"** In other words, we should always "be becoming" something better by allowing the Spirit to fill us and guide us. Ruth was always becoming a better daughter-in-law, and she ended up getting more than she bargained for.

Search Your Heart, Thank God, and Pray

What are you becoming? Does the Holy Spirit of God rule your life? Would you humble yourself to the Lord in the way Ruth did to Boaz? Pray to the Lord to help you to resolve to become what He wants you to become.

Day 6

Ruth
Wife of Boaz—King David's Great-Grandmother

Ruth 1–4

Now Ruth was in a period of waiting. Naomi encouraged Ruth by saying to her, "Wait, my daughter, until you know how the matter turns out; for the man will not rest until he has settled it today" (Ruth 3:18). Naomi was talking about Boaz, a man to whom Naomi had entrusted her beloved Ruth. Ruth was never ashamed of going to make her request to Boaz. Ruth, in her quest to love Naomi, reminds me of the book *Horton Hatches the Egg* by Dr. Seuss. Horton is an elephant that accepted a baby-sitting job for an egg on top of a tree. He got cold, hungry, and tired and was ridiculed, but he never stopped sitting on that egg. He always said to himself, "I meant what I said, and said what I meant … an elephant is faithful 100 percent." Ruth was faithful to Naomi 100 percent. Horton and Ruth were both rewarded at the end of their faithful quest.

Boaz started the process of redeeming Ruth because all of a sudden she became an important issue in his life. He went to the gate of the town in search of the nearest relative of Ruth and found him. Boaz requested that the closest relative of Ruth sit down with him at the gate. Then "he took ten men of the elders of the city" to be witnesses for him. Boaz stated his case. "Naomi, who has come back from the land of Moab, has to sell the piece of land which belonged to our brother Elimelech. So I thought to inform you, saying, buy it before those who are sitting here, and before the elders of my people" (Ruth 4:4). The relative said yes. Boaz said, "On the day you buy the field from the hand of Naomi, you must also acquire Ruth the Moabite, the widow of the deceased, in order to raise up the name of the deceased on his inheritance" (Ruth 4:5). The closest relative changed his mind because he realized something else: if he redeemed the land, it would jeopardize his own inheritance, have children for someone else, and marry someone from another culture. He said to Boaz, "Redeem it for yourself; you may have my right of redemption, for I cannot redeem it. Now this was the custom in former times in Israel concerning the redemption and the exchange of land to confirm any matter: a man removed his sandals and gave it to the one he was dealing with; and this was the manner of attestation in Israel" (Ruth 4:7). This was like signing on the dotted line. They exchanged sandals, and Boaz became the owner of Naomi's land and Ruth (4:10). *The unselfishness of Boaz to raise children for another man was a result of Ruth dedication to Naomi and Boaz's admiration for Ruth* (2:11–12; 3:10–11).

The people were witnesses to the deal between the two men, and after the talk was over, the people who were in the court and the elders also blessed Boaz, saying:

> We are witnesses. May the Lord make the woman who is coming into your home like Rachel and Leah, both whom built the house of Israel; and may you achieve wealth. Moreover, may your house be like the house of Perez whom Tamar bore to Judah, through the offspring, which the Lord shall give you by this young woman. (Ruth 4:11–12)

Boaz made Ruth his wife, and "The Lord enabled her to conceive, and she gave birth to a son." Then "Naomi took the child and laid him in her lap, and became his nurse. And the neighboring women gave him a name, saying, 'A son has been born to Naomi!' So they called him Obed. He is the father of Jesse, the father of David" (Ruth 4:16–17). Jesus came from the lineage of David (Matt. 1:1–17).

When Naomi came back to Bethlehem, she was very sad because she had lost her husband and sons. Now Ruth had blessed Naomi with a child who would carry the name of the husband she lost. Naomi really understood when the neighboring women said to her, "Blessed is the Lord who has not left you without a redeemer today, and may his name become famous in Israel." The lives of Naomi and Boaz changed because of the faithfulness of one woman: Ruth. Ruth's wisdom is immeasurable. Not only was she able to survive, but she also helped her mother-in-law, Naomi. She humbled herself and was willing to marry an older man to save her family, and God blessed her. She loved her mother-in-law so much that she was willing to move to a foreign land and start all over again. Ruth left a legacy of wisdom by listening to Naomi, as well as dedication, determination, commitment, and love.

Search Your Heart, Thank God, and Pray

Do you think Ruth gave Naomi her son with joy? Are you committed to God 100 percent? If you want to make something of your life, give God the opportunity by trusting in Him.

Day 7

Merab
Promised to King David
But Wife of Ariel

1 Samuel 14:49, 17:25, 18:17–19, 2 Samuel 21:8

King Saul was the first king of Israel (1 Sam 9–12). He had two daughters (1 Sam 14:49), and Merab was the oldest daughter. Their mother's name was Ahinoam, and she was the mother of all five of Saul's children (1 Sam 14:49). Merab must have been a beautiful woman because her father is described as the handsomest man in all of Israel (1 Sam 9:2). Saul used Merab's beauty and promised her as wife to the man who was brave enough to kill Goliath. "And it will be that the king will enrich the man who kills him with great riches and will give him his daughter and make his father's house free in Israel" (1 Sam 17:25). David came forward and took the challenge. He went to King Saul and assured him that he would go and kill Goliath. He was a young man with a lot of courage but King Saul was afraid for David's life because David was young and had no experience in battle. David convinced Saul by telling him he had killed a lion and a bear, God had protected him, and that God would do the same with his fight with Goliath.

Saul was not convinced, but he honored the boy's courage and said "go and the Lord be with you" (1 Sam 17:37). Saul took extra precautions: "Saul dressed David with his garments and placed a bronze helmet on his head, and clothed him with armor." Well, it was a bad idea because poor David could not even walk with all the stuff he had on. He simply had to go without the armor of men and put on the armor of God. David took with him "five smooth stones from the brook, and put them in the shepherd's bag, which he had, even in his pouch, and his sling was in his hand; and he approached the Philistine" (1 Sam 17:40). Every time I read this, I can imagine Saul getting ready for David's funeral! Saul probably did not think that David would come back from his fight with Goliath. I can imagine Saul's surprise when he found out that David finished the job by cutting of Goliath's head with Goliath's own sword!

After David killed Goliath, Saul held back Merab from David. Saul became very jealous of David's success. Saul decided that David should go out and fight another battle and then he could have Merab. He wanted David to die. David accepted the new challenge. Merab missed out on the glory of being married to the man of the hour, the catch of the day, the one who was able to do what all others could not—kill Goliath—because Saul did not keep his word. She was given to "Adriel the Meholathite for a wife." Merab had five sons with Adriel. Later on her five sons were hanged together with the sons of Rizpah, a concubine of Saul, by the Gibeonites (2 Sam 21:1–14).

It was probably good for her to be married to Adriel because that way her father couldn't play the game again of offering her to someone else. There is no indication of Merab's love for David. She was a prize to be won by the bravest of the city; it didn't matter who he was. This is one of the women in the Bible that you wish you were there to see her life evolve and console her when necessary. She was made famous only because David, king of Israel, was almost her husband and because her father, King Saul, didn't keep a promise he made. Unlike Saul, we have a heavenly Father who is known for keeping His promises to all His children.

Search Your Heart, Thank God, and Pray

Are you a person who keeps your word? Have you been cheated of something you thought you deserved? Have you ever overcome a trial in your life that you thought was too much for you to handle? The Lord is perfect, and He is the only one who always keeps His word. David was sure of the power of God, and David trusted Him. Read what David's Son wrote about trusting God on Proverbs 3:1-4.

Day 8

Michal

King David's First Wife and Daughter of King Saul

1 Samuel 14:49, 18:20–29, 19:11–17, 25:44; 2 Samuel 3:13–16, 6:16–23; 1 Chronicles 15:29

Michal was the first wife of David, the youngest daughter of King Saul. When Saul found out his daughter Michal loved David, he was happy. He tried to use her to kill David. Because of what happened with Merab, David probably thought he was not worthy of marrying the king's daughter. When David found out by Saul's servants that Michal was in love with him, he said: "Is it trivial in your sight to become the king's son-in-law, since I am a poor man and lightly esteemed?" Saul had a plan to get David killed again, so he told his servants to tell David, "The king does not desire any dowry except a hundred foreskins of the Philistines, to take vengeance on the king's enemies."

The proposal made David happy. The Bible says, "It pleased David to become the king's son-in-law." This doesn't necessarily mean David loved Michal, but like Saul told David, "For a second time you may be my son-in-law today." It was a challenge for the mighty David, killer of Goliath. The next day David went out and killed two hundred of the Philistines and sent the foreskins to the king. He did twice the requirement of Saul. Now there was no way out for Saul. He had to keep his promise. Michal became David's wife. She was given a very expensive and painful dowry! ". . . Saul saw and knew that the Lord was with David, and that Michal, Saul's daughter, loved him" (1 Samuel 19:28-29). Saul was afraid of David. In Saul's eyes, David was a strong threat to his kingdom. Not only did David have Michal's love, and the love and friendship of Saul's son Jonathan, but most importantly, he had the unconditional love of God.

Saul's hate for David became so strong that Michal had to save David's life. Saul was so determined to kill David that he sent his messengers to his home to kill him. Michal knew her father was going to send killers to her house, so "Michal let David down through a window, and he went out and fled and escaped." Michal "took the household idol and laid it on the bed, and put a quilt of goats' hair at its head, and covered it with clothes." When they came to get David, he was long gone. When Saul's men came to get David, Michal lied and said, "He is sick." So Saul sent messengers again asking them to "bring him up to me on his bed, that I may put him to death." The messengers returned to Saul in shame, because Michal deceived them with another lie. Saul forgot that Michal's loyalty was for David, and he was really angry. When he questioned her, she blamed David and said to Saul, "He said to me, 'Let me go! Why should I put you to death?" (1 Sam 19:17). She was smart and had a lot of courage to face her father, the king; she probably loved David a lot to disobey her father.

She helped save David's life, the future king of Israel. Saul wanted to kill David but Michal's determination was strong. Her priority was no longer her father but her husband, who was in danger. After becoming the wife of the greatest man in Israel, she became the wife of the biggest fugitive her father ever pursued. She loved both her father and her husband, but she made it her business to save David. She knew that she would always have her father, but what was she going to do with a dead husband? Perhaps she hoped that David would come back and take her with him.

Search Your Heart, Thank God, and Pray

Michal protected David because it was God's will. Have you ever been abandoned by someone you love? I was abandon by my earthly father but not by God, my Father in heaven. God will be with us no matter where we go (Joshua 1:9). Read Matthew 28:20, Acts 18:10, and Proverbs 3:3-4.

Day 9

Michal King David's First Wife and Daughter of King Saul—Her Sin

1 Samuel 14:49, 18:20–29, 19:11–17, 25:44; 2 Samuel 3:13–16, 6:16–23; 1 Chronicles 15:29

Michal was left behind in her father Saul's household by her husband David. Michal's father's house was the best place to leave her, but not in the eyes of Saul. Saul decided to give "Michal, his daughter, David's wife to Paltiel the son of Laish, who was from Gallim" (1 Sam 25:44). This union was not legitimate because David was still alive. There are no written complaints from Michal about this incident. Meanwhile, David had established himself very well. He had a strong army, a big household, six wives (2 Sam 3:3–4), and children, but he never forgot his first wife, Michal.

While Ish-bosheth, the son of Saul, was ruler, Abner, next in command, sent messengers to David requesting to make an "arrangement to assist David to take over the kinship of the nation," including Israel and Judah. Saul's son was afraid of Abner because Abner could have delivered him into the hands of David. Abner knew that eventually they would lose the fight with David. David took advantage of the situation and sent a message back to Abner and Ish-bosheth, saying first, "Give me my wife Michal, to whom I was betrothed for a hundred foreskins of the Philistines" (2 Sam 3:13-16).

As you remember from reading the verses above, David killed two hundred men, instead of a hundred, and then circumcised them, and brought their foreskins to King Saul as payment for Michal's hand in marriage! The son of Saul did as David requested, and Michal was taken from her husband Paltiel and brought back to David.

I can never forget reading the scene where Paltiel gets separated from Michal. Paltiel is crying like a baby for his wife Michal. He loved her so much that he went out "weeping as he went" on the way to take her back to David (2 Sam 3:16). "Then Abner said to him, 'Go, return.'" Paltiel's crying was so bad that not even Abner could handle it. Even though she had a relationship with Paltiel, there were no signs of Michal's love for him. There are no records of her crying or feeling sorry for him or herself. Perhaps David loved Michal or was grateful to her for saving his life. Whatever the reason was, he went to extremes to win her to himself.

Michal made a **mistake**: "Then it happened as the ark of the Lord came into the city of David [Jerusalem] that Michal the daughter of Saul looked out of the window and saw King David leaping and dancing before the Lord; and she despised him in her heart" (2 Sam 6:16). When David came into the house, she rebuked him: "How the king of Israel distinguished himself today! He uncovered himself today in the eyes of his servants' maids as one of the foolish ones shamelessly uncovers himself" (2 Sam 6:20). David was "dancing before the Lord with all his might, and David was wearing a lined ephod." An ephod was a sleeveless priestly garment that was made of fine linen; Michal did not like the fact that David was wearing it! She preferred to see him in royal clothing worthy of the king. David explained to her that God had put him above her father and his entire house and on top of it made him king. He could celebrate before the Lord however he chose. The fact that he went out dancing the way that he did would make him "distinguished" before his maids and servants not government officials. David was happy to please those who placed him in office, the people! (2 Samuel 21-22). Right after this incident, the Bible records in 2 Samuel 6:23 that, ". . . Michal the daughter of Saul had no child to the day of her death."

Michal's heart was probably full of resentment towards David. She loved him and defended him before her father but maybe her love for David diminished to the point that she dared to challenge him when he made the decision on how he was going to worship God. Eugenia Price called Michal "David's insensitive wife," and she showed this insensitivity by criticizing David's worship methods. In her lack of wisdom and in a moment of insensitivity, Michal lost any chance she had to renew her relationship with King David.

David's and Michal separation was long and by the time David rescued her; it is probable that she loved her husband Paltiel. Maybe Michal did not forget that David did not come back to get her and she had to live with another man. Perhaps, she lost respect for him out of resentment. In her arrogance, she lost David, and she even missed the blessing of having children.

Search Your Heart, Thank God, and Pray

Have you ever been a stumbling block to someone who wants to serve the Lord? The Lord God is there for you at all times. Do not miss knowing Him. Pray that He will reveal Himself to you, so you, like David, can worship Him freely. Read Ephesians 5:15-17 and Psalm 24.

[1] Eugenia Price, The *Unique World of Women (*Grand Rapids: Zondervan, 1969), 95

Day 10

Abigail
A Wife of King David and a Woman of Wisdom

1 Samuel 25:1–44, 30:1–18; 2 Samuel 2:2, 3:3; 1 Chronicles 3:1

Abigail was one of the eight named wives of King David. She was "intelligent and beautiful in appearance" She became the wife of David after her husband Nabal died. She is mostly known for her great wisdom in the way she helped David stop the bloodshed of innocent people when he wanted to take revenge on Nabal because of Nabal's injustice to David's men. We don't know much about Abigail's life prior to meeting David. All we know is that she was from a place called Carmel.

She was married to Nabal, a man described in the Bible as "harsh and evil in his dealings." When I think of these two, I remember the movie *Beauty and the Beast*. Nabal seemed to be ugly inside as well as outside. Besides the above, he was also an alcoholic. The problem between David and Nabal started when Nabal wouldn't help David and his men. David and his men watched over the safety of Nabal's flocks and possessions for provisions, and when it was time for Nabal to be gracious to David, he refused (1 Sam 25:15, 21-22). David prepared to battle with Nabal and took four hundred men with him, ready to fight. One of Nabal's servants came to the rescue, "but one of the young men told Abigail" what David was planning to do. After the servant explained to Abigail the reason for the anger of the attackers, the servant reminded her of the fact that her husband was such ". . . a worthless man that no one can speak to him" (1 Sam 25:17). If you are married, can you imagine someone talking about your husband like that, and in this case a servant! Abigail took matters into her own hands and didn't tell her husband. She took two hundred loaves of bread, two jugs of wine, five sheep, roasted grain, one hundred clusters of raisins, and two hundred cakes of figs and loaded all these things on donkeys and went to meet David and his men. She met David and "she fell at his feet," telling him to put the blame on her and asked him to please listen to her. She said, "Please do not let my lord pay attention to this worthless [fool] man, Nabal, for as his name is, so is he" (1 Sam 25:25). With a very eloquent speech, Abigail prevented David from killing a bunch of innocent men.

Abigail was a very wise woman. During all the time she was speaking to David, she talked to him in a very humbling and honoring way. She even called him lord. Abigail credited the Lord for keeping David from killing Nabal's men. She reminded David that he "is fighting the battles of the Lord, and evil shall not be found" (1 Sam 25:28) in him. She even looked into David's future. She said to him, "And it shall come about when the Lord shall do for my lord according to all the good that He has spoken concerning you, and shall appoint you ruler over Israel." She said, "This will not cause grief or trouble heart to my lord, both by having shed blood without cause and by my lord having avenged himself" (1 Sam 25: 29). Abigail then asked David to remember her. "When the Lord shall deal well with my lord, then remember your maidservant" (1 Sam 25:30), David did remember her request.

Abigail accepted her life the way it was without complaining, but she saw a future for her with David. Not only did she save her worthless husband but she also saved herself. Abigail accomplished what she set out to do. She convinced David to forgive her worthless husband, who could have been killed, an act that shows her loyalty and commitment to the undeserving Nabal. She saved the life of innocent men, which shows her compassion; she fed David's men, which shows justice and service; and she also saved David's future reputation, which shows wisdom. She achieved something really important, David's respect and admiration.

Search Your Heart, Thank God, and Pray

Have you made a difference in someone's life lately? Like Abigail, a wife, are you honoring a man who seems worthless? Do you live with a husband who to the world seems to be worthless? Abigail was not happy serving Nabal but she did and as you will see in the next page, God honored her. Remember that you *cannot* dislike a person you are praying for! Pray for him as you serve him and God will rescue you or change that person (Jeremiah 33:3). Only God changes individuals.

Day 11

Abigail
Wife of King David—
Rescued by David

When Abigail spoke to David, she humbled herself, but she never lost her dignity before him. When it was David's turn to speak to her, he also humbled himself. He said, "Blessed be the Lord God of Israel who sent you this day to meet me, and blessed be your discernment, and blessed be you, who have kept me this day from bloodshed, and from avenging myself by my own hand." What a beautiful expression came out of David's lips! He accepted all the provisions and gifts she brought for him and he called her blessed. Because of Abigail's actions, David knew she was not an ordinary woman.

Edith Deen said, "Certainly of all the women in the Old Testament she was the wisest." She says that "all of the greatness which she predicted would come to David she attributed to the only source of Good, God himself."[1] Herbert Lockyer wrote, "She had brains as well as beauty. Her plea before David also reveals her understanding of the events of her own world." [2] Besides having brains, beauty, and wisdom, she was also a woman of courage, vision, and character. What woman in those days would go and do what she did? I really recommend you read her story so that you do not miss anything.

After she finished confronting David, he said to her, "Go up to your house in peace. See, I have listened to you and granted your request." Abigail went home to her terrible husband and did not tell him about what she had done until the next morning, because when she got home Nabal was drunk. The next day she told Nabal and "his heart died within him so that he became as a stone. And about ten days after it happened, the Lord struck Nabal, and he died." David was really happy to hear of Nabal's death because he felt that God took revenge for him but David remembered the beautiful Abigail. He sent "a proposal to Abigail, to take her as his wife." My pastor once said that with David's request Abigail became the "Petitioned and not the petitioner". Her answer to David's request is beautiful. She said to David's messengers, "Behold, your maidservant is a maid to wash the feet of my lord's servants" (1 Sam 25:41). In a matter of days from Abigail's petition to David, of remembering her, she became his wife! She considered it an honor to just wash David's feet and for her to be married to such a man was a new beginning. David, as we all know, practiced polygamy, and Abigail went to form part of David's harem. She gave David a son named Daniel (1 Chronicles 3:1 also known as Chileab in 2 Samuel 3:3), a son who didn't give David any trouble, unlike his other sons.

David went to a city named Ziklag and Abigail and Ahinoam, his wives, were with him. After being there for three days, and David had gone out of the city, the Amalekites "made a raid on Ziklag, and had overthrown Ziklag and burned it with fire." They took captive everybody, including David's two wives. David and his men came back into an empty, burned city. David and his men "wept until there was no strength in them to weep" (1 Sam 30:3-5). David was so hurt that he didn't know what to do, so he went back to his main source: God. He asked God what to do, and God answered him and told him that he would succeed in the battle with the Amalekites. "So David recovered all that the Amalekites had taken, and rescued his two wives" (2 Sam 30:18). With great longing, David wanted to save his wife and his people, and with great longing God wants to save our souls for eternal life through Christ Jesus.

Why did Abigail marry Nabal? We will never know, it was probably arranged; who she married was not a choice a woman was able to make back then and she had to accept her circumstances. She was also submissive to him, and God blessed her by making her David's wife, a man after

God's own heart (1 Kings 11:4), and the opposite of what she had in Nabal. Abigail's big challenge was to share David with other women, with his people, with his army, with his children, and more importantly with the only true God.

Search Your Heart, Thank God, and Pray

Has God taken you out of one bad situation and taken you to a better one? Like Abigail, have you trusted God and accepted the situation you find yourself in today? It is hard to endure trials but remember that all trials come to an end and often reveals God's will for our lives. Read James 1:12

1 Edith Deen, *All the Women of the Bible* (New York: HarperCollins, 1983), 101.

2 Herbert Lockyer, All *the Women of the Bible (*Grand Rapids: Zondervan Publishing House, 1995), 23

Day 12

Bathsheba
A Wife of King David

2 Samuel 11, 12:1–25; 1 Kings 1:11–31, 2:13–25; 1 Chronicles 3:5

Bathsheba, daughter of Ammiel, was the most famous wife David ever had. She was the cause of David's great sin of adultery against God. She was the daughter of Eliam and the widow of Uriah the Hittite, who was a loyal soldier to David and his kingdom. One day David decided to stay home "at the time when kings go out to battle." Instead, he sent one of his men, Joab, with his army to battle. David decided to go for a walk "on the roof top of the king's castle, and from the roof he saw a woman bathing; and the woman was very beautiful in appearance" (2 Sam 11:2-3). David liked what he saw and he planned his next step. David's temptation started like Eve's: David saw, he liked, and he allowed temptation to take its course. He did his research and what he found out he did not like. She was married, but his desire for Bathsheba became uncontrollable.

This is where David's troubles began. He found that Bathsheba was married, and even though he knew she was married, he sent for her anyway and he had intercourse with her. Could Bathsheba say *no* to the king? It probably would not have made a difference, David was the king! She "purified" herself after her encounter with David and went home (2 Sam 11:4). When Bathsheba found out that she was pregnant, she informed David right away. Now the king had to figure out how to solve this problem. David tried to get Uriah home to his wife, Bathsheba, right away. This way the child could be blamed on him. David said to him, "Go home to your house, and wash your feet." Instead he "slept at the door of the king's house with all the servants of his lord [David]." When David found out, he asked why. Uriah said:

> The ark and Israel and Judah are staying in temporary shelters, and my lord Joab and the servants of my lord are camping in the open field. Shall I then go to my house to eat and to drink and to lie with my wife? By your life and the life of your soul, I will not do this.

Uriah was a true soldier. David agreed with him and allowed him to stay there for a few days. Then David brought him into his house to eat and got him drunk, but Uriah still did not go home. So David wrote a letter to Joab and sent it with Uriah himself! It said, "Place Uriah in the front line of the fiercest battle and withdraw from him, so that he may be struck down and die" (2 Sam 11:15). Uriah was killed in the line of duty. It was the perfect crime but not in the eyes of God.

Bathsheba mourned for her Uriah, and when the time of mourning was over, "David sent and brought her to his house and she became his wife; then she bore him a son. But the things David had done were evil in the sight of the Lord" (2 Sam 11:26). God sent David a message, through the prophet Nathan, that He was not happy with his behavior. David needed to repent. Nathan told him of God's judgment against him, and finally David said, "I have sinned against the Lord." David was supposed to die for his sin, but Nathan told him, "The Lord has also taken away your sin, you shall not die." Read Psalm 51 so you can really understand David's pain because of his sin. God forgave him of his sin, and a new relationship started between them. Today we can have a reconciled relationship with God as well. If we confess our sins, believe in Jesus as Lord, and accept the fact that we are sinners, the Lord will give us eternal life. The blood of Jesus washes away all our sins, and God forgets all. A reconciled relationship with God can then begin.

God forgave David, and then He revealed to the prophet Nathan that the child David had with Bathsheba was going to die and Nathan told David. "Then the Lord struck the child that Uriah's widow bore to David, so that he was very sick" (2 Sam 12:14). Even though David prayed fasted, wept, and lay all night on the ground, seven days later the child died. After the child died, David got up, cleaned himself up, anointed himself, and went into the Lord's house to worship. He restored his relationship with God. Even the mighty David, a man after God's own heart, the chosen king, sinned. David and Bathsheba paid for their sin of adultery with the life of their son. Our God is so merciful that He gave Bathsheba a new life with David free of the sin that put them together. They had more children, including the great Solomon.

Sometimes suffering strengthens people. Bathsheba lost her first husband; committed adultery with David; lost her first child; but was blessed and forgiven by God.

Search Your Heart, Thank God, and Pray

David did all the things he thought that would change God's mind in order to save his love child with Bathsheba. But God, in His holiness, had to have David and Bathsheba face their sin and repent. David was aware of God's command of not committing adultery, and he did it anyway. If you find yourself in the same circumstance, repent and call on the God of David, my God and yours, the only God, to rescue you in Jesus' name. Read Psalm 51, 1 John 1:9, Romans 8:1

Day 13

Bathsheba
A Wife of King David and Mother of Solomon

2 Samuel 11, 12:1–25; 1 Kings 1:11–31, 2:13–25; 1 Chronicles 3:5

Bathsheba was in pain for the loss of her firstborn son. David could see her pain. "Then David comforted his wife Bathsheba, and went in to her and lay with her; and she gave birth to a son, and he named him Solomon. Now the Lord loved him" (2 Sam 12: 24). The Lord erased their sin from His memory and blessed them with a new life together and a new family, starting with their new son, Solomon. When the prophet Nathan heard of Solomon's birth, he named the child "Jedidiah for the Lord's sake," which means "beloved of the Lord." Solomon was the son God promised to David, the son who was going to build the house of the Lord (1 Chron 22:6–10). Bathsheba lived in David's household as his wife until he died. She gave David more children than all of David's other wives. She had five sons: the one who died, Solomon, Shimea, Shobab, and Nathan.

When David got very old, Bathsheba had to fight for her son Solomon's kingdom. Adonijah, one of David's sons (the oldest living son) decided he was the one to be king. He proclaimed himself king and made himself a big party. But he did not invite his brother Solomon or Nathan the prophet. Then Nathan spoke to Bathsheba and asked her to go to David and remind him of the promise he made to her of making Solomon the king. Nathan told her what to say. She went to David, bowed down to him, and said to David, "My lord, you swore to your maidservant by the Lord your God, saying, 'Surely your son Solomon shall be king after me and he shall sit on my throne'" (1 Kings 1:17). She told him that Adonijah had proclaimed himself king and all of Israel was waiting for David to approve or disapprove of Adonijah's decision (1 Kings 1:1-27).

Bathsheba went beyond the word Nathan told her to say. She was convinced that if David died and Solomon did not become the king, he would be killed. Nathan came in right after her and added more to the conversation by telling David the same story. David called upon Bathsheba, and as she stood before him, David bowed down to her. He said to her, "As the Lord lives, who has redeemed my life from all distress, surely as I vowed to you by the Lord God of Israel, saying your son Solomon shall be king after me, and he shall sit on my throne in my place'; I will indeed do so this day" (1 Kings 1:30).

This is a beautiful scene. Here is King David, who was very sick, making a big effort to bow down to his own wife (he did not do this with any other) to fulfill his promise. She returned his honor by bowing down to the ground and saying to him, "May my lord King David live forever." David proclaimed Solomon the king of Israel and Judah by having him ride David's mule, **anointing** him, blowing the royal trumpet, and having the people say, "Long live King Solomon." The coronation of Solomon made Bathsheba very happy. She was very loved and respected by her son Solomon. He made his mother very proud. Solomon even had a throne just for his mother to sit by him.

Even though David and Bathsheba's relationship started on the wrong foot, there was mutual respect in their relationship. Based on the fact that Nathan trusted her with the future of God's people, Bathsheba must have been a trustworthy, intelligent, God-fearing woman. She left a legacy with her son Solomon. David taught Solomon God's ways and encouraged him to acquire wisdom, which he did. Solomon reminded his own sons of the words that his father told him. Solomon said to them: "When I was a son to my father, tender and only son of my mother, then he taught me and said to me, 'Let your heart hold fast my words; keep my commandments and live; acquire wisdom!

Acquire understanding! Do not forget, nor turn away from the words of my mouth'" (Prov 4:3–9). Solomon had more wisdom than any other man in the world.

Search Your Heart, Thank God, and Pray
Have you ever experienced the peace of forgiveness? Have you saved a sin in your heart that you need to confess? The confession of sin to the Lord and to the person we offended usually brings peace and order to our lives, just as He did with David and Bathsheba. Read Romans 10:9; Isaiah 62:2-3

Day 14

Ahinoam
A Wife of King David and Mother of Amnon

1 Samuel 25:43, 27:3, 30:5, 18; 2 Samuel 2:2, 3:2; 1 Chronicles 3:1

Ahinoam was from Jezreel and was one of David's wives. After David married her, he used to take her with him on his journeys. Unfortunately, during one of those journeys at Ziklag, the Amalekites captured Ahinoam and Abigail, David's other wife, and David had to fight to get them back. It seems to me that after Saul gave Michal away and David ran away from Saul, David decided to keep his wives as close to him as possible.

While Michal loved David and Abigail admired him, we have no idea what Ahinoam thought of him or felt for him. Ahinoam had the honor of giving David his firstborn, Amnon. Amnon means "trustworthy," and he didn't live up to the meaning of his name because he was wicked (2 Sam 13). Amnon fell in love with his own sister, Tamar (see "Tamar, David's Daughter" for the story), and he decided he had to have her. His lust and desire for his sister was so intense that he raped her. This is the way the sin of incest entered into the family of David.

Amnon knew that according to the Mosaic laws, he could not marry his half-sister (Lev 18:11), so he decided to take her anyway. By now, David had sinned against God with Bathsheba, and his children started the fulfillment of God's judgment on David: "Thus says the Lord, 'Behold, I will raise up evil against you from your own household'" (2 Sam 12:9–12). God had mercy on David and forgave him because he had a plan for him. Unlike God, David did not have a plan for Amnon, and he did not kill him like he was supposed to according to Mosaic laws. This may be due to the fact that Amnon was David's firstborn and would be expected to inherit the throne. So David's son Absalom made sure justice was done by having Amnon killed by his servants (2 Sam 13:29).

Ahinoam is not mentioned in the story of her son's actions, and there is no mention of her having other children with David. We are led to assume that Ahinoam was devastated by the death of her son. She lost her son and the chance of becoming the mother of the future king of Israel. Even though Ahinoam was from Jezreel, there is no indication she believed in God. Ahinoam had to be special in some way in order for her to become the wife of David. As a mother, Ahinoam had to live with the fact that she was the mother of the heir to David's throne and she lost the opportunity to become the mother of the king! Her upbringing methods were probably not taken into consideration by the king. Her son's behavior probably shamed her reputation by having her live with the shame of him raping his sister. Unfortunately for Ahinoam, Ammon is her call to fame.

Proverbs 29:15 says, "The rod of reproof gives wisdom, but a child who gets his own way brings shame to his mother." Solomon, David's own son, wrote in one of his proverbs, "A wise son makes a father glad, but a foolish son is a grief to his mother" (Prov 10:1). Amnon got in his own way. His acts were foolish, and he brought shame and grief to his parents. He is a clear example of a spoiled child who has to get his own way no matter what the cause.

Look around you and evaluate your children. See if the legacy you are leaving behind in them will shame your memory and theirs.

Search Your Heart, Thank, and Pray

Do you have a child you are not giving enough discipline? Did you know that God disciplines those He loves? The Lord gave us His Word, and in it you will find how to raise a family.

If you have young children, use the Bible as the only handbook for child rearing. If your children are already grown, pray that God will lead their homes as they follow the Bible. Read Deuteronomy 6: 1-6).

Day 15

Maacah
A Wife of King David and Mother of Absalom

2 Samuel 3:3; 1 Chronicles 3:2

Maacah was one of the wives of David and the mother of David's third son, Absalom. She must have been a beautiful woman because she had David's most handsome son. 2 Samuel 14:25 says, "Now in all Israel was no one as handsome as Absalom, so highly praised; from the sole of his foot to the crown of his head there was no defect in him." He was David's beloved son. Maacah was also the mother of David's daughter Tamar. She was the daughter of Talmai, king of Geshur. Maacah became David's wife for political reasons, "to consummate a political alliance with the Geshurite king Talmai." Like many of David's wives, very little is known about Maacah except for the fact that she came from a royal family.

Absalom, Maacah's son, had his older half-brother Amnon killed to avenge the rape of his sister Tamar. Absalom loved his sister so much that he even named his daughter after her. After he had his own brother killed, he ran away and hid in his grandfather Talmai's house (2 Sam 13:37-38; 2 Samuel 3:3) for three years and while there, he got really bitter toward his father, David. "David mourned for his son every day . . . the "heart of King David longed to go out to Absalom" because he had just lost his first born Amnon (2 Sam 13:39). Joab, the son of David's sister Zeruiah and head of

David's army, convinced David to bring Absalom back to Jerusalem but not to David's house.

It was good enough to David to bring his son back to Maacah and also enjoy knowing the fact that he was close by and know that he was safe. It took him two years to restore Absalom into the kingdom again. Absalom turned out to be one of the biggest threats David ever faced.

Absalom revolted against his father and forced David to leave Jerusalem by assuming the throne. When David fled, he left ten of his concubines in his house (2 Sam 15:15). While Absalom was ruling in Jerusalem, not being officially named king, Ahithophel, who was David's counselor and the grandfather of Bathsheba, revolted against David and advised Absalom to publicly take his father's concubines and have sex with them. "Then all Israel will hear that you have made yourself odious to your father" (2 Sam 16:21-22). Absalom was even counseled by Ahithophel to allow him to go with twelve thousand men and kill David.

David wanted Absalom to be captured alive. God had other plans. The word of God says, "For Absalom was riding on his mule, and the mule went under the thick branches of a great oak. And his head caught fast in the oak. So he was left hanging between heaven and the earth, while the mule that was under him kept going." Joab disobeyed David and took "three spears in his hand and thrust them through the heart of Absalom" (2 Sam 18:14-17). Then, ten of Joab's men finished killing him. David had now lost two sons.

After Absalom died there is nothing written in the Bible about how Maacah felt, but we know that David wept when he found out what happened to his son. He said, "O my son Absalom, my son, my son Absalom! Would I have died instead of you, O Absalom, my son, my son!" (2 Sam 18:33). Joab rebuked David for mourning and crying in front of the people for his son, the traitor of his kingdom (2 Sam 19:1-8). Then David got himself together and returned to the position of respect he had with his people. Solomon learned from his father's mistakes and wrote in Proverbs 22:6, "Train up a child in the way he should go, even when he is old he will not depart from it." Hebrews 12:6 says, "Whom the Lord loves He disciplines." Obviously, Absalom did not receive discipline, training in righteousness, or loyalty from his parents, and if he did he did, it was not expressed through his behavior. Maacah's son was rebellious, a weak-minded avenger, selfish, and an outright spoiled child, but David, his father, loved him unconditionally just as God, The Father, loves us (John 3:16).

Search Your Heart, Thank God, and Pray

Do you have someone who you trust, and who has counseled you to do the wrong things? Do you love your children unconditionally, regardless of how they turn out? If you are withholding discipline from your child, pray that is not too late for you to start guiding that child toward the Word of God and His ways. Read Joshua 1:8-9, Deuteronomy 6:1-7.

Day 16

Haggith
A Wife of King David and Mother of Adonijah

2 Samuel 3:4; 1 Chronicles 3:2; 1 Kings 1:5, 11, 2:13

Haggith was David's fifth wife and the mother of his fourth son, Adonijah (1 Kings 1:5–53, 2:13–28) born in Hebron. Haggith is always described as "the mother of Adonijah." There is no reference of her doing anything out of the ordinary. Her son Adonijah was an opportunist. He realized that his father David was really old and that his older brothers, Amnon and Absalom, were dead, so he took the opportunity to proclaim himself king. "Now Adonijah, the son of Haggith exalted himself, saying 'I will be king'" (I Kings 1:5). Adonijah was another spoiled child of David's. The Bible says, "His father never crossed him" (1 Kings 1:6), which means David did not discipline Adonijah. Adonijah was more powerful than his brother Absalom because he had the commander of David's army, Joab, as a follower.

Adonijah was really handsome and devious. His plans to take over the throne were great. He even gave himself a great party to celebrate his kingship, but he failed to invite the mighty men of David's army, Nathan the prophet, and his brother Solomon. "He apparently was planning to kill them, for had they eaten together, he would have obliged to protect them."[1] Adonijah was so strong that Nathan the prophet had to go David's wife Bathsheba to help David appoint the rightful king to the throne. He knew that if Adonijah became king of Jerusalem, the city would be in trouble! David honored his wife and Nathan's request of making Solomon king. David skipped all the preliminary work that was needed to make Solomon king, which Adonijah had already done, and went right into the coronation. When Adonijah found out what happened, all the men who backed him up abandoned him! "And Adonijah was afraid of Solomon, and he arose, went and took hold of the horns of the altar" (1 Kings 1:50). This was a "claim to protection" from the new king, which was not guaranteed. Solomon sent for Adonijah, and after having an audience with him, he sent Adonijah home. Solomon spared his life. After Adonijah was forgiven by Solomon, he, being the oldest at that time, went to Solomon's mother, Bathsheba. He said to her, "You know that the kingdom was mine and that all Israel expected me to be king; however, the kingdom has turned about and become my brother's, for it was his from the Lord. And now I'm making one request of you; please do not refuse me" (1 Kings 2:13-16). Adonijah wanted her to ask Solomon to allow him to marry Abishag, the widow of his father, David. This was his last try to overthrow the kingdom! Solomon said to her, "Ask for him also the kingdom, for he is my older brother" (1 Kings 2:22). Solomon noticed the scheme from Adonijah. He knew that if Adonijah married his father's widow, he would have a better chance to take the throne. Solomon had him killed (1 Kings 2:24-25).

David was dead, and so were his three older sons. Absalom had Amnon killed, Absalom was killed by his uncle Joab, and Solomon had Adonijah killed. Each of the three dead sons were wicked. Haggith was another mother in pain because of the behavior of her son. "In the five places that Haggith is mentioned [in the Bible] it is always as the mother of Adonijah. Immediately after the name of Haggith in 1 Kings 1:5, is the passage that Adonijah was a man who "exalted himself, saying I will be king."[2] Her son's legacy of bad behavior tagged on to his mother forever because we are still reading about it today. A child full of pride fighting for what he wanted and actually belonged to him, but going about it the wrong way. The wages of sin is spiritual death, but in Haggith's son case, it also cost him his physical life.

Search Your Heart, Thank God, and Pray

Adonijah was known as his mother's son. Will your child be recognized the same way as Adonijah? Do you step over anybody to get what you want? Adonijah learned from somebody! Read Proverbs 29:15; 29:23; 22:15, 17; 16:25

1 *The Ryrie Study Bible* (Chicago: The Moody Institute of Chicago, 1978), 505.

2 Edith Deen, *All the Women of the Bible* (New York: HarperCollins, 1983), 266.

Day 17

Abital, Eglah, and Abishag Wives of King David

Abital: 2 Samuel 3:4; 1 Chronicles 3:3
Eglah: 2 Samuel 3:5; 1 Chronicles 3:3
Abishag: 1 Kings 1:1–4, 15, 2:13–25

Abital was the mother of David's fifth son, Shephatiah. Eglah was the mother of David's sixth son, Ithream. These two wives of David are only mentioned by name in the Bible as part of the eight who are named as his wives. The appearance of these women in the Bible is short and there are no records of their lives or the lives of their sons. The fact that there are no bad deeds recorded about them means a lot. These two women found favor in the eyes of David and his feelings for them were strong enough for him to make them part of his harem.

Abishag, on the other hand, had a small piece of history in the life of King David. Even though David never had a physical relationship with her, she became part of his harem. When David got old, his wives were no longer his bedmates, so he slept alone and was cold. David's servants suggested to "Let them [servants] seek a young virgin for my lord the king, and let her attend the king and become his nurse; and let her lie in your bosom, that my lord the king may keep warm" (1 Kings 1:4).

David had eight queens and a bunch of concubines, and none of them was available to keep him warm and give him the companionship that he needed. The mighty David, who was worth ten thousand soldiers (2 Sam 18:3), was old, cold, and lonely. The search started in Israel for a beautiful girl throughout the whole land. The girl found was Abishag the Shunammite. She "was chosen for the task with great care on account of her virginity, youth, beauty, and physical vigor, and as a practical nurse for the aging king. The prescribed method was not successful, for David died soon after Abishag had taken on her duties."[1] David's servants brought her to him, and she became his nurse, but "the king did not cohabit with her" (1 Kings 1:4).

Because of her role in the final days of David's life, she was probably a witness to a lot of decisions and events in the life of David. She may have been present when Bathsheba and Nathan went into David's room to remind him of his promise of making Solomon king.

Abishag was the woman Adonijah, a son of David, wanted as a wife. Abishag's future was already designed for her. She was always going to be part of David's harem, even after his death, and Adonijah knew that. If you remember from yesterday's reading, Adonijah wanted take over his father' kingdom, and he wanted to use her to achieve it. Without Abishag even knowing it, she was the final reason why Adonijah was killed.

Even though Abishag did not choose to, she gave her young life, her beauty, and any chance of marrying and having children, to be a nurse and to serve a king who did not take his rights as a man because he was too old. While everybody was waiting for David to die, she was loving, comforting, warming, and taking care of her dying king. She was chosen to do a job that only she could have done, and she did it with excellence.

Search Your Heart, Thank God, and Pray

Would you be bitter if you had Abishag's life? Why? Do you think her life was unfair? Pray for the Lord to give acceptance and contentment in whatever situation you find yourself today. Read Romans 8: 28-29

1 Herbert Lockyer, All *the Women of the Bible (*Grand Rapids: Zondervan Publishing House, 1995).

Day 18

Tamar #2
King David's Daughter

2 Samuel 13:1–39; 1 Chronicles 3:9

This Tamar was the daughter of David and Maacah, and she was the sister of Absalom. It is really sad to recall Tamar's story because incest and rape are two very hurtful subjects of discussion but one that is often ignored and forgotten by society. The Bible says, "Absalom the son of David had a beautiful sister whose name was Tamar, and Amnon the son of David loved her" (2 Sam 13:1). Amnon, her half-brother, didn't love her as a sister but as a woman who he sexually desired. He desired her so much that he "made himself ill for she was a virgin, and it seemed hard to Amnon to do anything to her" (2 Sam 13:2). Here we see a brother with sexual desire, or perhaps love, towards his own sister.

Jonadab, Amnon's friend, was a bad influence in his life, because he advised him to fool his father, King David, to bring Tamar to his house. Amnon, David's firstborn, pretended that he was sick so his father would come and see him. When David went to see him, he asked David, "Please let my sister Tamar come and make me a couple of cakes in my sight that I may eat from her hand" (2 Sam 13:5). David didn't even think about it twice. He wasn't about to say no to his sick son! So he ordered Tamar to go and serve her brother.

After Tamar finished baking and cooking for Amnon, she brought the cakes to Amnon, but he did not eat. He made sure all his servants left his bedroom. "Then Amnon said to Tamar, 'Bring the food into my bedroom that I may eat from your hands.'" So Tamar took the cakes she had made and brought them into the bedroom to her brother Amnon. When she brought them to him to eat, he took hold of her and said to her, "Come, lie with me, my sister" (2 Sam 13:10–11). She said no to him and begged him, "Do not violate me, for such a thing is not done in Israel; do not do this disgraceful thing" (2 Sam 13:12). She even suggested Amnon to go and ask King David to give her to him, "for he would not withhold me from you" (2 Sam 13:13). She knew her brother was used to getting his own way.

Amnon did not listen to her and raped her anyway. Amnon hated Tamar after he raped her; his hate became greater than the lust he had for her before he raped her. He did not really love her because he did not respect her. After he realized his actions, he told her to go away. Tamar told Amnon that it hurt her more to be told to go away than what he did to her, but again he did not listen to her words. He was cruel. He asked one of his servants: "Throw this woman out of my presence, and lock the door behind her" (2 Sam 13:17).

She was wearing a long-sleeved garment worn by the virgin daughters of the king, and Tamar "put ashes on her head, and tore her long sleeved garment which was on her; and she put her hand on her head and went away, crying aloud as she went" (2 Sam 13:18–19). She met her brother Absalom in her walk of pain, and he tried to comfort her, but Absalom did not take it well. He loved his sister. He loved his sister so much that he named his own beautiful daughter after her (2 Sam 14:27).

Even though Amnon deserved death for his actions, David did not cut him off from the presence of all the people, like he was supposed to do according to the law (Lev 20:17). This may be due to the fact that Ammon was David's firstborn and would be expected to inherit the throne."[1] There was very little done to Ammon, but tragedy hit David's household again when justice came to Tamar a couple of years later. Absalom had Amnon, his half-brother, killed (2 Sam 13:32). Incest and rape is not new. They have been happening for hundreds of years, and only God can provide a victim healing and the ability to forgive the offender for this type of crime. One thing victims of this type of crime have to remember is that it is *not* their fault but the attacker's. Many women go around without telling about a wrong like this done to them because they think that it is their fault. No one can take responsibility for the sins of others. A violated woman like Tamar could find justice in her heart by first forgiving the attacker and second by helping put the offender in jail, when possible, so that the crime is not repeated with someone else. Every woman who has been violated like Tamar and Dinah (Jacob's daughter) has to do just like they did: come out and tell someone and let justice prevail. Remember that God will do His own judging as well. "Never take your own revenge, beloved, but leave room for the wrath of God, for it is written, 'Revenge is Mine, I will repay' says the Lord" (Rom. 12:19).

Search Your Heart, Thank God, and Pray

Has there been incest in your family? Was it done to you? Have you found healing? The subject matter today is really tough to read about and especially if you, the reader, have been a victim of this kind of abuse. The Lord God can comfort your heart and also give you the gift of forgiveness. Read Isaiah 41:10 Psalm 119:50, Matthew 18:22.

[1] *The Ryrie Study Bible* (Chicago: The Moody Institute of Chicago, 1978), 481.

Day 19

Ten Concubines From King David's Harem

2 Samuel 15:16, 16:21–22, 20:3

According to the *Eerdmans Bible Dictionary,* a concubine was "a female slave responsible primarily for bearing children to insure continuation of the family name."[1] She was someone who was "regarded as a member of the family and as a legitimate avenue for succession and inheritance. Access to the royal concubine was viewed as a legal claim to the throne. . . [concubines where view as property and were acquired by males mostly for sexual enjoyment] they were viewed with affection by their husbands, and any assault on their well-being might be a cause for revenge."[2] David had many concubines, but ten of them became famous because David's son Absalom sexually abused them.

When David was running away for his life from his son Absalom, he left his house, but "the king went out and all his household with him. But the king left ten concubines to keep the house" (2 Sam 15:16). David only left temporarily; he knew he was going to come back. David's children knew what a concubine represented, and so did David's advisers. Ahithophel, one of David's advisers, counseled Absalom. Ahithophel was really against David. For Absalom to really show Israel that he was the new boss in town, he was advised by Ahithophel to take, or openly rape, the ten concubines David left tending his house (2 Sam 16:20-23).

They both knew this act would show Absalom's possession of the throne. This added more pain and distance between David and his son. Ahithophel later on committed suicide (2 Sam 17:23) because he knew he did wrong and David was going to win the battle against his son. These ten women were humiliated before all of Israel. "So they pitched a tent for Absalom on the roof" on top of the house where everybody would know what he was doing . . . And Absalom went in to his father's concubines in the sight of all Israel" (2 Sam 16:22). Absalom had his brother killed because he raped his sister, and now he committed the same crime ten times. By doing this awful act, Absalom made himself like his dead brother. In his desire for power, Absalom raped ten women while forgetting the pain rape created in his sister's life.

After Absalom was defeated and killed, David returned to his kingdom. The Bible says, "Then David came to his house at Jerusalem, and the king took the ten women, the concubines whom he had left to keep the house, and placed them under guard and provided them with sustenance, but did not go in to them." The king couldn't touch them anymore "so they were shut up until the day of their death, living as widows" (2 Sam 20:3). David provided security and a safe haven for these ladies.

Sometimes innocent people get hurt, and that is the case with these ten women. Some of David's wives were taken during war but were never touched by other men like these concubines were. When David left these women in charge of his house, he never imagined that his son would do what he did. These women lived with the shame of Absalom's actions over them for the rest of their life, away from their king, and separated from the rest of the harem, and the world. Putting them away was David's way of offering them the protection he couldn't give them before. He was now protecting them from other offenders and gossips. Sometimes others make decisions that lead to bad consequences and we need to pick up the pieces and start all over again.

Search Your Heart, Thank God, and Pray

Have you ever been hurt because of some else's greed? Have you ever hurt an innocent person in order for you to get your way? David had to face that what is done cannot be undone so he took care of these ladies and allowed them to have a private decent life. Christ, our Redeemer, offers that kind of private, decent, but new life. Read Colossians 1:13-14

[1] Allen C. Myers, The *Eerdmans Bible Dictionary (*Grand Rapids: WM. B. Eerdmans Publishing Co, 1987), 137

[2] Ibid.

Day 20

Zeruiah
A Sister of King David

1Samuel 26:6; 2 Samuel 2:13, 18, 3:39, 8:16, 14:1, 16:9–10, 17:25, 18:2, 19:21–22, 21:17, 23:18, 37; 1 Kings 1:7, 2:5, 22; 1 Chronicles 2:16, 11:6, 39, 18:12, 15, 26:28, 27:24

Zeruiah was King David's half-sister and was the mother of three sons: Abshai, Joab, and Asahel. She was a widow, and all we know about her husband is that he died and his son Asahel, who was killed by Abner, the commander of the army of Saul, was buried in the same grave in Bethlehem (2 Sam 2:32). We don't know why her sons are always described as "the sons of Zeruiah." Every time there is a reference to them, her name also appears. That is why she is mentioned so much in the Bible. Edith Deen said, "The fact that her name appears twenty-five times beside that of her sons is sufficient proof that she was a mother of distinction who had a marked influence over the lives of her sons."[1]

Her other two sons, Joab and Abishai, were great warriors. They became important figures in David's army. Abishai was well known. He defeated thousands of men, but the most famous of both of them was Joab. Joab became the commander of his uncle David's army. He was very loyal to David while he served him but ended up turning against David. He was the one who helped David make peace with Absalom, and the one who saw the big threat to the king posed by Absalom and because of it killed Absalom without David's consent. Joab also was the one to bring David back to reality when he was grieving for Absalom. Joab "warned that David's unrestrained grief could lead to political disaster." [2] Tragically in disobedience to King David and behind David's back, Joab kills David's son Absalom (2 Sam18:9-18).

Killing was not new to Joab, he also killed Abner, the commander of King Saul's army, because he killed his brother Asahel, and again, he did it without David's consent (2 Sam 3:27). Even though Abner was serving Saul, he was the son of David's Uncle Ner (1 Sam 14:50). David "lifted his voice and wept at the grave of Abner, and all the people wept" (2 Sam 3:32). Abner was a great warrior and David made sure all of the people knew that he had nothing to do with his death (2 Sam 3:28-30).

Zeruiah's son Joab was a vindictive premeditated killer. Joab did whatever was necessary to achieve his goals, even if the one killed was a family member. Such was the case with Amasa his former commander. For political reasons David had replaced Joab with Amasa as his army's commander and Joab killed him the first chance he had because Amasa became his rival (2 Sam 20:9–12). As a mother, I often wonder if Zeruiah knew of the life her son lived or if she agreed with the life he lived.

Joab had great plans. He decided to follow David's son Adonijah to try to get the kingdom from David. The Word of God records that Adonijah "conferred with Joab the son of Zeruiah and with Abithar the priest," who David had taken into his household as one of the family (1 Sam 22:20–23), "and following Adonijah they helped him." Joab became so strong that David on his deathbed, warned Solomon about Joab. He was not to be trusted because he was guilty of killing Amasa and Abner during times of peace (1 Kings 2:5-6).

And sure enough, Joab decided to side with another jealous, selfish, power hungry man, David's son Adonijah. After Solomon was anointed king, Adonijah tried again to take over David's kingdom, but now he was facing Solomon and his wisdom, and he lost the fight and his life. Adonijah gets killed and Joab found himself without backup because Adonijah was dead. "And Joab fled to the tent of the Lord and took hold of the horns of the altar." Solomon asked for him to come out, but he said, "No, for I will die here." Solomon said to his men, "Do as he has spoken and fall upon him and bury him that you may remove from me and from my father's house the blood, which Joab shed without cause." (Read 1 Kings 2:28–33).

Zeruiah's son gave David a lot of good advice and was very helpful (1 Chron 11: 4-9), but he also gave him a lot of grief and caused him a lot of pain. We will never know the amount of influence Zeruiah had on her sons, but regardless of that, her name, like the names of many other biblical women, made history because of the deeds of their sons.

Search Your Heart, Thank God, and Pray

Zeruiah's legacy is based only on the bad behavior of her sons. There are many women out there that pray for their children every day and should not stop doing so. I once met a lady who had three sons in jail and we prayed for them. She was a godly woman with children who did not know God. She did not and would not give up her hope that God would take hold of her children's lives and turn them around. If you are in a similar situation, stay close to God and do not lose hope and faith. Read Hebrews 11:1.

[1] Edith Deen, *All the Women of the Bible* (New York: HarperCollins, 1983), 301.

Day 21

Abigail #2
Sister of King David and Mother of Amasa

2 Samuel 17:25, 1 Chronicles 2:13–17

This Abigail was the other sister of the David. David had only two sisters named in the Bible, Abigail and Zeruiah. Abigail was the wife of Jether the Ishmaelite. She was the mother of Amasa who became part of his uncle David's army. After Absalom was defeated, David decided that it was better to make Amasa head of the army and remove Joab. This was very smart of David because in David's case it was better to have his enemy closer to him than far away from him. Amasa would bring his rebel army with him. At this point Amasa had proven he could do the job because of the job he did while following Absalom.

David was very careful to remind Amasa who he was and who David was by claiming the blood that was between them (2 Sam 19:11-13). Amasa was faithful to David. After David settled back into his house and put everything in order, David said to Amasa, "Call the men of Judah for me within three days, and be present here yourself" (2 Sam 20:4). Amasa took longer than expected to gather the men of Judah and failed to follow David's order, so David sent Abishai, his other nephew and Joab's brother, to lead the army in pursue of another enemy of David, Sheba. Unfortunately, Joab went out to pursue the same enemy David had asked

Abishai to pursue. Amasa met with Joab on the way to gather the men of Judah.

> Now Joab was dressed in his military attire, and over it was a belt with a sword in its sheath fastened at his waist; and as he went forward, it fell out. And Joab said to Amasa "It is well with you, my brother?" And Joab took Amasa by the beard with his right hand to kiss him. But Amasa was not on guard against the sword which was in Joab's hand so he struck him in the belly with it and poured out his inwards parts on the ground. (2 Sam 20:8-10).

Joab had it all planned, and it looks like his brother Abishai, was unaware of his brother's plans because after this they both pursued Sheba together and were victorious the troops made Joab commander (2 Sam 20:11-23). Joab was even dressed for the occasion! This was how Joab got himself back into David's army as commander! David had no choice because the army was with Joab.

I'm thinking of these two sisters, Abigail and Zeruiah, and I wonder what happened to their relationship when they found out one of their sons killed the other. The choices their sons made in their lives created a lot of pain for both of them and other people. The price that these sons paid for their hunger for power was very high: their lives. Amasa started his military life on the wrong foot, but after being taken under his uncle's wings, he changed and was loyal, but Joab changed to be wicked.

Amasa and Joab did not honor their mothers and were not serving God; they were serving themselves and their hunger for power. I'm sure that if God had been the focus of their service, their lives would have been different. Zechariah 4:6b says, "Not by might nor by power, but by My Spirit says the Lord of hosts." Whether we are building a house, starting a family, starting a church, or simply trying to start a new job, we need the Spirit of God to guide our steps.

Search Your Heart, Thank God, and Pray

Joab was ready and dressed inside and out to receive his victim, Amasa. Are you properly dressed with the *opposite* clothing of Joab (salvation, love, kindness, self-control, etc.) to meet the Savior? Is the Spirit of God in your life now? If having power is what guides your life, you should know that power will not take you to heaven; Jesus will! Read Ephesians 6:10-18.

Day 22

The Wives of King David and Their Children

You have been reading for most of this time about all the women in the life of David, and I felt you should have a review of all of them and all the children David had (2 Sam 3:2–5; 1 Chron 3:1–9).

- *Michal* was David's first wife, with whom he didn't have any children.
- *Ahinoam* was the mother of David's son Amnon (first son).
- *Abigail* (#1) was the mother of David's son Daniel, also known as Chileab (second son).
- *Maacah* (#1) was the mother of Absalom (third son) and Tamar, David's only daughter named in the Bible.
- *Haggith* was the mother of Adonijah (fourth son).
- *Abital* was the mother of Shephatiah (fifth son).
- *Eglah* was the mother of Ithream (sixth son).
- *Bathsheba* was the mother of Shimea, Shobab, Nathan, Solomon, and the first baby who died after the Lord confronted David with his sin with Bathsheba. This child's name is never mentioned in the Scriptures.
- *Abihail* (not Abigail) is not mentioned as wife but was the mother of David's son Jerimoth. She was David niece (2 Chronicles 11:18-19).

According to 1 Chronicles 3:1–9, we can find all the above names of the sons of David plus nine more, Ibhar, Elishama, Eliphelet, Nogah, Nepheg, Japhia, Elishama (#2), Eliada, and Eliphelet. There is no indication of which of the above wives had these other sons of David. All we know is that they were born from his legal wives. After the list is over the Bible says, "All these were the sons of David, **besides** [not included] the sons of the concubines; and Tamar was their sister" (1 Chron 3:9). This could possibly mean that Tamar was his only daughter or the only daughter from one of his legal wives. David was king over Hebron for seven years, and during that time he had the first six sons. Then he had the others in Jerusalem, where he reigned for thirty years. His son Solomon, Bathsheba's son, was the most famous of all of David's sons. When we read the story of Solomon's birth (2 Sam. 12:24), he appears to be son number eight, but according to Chronicles he seems to be son number ten. In Proverbs 4:3 Solomon assures us that he was the first surviving son of David and Bathsheba.

As we discussed earlier, there was a lot of tragedy in life of David, his sons, and his family. Amnon was killed on the orders of his brother Absalom. Absalom was killed by his cousin Joab. Joab was ordered to be killed by Solomon for killing his cousin Amasa and David's nephew Abner. Solomon also ordered his brother Adonijah killed to save the kingdom. David, the husband of all these wives and father of all these children, was a man who loved God. David was always seeking God's help in times of trouble because he knew God was reliable. He even looked for God after his heart was convicted of breaking one of the Ten Commandments (Ex. 20), "You shall not commit adultery." He committed adultery with Bathsheba and then had her husband killed. The Lord disciplined him for his sins through his sons but forgave him and then blessed him with Solomon.

There are seventy-three psalms of David, and in Psalm 4, like in many of his psalms, no matter what was happening around him or in his life, David knew God was there. David was sure of this and he expresses it in Psalm 4:8, "In peace I will lie down and sleep, for you alone, Lord, make me dwell in safety." David knew the Lord's presence was with him always and that God always knew the status of his soul.

None of the women in David's life are known for their walk with God or their faith in God. None of his wives left a specific legacy of a pattern of godliness for women to follow today except for Abigail display of wisdom and Bathsheba was also wise in raising the godly Solomon. In the Bible we mostly learn more about the life of David's children not his wives.

David was the husband of many wives and the father of many children, but none of his wives or children were able to separate him from having a relationship with almighty God.

Search Your Heart, Thank God, and Pray

Are you a woman who loves God? Is there anything keeping you from God? Do you have trust in the Lord like David did? In David's psalms, you will learn how to pray. He has psalms of praise, of supplication, of confession, of forgiveness, of victory over sin, and of the mercy of God. Read them and pray your favorite! Read Psalm 23 to start!

King Solomon

(Jedidiah)

Then David comforted his wife Bathsheba, and went in to her and lay with her; and she gave birth to a son, and he named him Solomon. Now the LORD loved him and sent word through Nathan the prophet and he named him Jedidiah for the LORD's sake" (2 Sam 12:24-25 NASB).

Day 1

The Daughter of Pharaoh and the First Wife of King Solomon

1 Kings 3:1, 7:8, 9:16–17, 24; 2 Chronicles 8:11

The daughter of Pharaoh a princess of Egypt was Solomon's first wife. Solomon didn't marry the daughter of Pharaoh because he loved her but for business purposes. "Then Solomon formed a marriage alliance with Pharaoh king of Egypt, and took Pharaoh's daughter and brought her to the city of David, until he had finished building his own house and the house of the Lord and the wall around Jerusalem" (1 Kings 3:1).

She was a document of peace between the two kingdoms. Her god was not the true God of Solomon, and her entrance to the city of David brought idolatry into the city. The bringing of foreign women into his life was the main reason for Solomon's downfall (1 Kings 11:7-12). Pharaoh's daughter was really important to Solomon because he built a house, especially for her, something he did not do for any other women. He had three houses under construction at the same time, one of them for God. Before David died, he left everything ready for Solomon to build the house of the Lord, and Solomon's focus at this point was to obey his father's charge (1 Chron. 22:5–6). One house he built for himself and one for the daughter of Pharaoh (1 Kings 7:8). It took him thirteen years to build her the house (1 Kings 7:1). "Then Solomon brought Pharaoh's daughter up from the city of

David to the house, which he had built for her; for he said, 'My wife shall not dwell in the house of David king of Israel, because the places are holy where the ark of the Lord has entered'" (2 Chron 8:11). "After moving her he built the Millo [A Millo is a wall built for protection]" (1Kings 9:24). Out of respect to his father David, Solomon did not take her to live in Jerusalem.

When the Pharaoh's daughter married Solomon, her dowry was a city that her father destroyed to give to her. "For Pharaoh King of Egypt had gone up and captured Gezer, and burned it with fire, and killed the Canaanites who lived in the city, and had given it as a dowry to his daughter, Solomon's wife' (1 Kings 9:16-17). Solomon later rebuilt the city. She received a very costly dowry! It seems to me that she was one of the most beautiful women Solomon ever had, but even though she was special and spoiled by her father and Solomon, she was not the only woman or the only princess in the life of Solomon. Solomon was a very busy man, and the daughter of Pharaoh probably had to make an appointment to be with him or simply wait until he summoned her. "He had seven hundred wives of royal birth and three hundred concubines, and his wives led him astray" (1 Kings 11:3-NIV). There is no evidence that the daughter of Pharaoh and Solomon had any children.

Solomon, who was he the wealthiest, wisest man in biblical history, and one who found favor with God (1 Kings 3:3-15, lost his relationship and walk with God, and God was not pleased. 1 Kings 11:4 says, "For it came about when Solomon was old, his wives turned his heart away after other gods; and his heart was not wholly devoted to the Lord his God, as the heart of David his father had been." God said to Solomon, "Because you have done this, and you have not kept My covenant and My statutes, which I have commanded you, I will surely tear the kingdom from you, and will give it to you servant" (1 Kings 11:11).

But the Lord remembered David, and then He told Solomon:

> Nevertheless I will not do it in your days for the sake of your father David, but I will tear it out of the hands of

> your son. However I will not tear away all the kingdom, but I will give one tribe to your son for the sake of My Servant David and for the sake of Jerusalem which I have chosen. (1 Kings 11:12–13)

Pharaoh's daughter was a status symbol for Solomon and in the eyes of men, and because of her, he expanded the kingdom and became more powerful. Even though she had everything money could buy, she did not have Solomon for herself because he did not even consider her worthy of living in the same town as his father David.

Search Your Heart, Thank God, and Pray

Solomon allowed the women in his life to stand between him and the only true God. To please his wives Solomon allowed idolatry to come into his life. Have you ever allowed something or someone to take over your relationship with God? Pray that the Lord will give you the wisdom that you need so other beliefs do not change yours. Commit yourself to learn God's Word, and use it as a defense mechanism against false doctrine. Read 1 Peter 3:15-16.

Day 2

Naamah
Wife of King Solomon

1 Kings 14:21, 31; 2 Chronicles 12:13

Naamah was one of the many wives of Solomon. Even though he had so many she is the only one who is referred to by name in Bible. She was the mother of Solomon's son Rehoboam, the son who took over his kingdom after he died (1 Kings 11:43) and on whom the Lord discharged his wrath because of Solomon's sin of idolatry (1 Kings 11:13). This wife of Solomon kept her gods just like all the others (1 Kings 11:3-12).). There is no evidence that any of Solomon's wives accepted the God of Abraham, Isaac, and Jacob. The simple fact that Solomon's wives stayed with their own belief shows that Solomon, with all the wisdom he had, did not have the gift of evangelism.

Naamah was an Ammonite, and her god was Milcom, also known as Moloch, the god of the sons of Ammon (1 Kings 11:33). She was a descendent of Ammon, the son of the youngest daughter of Lot (Gen 19:38). Her sin of idolatry was brought into the city of David by a race conceived in sin and living in sin. The Bible said that Solomon went after her god who was "the detestable idol of the Ammonites" (l Kings 11:5). By being an Ammonites, Naamah had an evil influence on her son and probably Solomon because of the fact that Solomon allowed idolatry, and their son Rehoboam did evil before God (1 Kings 12:13-14). Solomon created a sense of confusion by building a house for God and also allowing altars of idolatry in Jerusalem. Her son Rehoboam followed the true God for a while, but he forsook Him and ended up also following false gods.

Naamah's son Rehoboam seems to be the firstborn of Solomon because he was the one to follow as king. He also followed after Solomon and his grandfather David when it came to women. Rehoboam had eighteen wives and sixteen concubines and fathered twenty-eight sons and sixty daughters (2 Chron 11:21). Naamah could not follow or teach anyone to follow God because she didn't know Him. As king Solomon could have made all his wives worship his God and not allowed any false gods to be worshiped in his kingdom.

No one will ever have perfect children. Only Mary, the mother of Jesus, had such an experience, but we can allow God to help us do our best. It is good to remember that little feet are copying our steps. Little hearts are worshipping what we worship. Little hands are doing what we are doing; little ears are memorizing what they hear. Little eyes are seeing what we are doing, and little hearts are being shaped the way ours is. Every day we should try to be like Christ, allow God to change us, and the Spirit to lead us. One of my favorite songs has words that are very appropriate to remember: "Change my heart, oh God, make it ever true. Change my heart, oh God, may I be like You. You are the potter, I am the clay, mold me and make me, this is what I pray."

Search Your Heart, Thank God, and Pray

There are many Naamahs out there who worship idols all the time, all day long, 24/7. What are you worshipping today? Are you worshipping your family, money, people, things, or God? If you feel that the life you live is not a good example for someone to follow, pray to the Lord to mold the clay of your life so you can be **the best God fearing, evangelist prayer vessel, and most beautiful pot ever made!** Read Psalm 139:13-14

1 Eddie Espinosa, *Change my Heart Oh God*, 1982 Mercy/Vineyard Publishing

Day 3

Two Harlots and a Child King Solomon's Wisdom Displayed

1 Kings 3:16–28

These two nameless women gave Solomon an opportunity to show his wisdom. Their story only appears in the book of 1 Kings and is an unforgettable example of selfishness and a great display of love at the same time. It is the story of two harlots who gave birth to children whose fathers were unknown. The Bible says in 1 Kings 3:17-18:

> The two women who were harlots came to the king and stood before him. And the first women said to Solomon, "Oh, my lord, this woman and I live in the same house; and I gave birth to a child while she was in the house. And it happened on the third day I gave birth, that this woman gave birth to a child, and were together. There was no stranger with us in the house, only the two of us in the house."

This woman made sure that Solomon knew there were no witnesses to the births of their children. She continued, saying, "And this woman's son died in the night, because she lay on it. So she arose in the middle of the night and took my son from beside me while your maidservant slept, and laid him in her bosom, and laid her dead son in my bosom."

The woman continued to tell Solomon that in the morning, she tried to breastfeed her son and she discovered that the baby was not hers and that the baby was dead. The second woman argued her point that the surviving baby was hers. They both went back and forth, claiming the living baby. In order to check for understanding, Solomon repeated their argument, and then he said, "Get me a sword. So they [his servants] brought a sword before the king" 1 Kings 3:24). Solomon used his wisdom to find out who was the real mother of the living child. He said, "Divide the living child in two, and give half to one and half to the other" (1 Kings 3:25).

> Then the woman whose child was the living one spoke to the king, for she was deeply stirred over her son and said, "Oh my lord give her the living child, and by no means kill him." But the other woman said, "He shall be neither mine nor yours; divide him!" Solomon then said "Give the first woman the living child, and by no means kill him. She is the mother." This decision by Solomon was a great witness of his own wisdom to the people of Israel, who admired him for such a tremendous display of wisdom."

The response of each woman to Solomon's decision brought out the real mother! Solomon knew the real mother would not allow her child to be cut in half to settle a dispute. The possibility of having her son killed allowed the real mother to give up the child, and this surrendering gave her the child back. Even though she lived a life of sin, there was also good in her, which allowed her to have wisdom and discernment to make the right choice.

What I like about this story is that these two women got an audience with the king, a very busy man, because their problem was such that it required the personal attention and wisdom of the king. *Two "worthless" women to society were treated with wisdom and respect by the king.* The selfishness of the one woman, who would have rather had the child killed, shows her lack of mercy and her desire for revenge. She could not accept the fact that she killed her son while sleeping and very selfishly reached out for someone else's baby to satisfy her loss. This story "has been the most frequently quoted example of Solomon's judicious judgment, and one of the Bible's most stirring examples of a mother's love put to a trying test."[1] These two women had a temporary problem that Solomon solved for them. Today, we have a problem with our souls that only Jesus can solve. Jesus, our King, did better than Solomon: He died to cleanse us of our sins. When we come to Him in repentance, we are restored before God as we acknowledge Him as our Lord.

Search Your Heart, Thank God, and Pray

Do you pray to the Lord to give you wisdom when you need to make crucial decisions in your life? Selfishness sometimes blinds us and makes us do what is wrong. Pray for the Lord to keep you alert to selfish thoughts and decisions. Read Psalm 37, Proverbs 1:7, James 1:5.

1 Edith Deen, All the Women of the Bible (New York: HarperCollins, 1983), 120

Day 4

The Queen of Sheba In Search of King Solomon's Wisdom

1 Kings 10:1–13; Chronicles 9:1–12; Matthew 12:42; Luke 11:31

The queen of Sheba was from Arabia. She decided she had to meet Solomon and inquire of his wisdom personally. She could have sent ambassadors instead of making a twelve hundred–mile trip, but she had to see for herself the kingdom of Solomon and the wonders that were spoken about Solomon's God. "Now when the queen of Sheba heard about the fame of Solomon concerning the name of the Lord, she came to test him with difficult questions." (1 King 10:1). What questions? Nobody knows! And by making the trip, she showed her own wisdom! She went to see and "Solomon answered all her questions; nothing was hidden from the king which he did not explain to her" (1Kings 10:3).

There are many legends based on the Queen of Sheba's visit to Solomon and none of them can be verified. The one thing we know is that the visit was real! The Lord Jesus assures us of her visit in the book of Matthew. When the Pharisees were asking Jesus for a sign, he said, "The Queen of the South will rise up with this generation at the judgment and will condemn it, because she came from the ends of the earth to hear the wisdom of Solomon; and behold, something greater than Solomon is here" (Matthew 12:42). Many of us completely ignore the fact that we have the freedom to seek for wisdom at any time and from anywhere. We do not need to travel like the Queen of Sheba traveled in search of wisdom. All we need to do ask for it! (James 1:5). She wanted wisdom so badly that's he was willing to make herself uncomfortable in order to seek it. She was prepared with difficult questions, questions that when answered would give her the wisdom she was seeking. God's wisdom is immeasurable and He is willing to give some of that wisdom to anyone who asks for it.

When she finally listened to Solomon and saw the world in which he lived, she praised him with honesty and admiration. She confessed that she did not believe what she had heard about him until she saw it herself. She said to Solomon, "You surpass the report that I heard… How blessed are your men, how blessed are your servants who stand before you continually and hear your wisdom" (1 Kings 10:8). She goes even further by recognizing the God of Solomon, who was the reason for her trip; she knew that only God could create such a kingdom and bless Solomon with such wisdom. Even though there is no evidence that she believed in God, she recognized God's existence. She said, "Blessed be the Lord your God who delighted in you to set you on the throne of Israel; because the Lord loved Israel forever, therefore He made you king, to do justice and righteousness" (1 Kings 10:9). She realized that wisdom was not an ability Solomon had but a gift from his God.

After her praises to Solomon, "Then she gave the king one hundred and twenty talents of gold, and a very great amount of spices and precious stones; there had never been spice like that which the queen of Sheba gave to King Solomon" (1 Kings 10:10). The beauty of her gifts is that she knew Solomon really did not need them, but she honored him with them anyway. Her visit to Solomon made him even richer than he already was. Her caravan to Solomon was an example of numerous other kings, who also sent caravans to honor Solomon. 2 Chronicles 9:22–23 says, "So King Solomon became greater than all the kings of the earth in riches and wisdom. And all the kings of the earth were seeking the presence of Solomon, to hear his wisdom which God had put in his heart."

The Queen of Sheba was a bold and determined woman who wanted to know firsthand the wonders of Solomon's wisdom and was blessed by seeking it. She was a rich woman trying to get nonfinancial richness. You can be blessed with wisdom also! James 1:5 says, "But if any of you lacks wisdom, let him ask of God, who gives to all men generously and without reproach, and it will be given to him."

Search Your Heart, Thank God, and Pray

Like the queen of Sheba, would you go out of your way to search for God's wisdom? Read Jeremiah 33:3 and Psalm 111:10

Day 5

Mahalath Wife of King Solomon's Son Rehoboam

2 Chronicles 11:18–19

Mahalath was one of the eighteen wives of King Rehoboam, the son of Solomon. She was King David's granddaughter. "Then Rehoboam took as a wife Mahalath the daughter of Jerimoth the son of David and of Abihail the daughter of Eliab the son of Jesse" (2 Chron 11:18–19). Jesse was David's father. Mahalath seems to be Rehoboam's first wife because she is named in the Bible before all of the other women in his life.

She gave King Rehoboam three sons, Jeush, Shemariah, and Zaham. Rehoboam married her during the days when he was following the Lord. The Bible tells us he later became corrupted with sin and moved away from God. It is interesting to note that of Solomon's children who are mentioned in the Bible, most end up marrying people who were around their father. Rehoboam married into his father's family, and his daughters married men who were part of Solomon's kingdom. His daughter Taphath (1 Kings 4:11) married one of Solomon's twelve deputies who were over Israel, Ben-abinadab. His other daughter, Basemath (1 Kings 4:15), also married one of her father's deputies, Ahimaaz.

Mahalath got to see her husband Rehoboam, the son of Solomon, reign in Judah. "He was forty-one years old when he became king, and he reigned for seventeen years in Jerusalem, the city which the Lord had chosen from all the tribes of Israel to put His name there" (1 Kings 14:21). She enjoyed the kingdom in which her husband Rehoboam lived, a kingdom King David raised from the ground and his son Solomon finished building which belonged to Rehoboam. Rehoboam only followed his father and grandfather for a while when it came to God. Later on, he forsook God and ended up making bad decisions that would affect all of Israel. He did his own thing (2 Chron 12). Rehoboam and the people of Israel became self-sufficient. God took a nonexistent place in their lives to the point where they stepped all over His Law. "This took place when the kingdom of Rehoboam was established and strong that he and all Israel with him forsook the law of the Lord" (2 Chron 12:1).

There is no evidence that Mahalath directly influenced Rehoboam to forsake God and follow her gods; the Bible says that he "did evil because he did not set his heart to seek the Lord" (2 Chron 12:14). Rehoboam is a great example that parents cannot pass down wisdom or salvation to their kids. We are all individuals and God made us as such. Solomon, a man of wisdom, was not able to bestow wisdom on his children, because no one can, not even the great Solomon. The previous verse gives Rehoboam sole responsibility for his actions. We are responsible for our actions before God regardless of who we follow. Every decision we make should be based on God's will for our lives. How do we know what God's will is? The Holy Spirit speaks to our hearts, but this only happens when we seek God day and night through reading the Bible, praying—and waiting on Him—after receiving Jesus as Savior. God lets us know His will by answering prayers and by opening doors in our lives that we considered closed.

When my older sister was a new believer in Christ, she asked me, "How do you know when God wants you to do something?" My answer to her was, "When it comes from God, you will know, but you have to seek Him first with all your heart." The real answer to her question was something she had to find out by herself. She knows now when God speaks to her, and she cannot explain it to me either! She just knows. Our God is an awesome

God! Jeremiah 33:3 says, "Call to Me, and I will answer you, and I will tell you great and mighty things, which you do not know." God is waiting for you to call on His name so He can answer you. He is a God of promise. God always knows what is good for us. Remember that, "It's "not by might nor by power, but by My Spirit, says the Lord of hosts" (Zech 4:6b).

Search Your Heart, Thank God, and Pray

Do you know God's will for your life? Are you seeking Him by calling on Him every day for everything? Set your heart to seek God. If you have pulled away from God remember that Jesus loves you, repent from any sin that keeps you captive, and pray to God to reveal Himself to you. Read Romans 10:13.

Day 6

Maacah

Wife of King Solomon's Son Rehoboam

2 Chronicles 11:20–23,

This Maacah was a wife of Solomon's son Rehoboam. She was the daughter of David's son Absalom (2 Chron 11:20) and she gave Rehoboam four children: Abijah, Attai, Ziza, and Shelomith. Rehoboam also practiced polygamy like his father Solomon (1 Kings 11:3), but out of the wives Rehoboam had, Maacah was his favorite. "And Rehoboam <u>loved</u> Maacah more than all his other wives and concubines" (2 Chron 11:21). The Bible doesn't specify why she was his favorite. We can imagine she was beautiful and very attractive or maybe she was just wise in her own way because of the eighteen wives he had he loved her the most. She was loved so much that "Rehoboam appointed Abijah the son of Maacah as head and leader among his brothers, for he intended to make him king" (2 Chron 11:22). Rehoboam also made sure Abijah was not threatened by his other brothers (twenty-eight of them), so "he acted wisely and distributed some of his sons through all the territories of Judah and Benjamin to all the fortified cities, and gave them food in abundance. And he sought many wives for them" (2 Chron 11:23). Eventually Abijah (also known as Abijam) became the king after his father died (2 Chron 13, 1 Kings 14:31).

Maacah was the favorite among eighteen wives and sixty concubines. She was the queen among queens, and she was guaranteed to be queen mother as well! Her husband Rehoboam reigned in Judah and all of Jerusalem for seventeen years (1 Kings 14:21). Maacah was married to a man who the Bible tells us was not a man after God's own heart (2 Chron 12:14). As a mother, she probably influenced the kingdom of her son Abijah/Abijam and tried to continue with her son's successor, Asa (2 Chron 15:8). Maacah was Asa's grandmother even though sometimes she is mentioned as his mother (1 Chron 15:13). Asa followed God as the king for forty-one years, and he removed the idols from Jerusalem after his father's death, and dear old grandmother was part of the cleanup. Asa "removed Maacah his mother [really his grandmother] from being queen mother, because she had made a horrid image of an Asherah. Asa cut down her horrid image and burned it" (1 Kings 15:13). She was a bad influence on her husband, her son, and her grandson. The favorite wife of Rehoboam, she was probably one of the reasons Rehoboam forsook the Lord. His love for her was so strong that it blinded him: and led him to worship her gods and bring up his son the same way. Her son Abijah was wicked, "and he walked in all the sins of his father which he had committed before him; and his heart was not wholly devoted to the Lord his God" (1 Kings 15:3). The legacy Rehoboam left for his son Abijah was the bad influence of his wife Maacah and his lack of conviction to do what was right in the sight of the Lord.

What a legacy! She had a wicked background, a wicked husband, and a wicked son. Maacah had a great thing in her hands—power—but she used it for evil instead of good. The Lord has given us gifts to use for His glory, and we also can turn them around and use them for evil. Our lives are examples for others to copy. In Maacah's situation, it was her son who copied and lived it. She made Rehoboam, a man God could have used, lose his focus, and she ruined the life of her son by modeling idolatry.

Search Your Heart, Thank God, and Pray

Are you determined to fight for God's way of life! God had mercy on David's generation by giving Asa into Maacah's genealogy and placing Himself as the center of Asa's life. Have you ever stopped to think that once you plant evil in the heart of a child, it is very difficult to take evil out? As women, we can help our family members direct their lives whether we are married or single. Where there is no wisdom the people will be unrestrained. Read Proverbs 29:18 and ask for wisdom.

Day 7

Wisdom—Female Food for the Soul the Main Desire of King Solomon's Heart

The word *wisdom* is referred to using feminine pronouns in the Bible, and Solomon always refers to all the descriptions of wisdom as female. This is why I put her in the category of women in Solomon's life. Even our Lord Jesus referred to wisdom as female (Matt 11:19). Wisdom was the heartfelt longing in Solomon's life. Even though Solomon had one thousand women in his life (1 Kings 11:3–5), we should not think Solomon desired wisdom like he desired women. He was able to get a woman any time he wanted but not wisdom, because wisdom is a gift from God. The desire of Solomon's soul for wisdom was stronger than the desire of his flesh for women.

The American Heritage Dictionary of the English describes wisdom as an "understanding of what is true, right, or lasting, common sense, sagacity; good judgment."[1] However, when Solomon refers to wisdom, he describes her as a unique and precious possession that would enrich his mind and guard his heart. He said, "She is more precious than jewels; and nothing you desire compares with her" (Prov 3:15). Solomon knew wisdom came from God. He wrote, "For the Lord gives wisdom" (Prov 2:6a). He knew, "The Lord by wisdom founded the earth" (Prov 3:19). He also knew wisdom could live in the heart: "Wisdom will enter your heart, and knowledge will be pleasant to your soul" (Prov 2:10). He loved the results wisdom gave him. Solomon felt blessed by having wisdom and made sure we knew how he felt. He wrote, "Blessed is the man who finds wisdom" (Prov 3:13) because he knew that wisdom was not easy to find. Wisdom only comes from following after God and asking God for it. He described her in the most loving way he could by saying, "She is a tree of life to those who take hold of her, and happy are all who hold her fast" (Prov 3:18). He knew that by possessing wisdom, he would be honored: "Prize her, and she will exalt you; she will honor you if you embrace her. She will place on your head a garland of grace; she will present you with a crown of beauty" (Prov 4:8–9). For Solomon, wisdom was everything!

This great king experienced that "wisdom gives understanding, understanding gives discernment, discernment gives knowledge, knowledge gives discretion, discretion produces diligence, diligence produces endurance and endurance results in righteousness" (Prov 8:1–12). When I realized this, I felt like begging the Lord for wisdom instead of just praying for it! The Word of God encourages us to seek wisdom because if we ask for it, God will give it: "But if any of you lacks wisdom, let him ask of God, who gives to all men generously and without reproach, and it will be given to him" (James 1:5).

When God told Solomon to ask Him for whatever he wanted, Solomon asked for wisdom (1 Kings 3:3–15). Wisdom will help you to "set your mind on the things above, not on the things that are on earth" (Col 3:2). Solomon also gave us a warning concerning wisdom. "Do not be wise in your own eyes; fear the Lord and turn away from evil" (Prov 3:7), because he knew that "The fear of the Lord is the beginning of wisdom, and knowledge of the Holy one is understanding" (Prov 9:10). He who has wisdom has the discretion not to boast about it. Wisdom is displayed in our lives by the way we walk with God. Wisdom says, "For he who finds me finds life, and obtains favor from the Lord" (Prov 8:35). By having so much wisdom, the wise king also discovered that "in much wisdom there is much grief, and increasing knowledge results in increasing pain" (Eccles 1:18).

Being wise does not erase the problems of everyday life. Even though God granted him wisdom, Solomon sinned against God. Nobody is perfect … even if they are wise! Solomon also knew that "wisdom is protection just as money is protection. But the advantage of knowledge is that wisdom preserves the lives of its possessors" (Eccles 7:12). Solomon even tried to convince his own son, to whom he wrote the book of Proverbs, to acquire wisdom (Prov. 4:7–9) because he was fully aware of its benefits. Solomon desired wisdom more than women, wealth, fame, material possessions, and power. It's interesting to note that wisdom was something our Lord Jesus acquired as He grew up (Luke 2:52), and later on Paul described Him as the wisdom of God and the wisdom from God (1 Corinthians 1:24, 30). The Son of God displayed wisdom and was wisdom. Solomon acquired wisdom. Praise be to God that we have access to both wisdom and Christ! [2]

Search Your Heart, Thank God, and Pray

Wisdom is only a prayer away for those who follow after God. It is a free gift! Free is good. Wisdom was the one request made to God from the great Solomon. Why can't you humble yourself and ask for it as well? God is generous and He will give you as much wisdom as you want. Read James 1:5, Matthew 7:7.

1 Houghton Mifflin Company, "Wisdom," in *The American Heritage Dictionary*, 2nd ed.

2 Clara Molina, "Wisdom: Female Food for the Soul (A Desire of Solomon's Heart)," *The Navigator's National Hispanic Prayer Ministry*, February/March, 2006.

Day 8

The Contentious Woman Disliked by King Solomon

Proverbs 19:13b, 21:9, 19, 25:24, 27:15

Solomon disliked the contentious woman very much, but to understand why he disliked her so much, we need to find out what contentious means. The American Heritage Dictionary describes contentious as follows: "A verbal struggling; dispute; controversy. A striving to win competition or an assertion put forward in argument."[1] The thesaurus's synonyms for "contends" are to fight, struggle, argue, and quarrel! The one called contentious is the one who is "given to contention." For obvious reasons, Solomon heated this argumentative, angry, aggressive, annoying kind of woman.

As you remember, I mentioned before Solomon had one thousand women in his harem, and I assure you that the ones who were contentious did not see much of him because of the way he described them! In Proverbs 21:9 he said, "It is better to live in a corner of a roof, than in a house shared with a contentious woman." He repeats the same words again in Proverbs 25:24. In Proverbs 21:19 he also said, "It is better to live in a desert land, than with a contentious and vexing woman." Vex means "1. To irritate or annoy, as with petty importunities, bother, pester. 2. To confuse, baffle, puzzle. 3. to debate (a problem) at length; bring up repeatedly for discussion." The English Standard Bible translated vexing as "quarrelsome." Do you want to be called vexing! Well! Start nagging your family today!

The most annoying description of the contentious woman by Solomon comes from Proverbs 27:15, where he said, "A constant **dripping** on a day of steady rain and a contentious woman are alike." Major nagging! Part of the next verse is even worse because it makes one feel that is impossible to control this kind of woman. He said in verse 16 of the same proverb, "**He who restrains her restrains the wind, and grasps oil with his right hand**." Have you ever tried to hold oil in your hands or control the wind? Well Solomon with all his wisdom could not do it either. He wanted you and me, and the world to know how difficult it is to live with this kind of woman. Solomon gave the contentious woman advice. He wrote, "Pleasant words are a honeycomb, sweet to the soul and healing to the bones" (Prov.16:24). "When there are many words, transgression is unavoidable, but he who restrains his lips is wise" (Prov. 10:19).

He is calling wives to be careful about what to say, when to say it, how often to say it, and how to say it. We need our speech to be honorable and discrete. Solomon wants us women to be wise. In Proverbs 14:1 he wrote, "The wise woman builds her house, but the foolish tears down with her own hands." Our speech can tear down our homes! How would you like your husband to think you are irritating and annoying? How would you like your husband to dread coming home because of fear of being nagged? I am sure the rooftops in the day of Solomon were very different than ours today. A rooftop today can be anything that would take your husband away from you and your home to avoid you (TV, friends, golf, and even sleeping). Listen to Solomon's advice; he really knew the problem first hand (1 Kings 11:3-5).

I am challenging you today, if you consider yourself a contentious woman, <u>do not</u> create a rooftop in your home. I want to challenge you to spoil your husband. My husband said to me one day, You've spoiled me so much I don't want any other woman." and I replied, "That's the point." I want to encourage you to consider what Solomon said in Ecclesiastes 3:1: "There is an appointed time for everything. And there is a time for every event under the sun." Part of his list of these events is "a time to be silent, and a time to speak" (Eccles 3:7a). We can always express our feelings, worries, discontentment, fears, and desires without nagging.

Search Your Heart, Thank God, and Pray

Are you a contentious woman? Do you have a rooftop in your house that your mate, children, friends, or family members escape to so they can be away from you? If the answer to the above questions is yes, pray for wisdom from the Lord to change you and to destroy the rooftop in your home. You cannot change yourself, but *God* can! Read Proverbs 31 and Psalm 19:7 for ideas, but not for perfection.

1 Houghton Mifflin Company, "Wisdom," in *The American Heritage Dictionary*, 2nd ed.

2 Ibid.

Day 9

The Harlot and the Adulterous Woman King Solomon Despised Their Sin

Proverbs 5:1–14, 20, 6:26, 7:10–27, 23:27, 29:3; Luke 15:30

Solomon was a man who loved women, but even though his love for them was so great, he also had space in his heart to despise the acts of a few. Yesterday we saw his dislike for contentious women, and today we will see how great his hate was for harlots and adulterous women. First, we need to know what a harlot is and what an adulterous woman is. A harlot is a prostitute. The Eerdmans Bible Dictionary describes her as:

> A female prostitute: in the general sense, one who engages in extramarital sexual relations for commercial purposes. Common throughout Palestine and Ancient Near East, they would dress enticingly and frequent public places, seeking to lure their customers back to the houses of their enterprise. Harlotry was condemned by the Israelites (Deut 22:21).[1]

The **adulteress** woman does not gain financial recompense however she violates the seventh commandment, which states, "You shall not commit adultery" (Ex 20:14). Adultery was considered a sin before the Ten Commandments were written (Gen 20:9, Lev 20:10, Gen 39:9) and it is still a sin today. An adulterer is a married person who has sexual relations with another person who is not his or her spouse. The only difference between the harlot and the adulteress is that the **harlot** (prostitute) gets paid. Both women commit the same sin; sex out of marriage, and like God, Solomon despises it. Solomon's advice to his sons is to avoid these kinds of women at all costs. I think that Solomon in his wisdom would have understood the truth of what Paul wrote in 1 Corinthians 6:16a, "Or do you not know that the one who joins himself to a harlot is one with her?" Solomon described the harlot as "boisterous and rebellious; her feet do not remain at home" (Prov 7:11). She is a woman out of control. Sometimes Solomon puts these two women in the same sentence to describe them even more graphically. In Proverbs 23:27 he said, "For a harlot is a deep pit, and an adulterous woman is a narrow well." When Jesus told the parable of the prodigal son, we can see that prostituting our bodies is not acceptable to God and it is destructive. The good son who stayed with his father was very angry because he didn't think his father should have made such a big deal about his prodigal son returning home. In his complaining, one of the things he said to his father was, "But when this son of yours came, who has devoured your wealth with harlots, you killed the fattened calf for him." The prodigal son did what Solomon told his sons not to do in Proverbs 29:3b: "He who keeps company with harlots wastes his wealth." Harlots were stoned for their sin (Deut 22:21) and it was and is an insult to a God fearing woman to be considered to be a harlot. Because of this reputation, Jacob's sons killed a whole city, including their leader, because their sister, Dinah, was treated like a harlot by one of them (Gen 34:26–31).

Now we all know the bad reputation a harlot had and still has, but we also should know that God can forgive any sin committed against Him, others, and ourselves when we confess them to Him. "If we confess our sins, He is faithful and righteous to forgive us our sins and to cleanse us from all unrighteousness" (1 John 1:9). So there is hope for the harlot, adulteress, and any other kind of sinner in Jesus our Lord! If you ever had this kind of lifestyle, remember that Jesus died for you too**. Prostitutes and adulterous women have access to Him just like anyone else** (Luke 19:10). Jesus forgives all who ask as for forgiveness, repent and confess their sins. Solomon hated these kinds of women because he knew the consequences of the sin they lived in, but Jesus hates the sin, and loves and died for the sinner. There is nothing in this world that would stop Him from giving you eternal life and forgiveness if you want it. "There is therefore now no condemnation for those who are in Christ Jesus" (Rom 8:1).

Search Your Heart, Thank God, and Pray

Have you ever exposed yourself to either of these kinds of life styles? Remember that God can forgive your sins when you accept Jesus as Lord and Savior. I pray that the Holy Spirit would open your eyes to the mercy of His love for you in Jesus Christ. If you never experienced this kind of life but you know someone that has, pray for him or her and share the love of Jesus. Read Matthew 18:1; Romans 6:23, 3:28, John 3:16

1 Allen C. Myers, The *Eerdmans Bible Dictionary (*Grand Rapids: WM. B. Eerdmans Publishing Co, 1987), 462.

2 *The Ryrie Study Bible* (Chicago: The Moody Institute of Chicago, 1978), 45.

The Lord Jesus

The angel said to her, "Do not be afraid, Mary; for you have found favor with God. and behold, you will conceive in your womb and bear a son, and you shall name Him Jesus. He will be great and will be called the Son of the Most High; and the Lord God will give Him the throne of His father David; and He will reign over the house of Jacob forever, and His kingdom will have no end" (Luke 1:30-33, NASB).

". . . He who is the blessed and only Sovereign, the King of kings and Lord of lords. . ."
(1 Tim 6:15b).

Day 1

Mary, the Mother of the Lord Jesus A Woman Chosen by God

Matthew 1:18–25, 2:1–23, 12:46–50, 13:55; Luke 1:26–56, 2:4–5, 28:19–21; Mark 6:3, 3:31–35; John 2:1–12, 19:25–27; Acts 1:14; Galatians 1:19; 1 Corinthians 9:5

This Mary is the best known of all the Marys in the Bible because she was the mother of our Lord Jesus Christ. She was the only woman in the world to give birth to a child who was born free of sin. She was the woman chosen by God to have His Son. She bore a Son for the sake of others. Jesus was the seed promised to save the world, and Mary ushered Him into the world. Jesus' birth was her contribution to the salvation of the world. Mary and her Son Jesus exchanged the most beautiful gift ever, life for life. She gave Him physical life, and He gave her spiritual life.

"Now in the sixth month the angel Gabriel was sent from God to a city in Galilee, called Nazareth, to a virgin engaged to Joseph, of the descendants of David; and the virgin's name was Mary. And coming in, he said to her, "Hail, favored one! The Lord is with you" (Luke 1:26–30). She was chosen for a great mission to be the mother of the Savior of the world because she "found favor with God." The angel said to her, "Behold, you will conceive in your womb, and bear a Son and you shall name Him Jesus" (Luke 1:31). There is no doubt that Mary was a special woman. It encourages me to imagine her relationship with God, the time she took to pray, and the time she took to memorize the Word of God.

She did have one question for the angel who visited her: "How can this be, since I am a virgin?" (Luke 1:34). She knew she had kept herself pure and that for her to get pregnant before she married Joseph would have to be a miracle. The angel answered her by saying "The Holy Spirit will come upon you, and the power of the Most High will overshadow you; and for that reason the holy offspring shall be called the Son of God" (Luke 1:35). A lot of people feel that Mary didn't have a choice in this matter, but she did. She could have said no to God or given Him excuses. She could have been so frightened as to run away from the presence of the angel, but she didn't. She felt honored to be used by God in this way and she placed herself in God's hands. She said to the angel, "Behold, the bondslave of the Lord; be it done to me according to your word" (Luke 1:38). The virgin birth of Jesus our Savior was not a result of the will of man, but the will of God.

If you read Luke 1:47–55, you will see that Mary was a godly woman. These verses are known as The Magnificat, and they show Mary's knowledge of the Old Testament and that fact that she memorized God's Word. In these famous verses she is speaking to her cousin Elizabeth, John the Baptist's mother, and she is expressing the joy and honor she feels about the mission she had been given.

My favorite verse from the Magnificat is where she said, "For He has had regard for the humble state of His bondslave; for behold, from this time on all generations will count me blessed" (Luke 1:48). She understood the honor that God had bestowed upon her, and she was humble about it. Mary didn't go running into town, alerting all her relatives and friends that she was going to be the mother of the Son of God. She kept it to herself. Many times we are chosen by God to do something special for His kingdom, and we fail to listen to Him and accept the challenge. In Mary's case, she was so ready to do God's work that she didn't even think twice about it. Why? Her heart was right with God, and it enabled her to do His will even when it was no socially unfavorable. She was a woman just like you and me, who was special to God, and who had a special calling from

God. She was chosen by God to do something out of the ordinary, to be the mother of His precious and perfect only Son.

Search Your Heart, Thank God, and Pray

How is your walk with God right now? Are you available to God like Mary was? Can God choose you to do His will right now and expect immediate obedience from you? Open your life to God's use. Read 2 Chron 7:14, Psalm 37.

Day 2

Mary, the Mother of the Lord Jesus Wife of Joseph and Mother

Mary was engaged to a man who followed and trusted God. He loved her so much that he was willing to hide what he thought was her shame of being pregnant by another man. Joseph was planning to quietly hide her until her baby was born. This is the most beautiful act of love from a man to a woman in the New Testament. Before the angel came to talk to Joseph, he showed how much he loved her by not shaming her.

> But when he had considered this, behold, an angel of the Lord appeared to him in a dream, saying, "Joseph, son of David, do not be afraid to take Mary as your wife; for that which has been conceived in her is of the Holy spirit. And she will bear a Son; and you shall call His Name Jesus, for it is He who will save His people from their sins." (Matt 1:20–21)

Mary married a man who had God's trust; otherwise God wouldn't have allowed him to be the stepfather to Jesus. He had to take care of her and the baby, and on top of all his responsibilities, Joseph "kept her a virgin until she gave birth to *His* Son" (Matt 1:25). Joseph was a man who obeyed the commands God gave him. The angel only spoke to Mary once. Subsequently, whenever the Lord wanted to communicate with this special family, he called only on Joseph and Joseph obeyed. Since Mary was a submissive wife to the Lord and to Joseph, she followed his lead.

She had her baby without a house, a finished nursery, or a simple crib. She didn't have a doctor or painkillers. There were no welcoming parties or cameras to receive the King of kings. He was born in a simple manger and, as a man; He never had a place of His own. Jesus said, "The foxes have holes, and the birds of the air have nests; but the Son of Man has nowhere to lay His head" (Matt 8:20). The KING of kings and LORD of lords, was **born homeless**! During his three-year of ministry, Jesus never really had a home.

Mary never got in the way of God's plans for His Son. Her attitude toward her child made me come to the understanding that my children don't belong to me; they are God's. They are here for me to love and enjoy, take care of, and guide towards God. Mary did just that until it was time for her baby, Jesus, to start doing the work for His Father in heaven. She enjoyed having the Son of God running around her house in diapers just like any mother would.

Once, for three days, Joseph and Mary thought that Jesus had gotten lost. They looked high and low for Him and, when they finally found Him, Mary asked Him, "Son, why have you treated us this way? Behold your father and I have been anxiously looking for You" (Luke 2:48). He said to them, "Why is it that you were looking for Me? Did you not know that I had to be in My Father's house?" (Luke 2:49). Mary forgot that her child was the Son of God. He was not lost. He was already doing God's work. After this, Jesus continued ". . . in subjection to them . . ." (Luke 2:51), and even though Mary did not understand everything about Him, she "treasured up all these things, pondering them in her heart" (Luke 2:51b), just like she did when He was born.

I like what happened at the wedding of Cana. It seems that Jesus didn't want to perform a miracle yet, but He did His first one and at the same time pleased His mother by turning water into wine (John 2:1–11). "This beginning of His signs Jesus did in Cana of Galilee, and manifested His glory, and His disciples believed in Him" (John 2:11).

After Jesus was born, Mary did not lose favor before God because she became Joseph's wife. She did what God commanded her to do, to give birth to God's precious Son, and now she had to be the wife she was supposed to be to Joseph. The Bible tells us that after the angel spoke to Joseph in a dream, "…**Joseph awoke from his sleep and did as the angel of the Lord commanded him, and took Mary as his wife, but kept her a virgin until she gave birth to a Son; and he called His name Jesus"** (Matt 1:24-25). God's command was that Joseph had to keep Mary a virgin *until* Jesus was born. Joseph obeyed. After that, they had to become what they were meant to be: husband and wife. God couldn't get angry with Mary because she was Joseph's wife and Joseph was obedient. Mary, a servant of God, the mother of our Savior, and the wife of a faithful man, was also a woman. We need to recognize how special she was to God, but we need to remember that she was also human. Many have made an idol out of her but she was not a god to be worshipped. She did not die on the cross for the sins of the world, Jesus did.

Search Your Heart, Thank God, and Pray

Would you follow your husband the same way Mary did? If you ever placed Mary above her Son, remember that she was a sinful human for whom Jesus also gave His life. Mary did not have a miraculous birth, she was also a daughter of Eve, and Eve was a sinner. Read Gen 3:16

Day 3

Mary, the Mother of The Lord Jesus The Woman Who Loved Her Son and Was Loved by Her Son

Mary was a patient, non-complaining woman who embraced her future by faith. She suffered great pain when she saw her Son die on the cross for the sake of others. Even though Mary's heart was hurting, she didn't go to the Lord in prayer and ask Him to stop the whole thing like we mothers do when something bad is happening to our children. She knew it had to happen, and she also knew He was going to rise from the dead. She knew the salvation of the world depended on the death and resurrection of her Son. She knew the truth, but oh how it hurt.

I remember the agony I experienced when I had my six-week-old son in the hospital for a hernia operation, which required him to have tubes and electrodes all over the place. It was painful, but in the middle of the whole thing, I trusted that God would take care of him like He had done previously. He prevented my son from dying while he was inside my womb because I almost lost him when I was five months pregnant. God also prevented my son from experiencing eternal death. My son accepted Mary's son as his Lord and Savior. I can never compare my pain to Mary's or to the pain of a woman who has lost a son, but going through what I went through is as close as I would like to get to losing a child. Mary's Son was dying for her, for you and for me. She couldn't save Him! She would have given her life not to see Him suffer, but she knew He had to do die. I can't imagine the sorrow and anguish she endured and the tears she shed after every nail was nailed to her Son's hands and feet, and after every drop of blood Jesus shed.

Mary was the mother of the only perfect Son ever born to a woman, the Lamb of God, and He loved her very much. Jesus showed His love for His mother on the cross at Calvary. Jesus was concerned for His mother's welfare. Can you imagine Jesus nailed on the cross, bearing the burden of all the sins of the world, yet taking the time to take care of His mother? Before He died at the cross, He placed her under the care of the apostle John, "whom He loved" (John 19:26–27). John was the only disciple who didn't abandon Jesus at the cross, and He knew that. Jesus was no longer going to be around His mother physically to love her, but He was going to ascend to heaven and **prepare a place there for her**. In John, Mary gained another son and earthly protector and provider because "the disciple took her into his household." We don't really know why Jesus had to make sure that He cared for his mother. Joseph was probably dead, and He, the oldest son, had to take care of her. He knew John would do a good job. Here we see Jesus giving His mother physical security while dying on the cross to give her eternal security.

Mary must have been a tremendous example to Jesus when He was a boy. Even though He was God, He was also human, and children learn by example. Mary and Joseph were the guides Jesus, God's only Son, needed in order to grow. Mary was a woman of prayer. She gathered with others to pray to God Almighty. Before I became a Christian, I used to put Mary right next to the seat of God because I thought she could intercede for me with the Father. I thought she had connections in heaven to help me because she was the mother of Jesus. However, her Son is the only one who can mediate between man and God. As 1 Timothy 2:5 says, "For there is one God, and one mediator also between God and men, the man Christ Jesus."

Search Your Heart, Thank God, and Pray

Just like Jesus trusted John with His mother, has God trusted you with something special? Have you received Mary's Son, Jesus, as Lord? If you do not know how to become a Christian, read the last chapter of this book for assurance of salvation. Read John 3:16

Day 4

Mary, the Mother of The Lord Jesus She Gave Birth to the Son of God

Mary, the mother of the Son of God, found favor in the eyes of God, and He blessed her. God knew that she would serve Him because He knew her heart. After giving birth to Jesus, I am sure that at times she probably forgot to whom she had given birth: For example, when little Jesus cried because He was hungry and needed to be breastfed, when He needed a diaper change, when He was cold and needed her arms to warm up His little body and feel secure, when He smiled at her when she satisfied his needs of hunger and care, when He took His first steps, and when He lost His first tooth. Mary would come to recognize her baby as:

- The Son of God (John 3:16)
- The Messiah and Savior so long expected by God's people (Isa. 7:14)
- The Prince of Peace (Isa 9:6h)
- The Light of the world (John 8:12)
- The Word of God (John 1:1, 14)
- The bridge that would lead all to heaven (John 14:6)
- The gift of God to all who believe (Rom 6:23)
- The King of Kings and Lord of Lords (1 Tim. 6:15)
- The second person of the trinity (Matt 3:16–17)
- The bright morning star (Rev 22:16)

- The Lamb that would be slain (1:29)
- The giver of eternal life (1 John 5:11–12)
- The Good Shepherd (John 10:11)
- The only sinless man to walk the earth perfectly (2 Cor 5:21)
- The best preacher who ever existed (Matt 4:17); He preached Himself.
- The perfect sacrifice to satisfy God's wrath on mankind, the Redeemer (Rom 3:24)
- The well of living water (eternal life) and the one to raise people from the dead (John 4:13–14)
- The Wonderful Counselor (Isa 9:6e)

Mary gave birth to our Lord Jesus who was born into the world just like one of us except without sin. He had a special purpose: to save the world from the fires of hell. Mary knew that her heart would hurt by having this special, unique Baby who would die for the world as she had been foretold. In Luke 2:34-35, Simeon tells Mary, "And a sword will pierce even your own soul." Seeing Him die was going to pierce her heart with pain. W*e need* to accept Christ as Savior, love and praise Him, bow down and adore Him, honor, and worship, serve Him, obey Him and imitate Him. Mary's baby was:

- Born homeless
- Born naked in a stable with no place to rest His head;
- Born to die for our sins;
- Punished for crimes He never committed and publicly humiliated
- Spit on, mocked, pierced, hanged on a cross at Calvary
- Persecuted, beaten, lacerated, and killed.

Mary's baby was the only one to raise Himself from the dead after His body was lifeless, thereby fulfilling God's Word. He ascended into heaven and we have His promise that He is coming again! Mary saw all these things happen to her baby! When Jesus died and suffered, not only did He give us the opportunity to go to heaven, but He also gave it to His precious mother as well.

Search Your Heart, Thank God, and Pray

Have you ever stopped to imagine Jesus as an ordinary newborn? Do you think Mary got overwhelmed with the responsibility of being the mother of Jesus? God never makes mistakes and Mary was chosen and given the responsibility of being the mother of His Son. Are you ready to be used by God? Read Psalm 42:1-2, 1 Peter 1:18-21

Day 5

Mary Magdalene
A Faithful Follower of the Lord Jesus

Matthew 27:56, 61, 28:1–10; Mark 15:40, 47, 16:1–10; Luke 8:2, 24:10; John 19:25, 20:1–18

This Mary was a servant of Jesus and had a tremendous love for Him. Jesus cured her wounded spirit by taking seven demons out of her body (Mark 16:9). He gave her the chance to become a lady by giving her a new life in Him. She was a walking witness of Jesus' power over evil. When I say Jesus made her a lady, I refer to her new life of order and respect that Jesus gave her by allowing her to be able to live in society as a "normal" person free of evil spirits. She was a sinner just like all of us, but one whom Jesus personally cured.

Here is Mary Magdalene: a demon-possessed woman who did not have a future and was trapped in a world of darkness. She was completely lost under the power of Satan, but *Jesus was able to* take her out of the pit and make something great out of her life. She had the honor of being the first woman to see Jesus after his resurrection from the dead and be the first messenger of this wonderful truth to the world (Mark 16:9). She was so excited to see Him come back from the dead that He had to say to her, "Stop clinging to Me, for I have not yet ascended to the Father; but go to

My brethren, and say to them, I ascend to my Father and your Father, and My God and your God" (John 20:17).

Mary Magdalene was committed to Jesus' ministry by being a faithful follower and believer. Even when the apostles fled while Jesus was dying on the cross, she remained faithful. She was at the cross (John 19:25) while He was dying, and she was very careful to learn where He was going to be buried (Mark 15:47). This would allow her to pay her final respects to Jesus by trying to go and anoint Him for burial. To her great surprise, she found a risen Lord. She was so determined to honor Him that she went very early in the morning when it was still dark. She knew His voice so well that, when He called her name after He was resurrected, there was no doubt in her mind who was calling (John 20:11-16).

There is not much documentation about her personal life in the Bible. All we know is that she was from Magdala and that Jesus rescued her from a world of darkness. There are strong rumors about her sexual life, which indicate that she was a prostitute before Jesus took out the seven demons that were living inside her, but there is no biblical foundation that supports this theory. Her reputation has been tainted without biblical support. She will probably continue to have a bad reputation in the eyes of many but not in the eyes of God.

Jesus paid the price for sins: hers, yours, and mine, and God placed these sins as far away as **the east is from the west** (Psalm 103:12). Sometimes we keep on reminding ourselves of our sins, forgetting that when we confess our sins and receive Jesus in our hearts as Lord and Savior, all is forgiven and forgotten. Jesus can remove what keeps you from Him if you allow Him to enter your heart by surrendering your soul to Him and accepting Him as Lord and Savior.

Mary Magdalene is named fourteen times in the gospels, and her faith will be remembered forever. "Mary is named in connection with other women, but she is always at the top of the list, implying that she occupied the place at the front in the line of service rendered by godly females."[1] There were three Mary's at the cross at Calvary, and Mary Magdalene was one of them. Jesus saved her soul and mended her heart because she gave Him her whole heart. **"The Lord will heal a broken heart, but first he must have all the pieces"** [2]

Mary went through a lot. She was possessed by demons and was restored by Christ. She thought she lost her Savior but He was raised from the dead; she thought her Savior was stolen from the grave, and she was devastated because she was not able to find Him at the tomb; and she lost Him again to the Father because she was not able to physically walk with Him when He went to heaven. She continued to walk with him in faith, and she is helping us walk with Him today by encouraging us with her story.

Search Your Heart, Thank, and Pray

Are you a faithful follower of our Lord Jesus? Are you committed to His ministry? Just like Mary went early in the morning to the tomb, are you seeking Him early in the morning? Have you given God your whole heart? Pray that the Lord will give you the strength to follow Him regardless of your circumstances. He can mend all parts of your heart, if you allow Him. Read Psalm 30:5

1 Herbert Lockyer, All *the Women of the Bible (*Grand Rapids: Zondervan Publishing House, 1995), 100.

2 Clasby Gretchen, *Heart*, 1991, Oklahoma City.

Day 6

Mary of Bethany
She Publicly Loved the Lord Jesus

Matthew 26:7–13; Mark 14:3–9; Luke 10:38–42; John 11:1–45, 12:1–8

This Mary is the sister of the famous Lazarus, who Jesus raised from the dead, and the sister of Martha who was also Lazarus' sister. Mary of Bethany was a perfect example of Psalm 46:10, "Be still and know that I am God," because she was calm enough to sit by Jesus' feet and listen to Him. Because of this, she is mostly known for being the one who didn't help her sister Martha in the kitchen when Martha was cooking for Jesus. She was the one who decided to spend her time listening to the Lord instead of cooking. Her sister Martha did a good job of serving, but she missed out on the blessing Mary received. There is a time for everything, and Mary of Bethany knew how to invest her time.

This is the Mary who anointed the Lord Jesus with a very expensive perfume. This perfume was worth three hundred denarii or the equivalent of almost a year's salary in Jesus' day. "Mary therefore took a pound of very costly perfume of pure nard, and anointed the feet of Jesus, and wiped His feet with her hair; and the house was filled with the fragrance of the perfume" (John 12:3). Mark wrote, "She broke the vial and poured it over His head." This beautiful scene took place while Jesus was a dinner guest at Simon the leper's house (Mark 14:3). Those who loved Jesus didn't care about the place He chose to visit, what the people around Him looked like, or with what diseases they were infected. For His followers, Jesus' presence was sufficient to risk it all. His followers were seeking His wisdom, and the simple pleasure of being around Him had more value than where they worshiped.

When Mary's brother died, like the loving sister that she was, she took his death very hard. She said to Jesus, "Lord, if You had been here, my brother would not have died" (John 11:32b). She knew of Jesus' power to heal the sick. Jesus knew how much Mary was suffering, and He felt her pain. The Word says, "When Jesus therefore saw her weeping, and the Jews who came with her, also weeping, He was deeply moved in spirit, and was troubled" (John 11:33). "Jesus wept" (John 1:35) because He loved Lazarus. Everyone realized His love to the point of saying, "Behold how He loved him." In this moment of sorrow, we can see that Mary was used by God to gain souls for the kingdom. After Jesus raised Lazarus from the dead, "Many of the Jews, who had come to Mary and beheld what He had done, believed in Him" (John 11:45). It is interesting to notice that people were coming to Mary not Martha.

Throughout Mary's life, she didn't care if people made fun of her or criticized her when it came to worshiping the King of Kings, and Jesus praised her for it. He said, "Truly I say to you, wherever this gospel is preached in the whole world, what this woman has done shall also be spoken of in memory of her" (Matt 26:13). She honored Him with the best she had in front of everybody, and Jesus honored her by making her name unforgettable.

There are many things that also made this Mary unforgettable. Besides anointing Jesus and preparing Him for burial, she was also able to discern what her priorities were before Him. She humbled herself in the sight of the Lord, and she was not ashamed.

Choosing to sit and listen to the King was wise, and anointing Him was humbling. She declared herself a servant of Jesus in public by listening to Him, honoring Him while He was alive, and worshiping Him in front of others. She had the opportunity all Christians would like to have and that is to have Him in front of us in person so we too can worship His majesty.

Mary left us a legacy of wisdom by giving us an example of what is the best thing to do as followers of Christ: to listen at the feet of Jesus.

Search Your Heart, Thank God, and Pray

Do you worship Jesus before the world? Can you offer Him what is most valuable to you? Do you take a stand for Jesus where you work or live or with your family members? If you don't like worshiping Jesus before others, pray for boldness. God deserves recognition before men. Give to Him something that is precious to you from the heart (In my heart I gave Him my children). Read Revelations 4:11 and 5:12.

Day 7

Mary, the Mother of James and Joseph Committed to the Lord Jesus

Matthew 27:56, 61, 28:1–10; Mark 15:40, 47, 16:1–8; Luke 24:10; John 19:25

There were many women committed to Jesus' ministry, and Mary, the mother of James and Joseph, was one of them. This Mary is also a witness of Jesus' resurrection; she and Mary Magdalene are usually found together in the Scriptures. She was faithful to follow the Lord Jesus. She was one of the three Mary's at the cross when Jesus was crucified (John 19:25). She was the wife of Clopas, a believer of Jesus' teachings who was also a witness to Jesus' resurrection. Jesus appeared to Clopas and another (Luke 24:13–35) on the way to a village called Emmaus.

She had the honor of having one of her sons, James or "James the less," as he was called, as one of the twelve men who became apostles of Jesus Christ. Mary, like other women who followed Jesus, kept a close look from a distance at our Lord, when He was being crucified, and even when His dead body was put to rest. This Mary, Mary Magdalene, and Salome are who I call "**The Three Amigas**" because they are usually always together involved in something to do with the Lord Jesus.

She also went to try to anoint Jesus' dead body as a symbol of love and reverence. She appears to be Mary's sister, the Lord Jesus' mother: "Therefore the soldiers did these things. But standing by the cross of Jesus were His mother, and His mother's sister, Mary the wife of Clopas, and Mary Magdalene" (John 19:25). This makes Mary the Lord's aunt, but there is no other reference to this idea anywhere else in the Bible. Even though Jesus didn't do a miracle in her life that was recorded in the Bible, her love and faithfulness toward Him moved her to honor Him. His lordship was good enough for her to commit herself to walk by Him for Him, and in Him.

At times we lose faith and strength to follow our Lord because we lose focus on our walk with Christ. There are events in our lives that make us stop serving God, reading God's Word, and having fellowship with our brothers and sisters in the Lord. This Mary had her whole family living around Jesus and His followers. She was always around someone who loved our Lord. She was with Jesus' mother at the cross; she was also with Mary Magdalene at the tomb. She is an example to us of the importance of fellowship. We need to have members of the body of Christ around us to walk and grow toward an abundant life with Christ. I am sure she had someone to pray with, someone to hold her when she cried, and someone whom she could comfort as well.

Mary Magdalene was a witness of the risen Lord and she is an example of persistence. She left a legacy in the world because of her service and love for Christ.

Search Your Heart, Thank God, and Pray

Do you have a friend who serves the Lord with you? Godly friendship is a necessity. Pray to the Lord to give you faithful friends in the body of Christ to help you with your walk. Confess any sin that is stopping you from serving God with a friend. Read Deuteronomy 6: 4-7

Day 8

Mary the Mother of John Mark A Lady of Hospitality Who Helped to Spread The Love of Jesus

Acts 12:12

This Mary is the mother of John Mark, the writer of the second gospel. This Mary was a woman who practiced the gift of hospitality. Traditionally it has been said that her house was the place Jesus used for the Last Supper and that her house was the center of the church in Jerusalem. Her house is the place where Peter went after he was rescued from prison by an angel of the Lord (Acts 12:1-18). God saved his life from the hands of Herod, and he ended up in a house of prayer where Christians were praying for him. Acts 12:12 says, "And when he realized this [Peter, knowing he was free], he went to the house of Mary, the mother of John who was also called Mark, where many were gathered together and were praying."

Mary knew that the power of prayer is the perfect line of communication we Christians have with our Lord and our Father. The line is never too busy! He will answer everybody's call. God's has requirements in order to answer and listen to prayer, and one of these requirements is a clean heart free from sin. When God sent Samuel out to find Israel's next king, Samuel had his own profile of the king in mind. When he saw David's brother Eliab, he thought he had found his man! "But the Lord said to Samuel, 'Do not look at his appearance or at the height of his stature, because I have rejected him; for God sees not as man sees, for man looks at the outward appearance, but the Lord looks at the heart'" (1 Sam 16:7). Then he found David, a young boy, one who became a man after God's own heart, and one who knew that he needed to have a clean heart to come before God in prayer. In Psalm 19:14 he said, "Let the words of my mouth and the meditation of my heart be acceptable in Thy sight o Lord, my rock and my redeemer." He also said in Psalm 51:10 after his sin with Bathsheba, "Create in me a clean heart, o God, and renew a steadfast spirit within me." He knew the Lord loves "he who has clean hands and a pure heart" (Psalm 24:4). I once read in prayer booklet, The Navigators-Daily Walk, a powerful statement about prayer that changed my prayer attitude that said, "Just as a doctor must scrub up before surgery, so must the Christian 'scrub up' before entering the presence of the Holy God in worship and prayer".

When I think of this Mary, I think of a woman who loved people because you will find that people who love people pray for people and always have people around them. I am sure many of the friends to whom she opened the doors of her house were saved. Christians met at her house to pray in the middle of controversy and some took spiritual refuge in it as well, like Peter.

Prayer is a very important part of our Christian life and is crucial for our spiritual growth. It is our way to communicate with God. Jesus gave us the power to ask of Him in prayer. "If you abide in me, and my words abide in you, ask whatever you wish, and it shall be done for you" (John 15:7). He showed us how to pray (Matt 6:5–15). He taught us to believe while we pray "and in all things you ask in prayer, believing, you shall receive" (Matt 21:22). He also said, "Where two or three have gathered in My name, there I am in their midst" (Matt 18:20).

In Mary's house, this last verse became a reality. Her heart for God gave her the ability to open the door of her home to the body of Christ regardless of the persecution Christians were facing in those days. She did this so Christians could gather and pray for the will of God to manifest itself through them. Think of the times when your home has been the center of prayer for Jesus. I am sure you can relate to Mary. If you have never had the experience of gathering brothers and sisters in the Lord in your home, try it. God is not concerned about what kind of furniture, dishes, or home you have, what kind of food you serve or clothing you wear. All that is important to Him is that you honor and worship Him, share your faith with others and love others as yourself.

Search Your Heart, Thank God, and Pray

Have you opened the door of your home to the Lord to use as He sees fit? Is prayer an important part of your household? If you have the desire to give your house to God, pray that He gives you the opportunity to offer it. Remember that God gave you the house and all you have belongs to Him anyway. Read Joshua 24:15.

Day 9

Elizabeth
Mother of John the Baptist, Wife of Zacharias, Touched by the Presence of the Lord Jesus

Luke 1:5–25, 36, 40–41, 57–80

Elizabeth was the wife of the priest Zacharias from the division of Abijah. She was a descendant of Aaron's family of priests, which was ordained by God, giving her godly roots. When referring to Elizabeth and Zacharias, the Bible says: "And they were both righteous in the sight of God, walking blamelessly in all the commandments and requirements of the Lord" (Luke 1:6). But there was a big disappointment in Elizabeth's life, she could not have children. A priest's wife who could not have children? It was embarrassing for her not to be able to produce more males to continue the line of priests for her husband. We know that it was Elizabeth who was not able to have children, because the Bible says, "And they had no child, because Elizabeth was barren" (Luke 1:7). They had given up any hope of having children because "…they were both advanced in years" (Luke 1:7).

The Lord God had a surprise for this couple. Zacharias was chosen by lots to go and burn incense in the temple of the Lord (Luke 1:9) which was an honor. This indicates that Zacharias was of the priesthood because he had the privilege of burning incense to the Lord and did not get killed by the Lord while performing priestly duties. While Zacharias was doing his service inside the temple, an angel appeared to him. It was the angel Gabriel and, of course, whenever he appears to people they get scared! (Luke 1:29–30; Dan 8:15-17). The angel Gabriel told him that God had listened to his prayers and that Elizabeth would have a son and he should name him John. Zacharias didn't really believe Gabriel because he was old and so was his wife. The angel Gabriel did not like what he heard and said, "I am Gabriel who stands in the presence of God; and I have been sent to speak to you, and to bring you this news" (Luke 1:19). Zacharias was disciplined for his lack of faith. The angel Gabriel said, "And behold you shall be silent and unable to speak until the day when these things take place, because you did not believe my words, which shall be fulfilled in their proper time" (Luke 1:20).

Elizabeth did not know what was going on until Zacharias was done with his priestly duties and went home. It is not clear if Elizabeth witnessed Zachariah's first mute encounter with the people, after being delayed inside the temple. "And after these days Elizabeth his wife became pregnant; and kept herself in seclusion for five months, saying, 'this is the way the Lord has dealt with me in the days when He looked with favor upon me, to take away my disgrace among men'" (Luke 1:24–25). Elizabeth enjoyed her pregnancy until she was ready to reveal it to the world. Five months was a long time to keep such a wonderful event as a secret! Maybe she was afraid of miscarrying or perhaps she was probably embarrassed that people would know that she had sexual relations with her husband being old. Sometimes I think that in those days, sex was discontinued after so many years of marriage! Elizabeth was finally going to contribute to the line of priests in her family! Or so she thought… She was going to give birth to John the Baptist, who was born to do just like the angel Gabriel said: to prepare the people for Jesus, the Messiah (Luke 1:17a).

When Elizabeth realized that Mary was pregnant with Jesus the long awaited Messiah, she felt her own child leap in her womb." Elizabeth "She cried out with a loud voice, and said, 'Blessed among women are you, and blessed is the fruit of your womb! And how has it happened to me that the mother of my Lord should come to me?'" (Luke 1:42–43). Elizabeth knew

Mary was special in the eyes of God. Jesus had not been born yet, but He was touching lives already!

Search Your Heart, Thank God, and Pray
Do you find yourself doubting God's Word at times? If you are not able to have children, would you be happy to have them when you are old like Elizabeth? If you have never had children and still resent it, search your heart and ask God for the peace that only He can give. As I wrote this, I prayed for you so that the Lord will help you accept His decisions for your life. If you still have time and energy, adoption is an option. We are all adopted into the family of God because of Jesus Christ. Read Romans 8:15, Ephesians 1:5; Acts 13:48

Day 10

Elizabeth
Her Son Loved the Lord Jesus

Elizabeth's joy was great, and the company she had was even better, "And Mary stayed with her about three months, and then returned to her home" (Luke 1:56). Mary, the mother of Jesus stayed with Elizabeth while she was pregnant of Jesus and Elizabeth commended Mary for her faith in God when she said, "Blessed is she who believed that there would be a fulfillment of what had been spoken to her by the Lord" (Luke 1:45). Mary believed what she couldn't see and was hopeful of things to come, just like Hebrews 11:1 challenges us to do: "Now faith is the assurance of things hoped for, the convictions of things not seen." Mary knew Elizabeth was pregnant because the angel Gabriel encouraged her with these words, "And behold even your relative Elizabeth has also conceived a son in her old age; and she who was barren is now in her sixth month" (Luke 1:36). So it was with great joy that Mary went to Elizabeth. They were both taking care of each other while they nourished their unborn babies for the glory of God. It seems that Mary had the pleasure to see John the Baptist as a new born baby (Elizabeth was six months when Gabriel told Mary and Mary stayed with her for three months!)

After John was born, his parents knew what name to give him because the angel Gabriel had already told them. In this way Gabriel went beyond the predictions of a sonogram. Zacharias said, "And you, child, will be called the prophet of the Most High; for you will go on before the Lord to prepare His ways" (Luke 1:76). John was loved, understood, and respected by Jesus. "I say to you, among those born of women, there is no one greater than John; yet he who is least in the kingdom of God is greater than he" (Luke 7:28). John never tried to pretend to be Jesus and he never got in the way of Jesus' ministry. In spite of his miraculous birth, and Jesus' kind comments, John still experienced spiritual doubt. John sent some of his disciples to make sure that Jesus really was the Messiah that he had preached about in the wilderness. For John Jesus was taking too long. Jesus performed miracles which were witnessed by John's messengers. They saw Jesus perform miracles like rescuing people from evil spirits, diseases, afflictions, and blindness and raising people from the dead (Luke 7:18–27). When they went back to John, their testimonies were all he needed to be convinced that Jesus was the Christ.

John was always focused on accomplishing his purpose: to exalt the name of Jesus. John said before Jesus showed Himself to the world as the Son of God, "One is coming who is mightier than I, and I am not fit to untie the thong of His sandals; He will baptize you with the Holy Spirit and fire" (Luke 3:16). John had the honor of baptizing the Savior of his soul even though he didn't consider himself worthy of such a job (Matt 3:13–17). John knew that Jesus was the Son of God and that people needed to take their eyes off of him when he said, "He [Jesus] must increase, but I must decrease" (John 3:30). The Bible doesn't say whether John's parents lived long enough to see his ministry and the results of the work they did with him. All we know is that he did what he was supposed to do according to the Word of God.

When I think of Elizabeth, I think of the holiness of God and how God prepared the way for Jesus' ministry. God selected a few key people to play an important role in His salvation plan, and Elizabeth was one of them. God blessed Elizabeth because He is gracious and He loves those who love Him and follow Him. The name John means "God is gracious," and that is exactly what God was to Elizabeth and Zacharias: gracious. John lived up to the meaning of his name.

Search Your Heart, Thank God, and Pray

Would God pick you to do His work because of your godliness? Do you know that you are called to the ministry of serving God? God always calls us to do things out of the ordinary like He did with John. Pray that the Lord will make ready your heart and your walk so He can guide you according to His will for His service. Read Psalm 32.

Day 11

The Giving Widow The Lord Jesus Used Her as an Example; She Gave All She Had

Mark 12:41–44; Luke 21:1–4

Our Lord Jesus took time to observe everything around Him, whether it was good or bad. Because of His observations, He blessed us with the short and powerful story of the giving widow. One day Jesus decided to observe the treasury where people were dropping off their monetary gifts for the house of the Lord.

> And He sat down opposite the treasury, and began observing how the multitude was putting money into the treasury; and many rich people were putting in large sums. And a poor widow came and put in two small copper coins, which amount to a cent. And calling His disciples to Him, He said to them, "Truly I say to you, this poor widow put in more than all the contributors to the treasury; for they all put in out of their surplus, but she, out of her poverty, put in all she owned, all she had to live on." (Mark 12:41–44)

Thousands and thousands of preachers and missionaries in search of financial support to keep churches and ministries going have used this observation by Christ. This nameless, poor, sacrificing widow became a symbol of a faithful giver who understood the law and the meaning of tithing. She was a symbol of an unselfish heart towards God.

God commanded Moses in the Old Testament that the sons of Israel had to give Him a tenth of all they produced from their flocks, land, and money (Lev 27:30–32). He required it, and it was the law. A tenth of all we have is no longer required by Levitical law, because we are under the lordship of Christ. Today this tenth is part of our worship to God during our gathering together as the body of Christ, the church. The monetary gifts we give God provides for those who serve Him and are taking the Gospel to unbelievers: our pastors and missionaries. **Giving is an honor** and a privilege that pleases God. You don't **have to** give, you **get to give**. In Christ, the believer understands that giving to the church is not only a blessing but a way to love God and others. Paul encouraged the people of Corinth to give. He said to them:

> Let each one do just as he has purposed in his heart; not grudgingly or under compulsion; for God loves a cheerful giver. And God is able to make all grace abound to you, that always having all sufficiency in everything; you may have an abundance for every good deed. (2 Cor 9:7–8)

We should not give to receive, but there is a promise that if you give, you will also receive beyond measure and you will please God at the same time. Jesus said, "Give, and it will be given to you; good measure, pressed down, shaken together, running over, they will pour into your lap. For by your standard of measure it will be measured to you in return" (Luke 6:38). The Lord loves those who give their best from the heart. Do you know that you honor God when you give and that you receive a blessing? Proverbs 3:9–10 reads, "Honor the Lord from your wealth and from the first of all your produce; so your barns will be filled with plenty, and your vats will overflow with new wine." Not only does the Lord love it when you give, but you also honor Him. Store up treasures in heaven by giving to the work of God. You may ask yourself, "To whom should I give my tithe, the portion of the money God gave me?" The Bible says we should tithe to the church. In Malachi 3:10a the Lord said, "Bring the whole tithe into the storehouse, so that there may be food in My house." So our first obligation is to the church. We also should financially support missionaries who dedicate their lives to help others to know Jesus. It is biblical and is my personal conviction that the people who give their lives to minister personally to us should benefit from our financial support!

The giving widow's gesture shows that she loved God and wanted to give Him her all. It shows that she wasn't attached to money. The great Solomon said, "He who loves money will not be satisfied with money, nor he who loves abundance with its income. This too is vanity" (Eccles 5:10). This widow had no vanity, only love of God in her heart. Many lessons have been taught because of this giving widow. My favorite is that we should always give from what we have, making sacrifices instead of giving from what is left over. The giving widow in this story gave all she had. She remained nameless because Jesus wanted to keep it that way; she could be any one of us. I like to put my name in the part where Jesus refers to her as "she" and "this" because it encourages me to give and to do it with love and surrender. She knew that what she had belonged to God anyway, and she was willing to give it right back to Him. Psalm 24:1 reads, "The earth is the Lord's, and all it contains, the world, and those who dwell in it."

Search Your Heart, Thank God, and Pray

God knows when you give, how you give, why you give, and the sacrifice you made to give. Did you know that the Lord is robed when you do not give Him what belongs to Him? God owns it all. Ask the Lord to help you understand the process of giving and to allow you to experience the results of faithfully surrendering your finances to Him. Read Malachi 3:8-15.

Day 12

The Adulterous Woman
The Lord Jesus Forgave Her Sins and Saved Her from Death

John 8:1–11

In today's society we have many means of catching people doing things that are wrong. A person can become famous these days because of social media and other media outlets. The adulterous woman didn't have a television camera installed in her house to catch her every move. She didn't have someone recording her life, a spy observing her all the time, as if she were on a reality television show. The simple fact of the matter is that if a person sins, sooner or later the sin will come out. This woman in our reading today was caught in the act of adultery. The Pharisees and the scribes used her sin to challenge Jesus, to test Him to find something wrong in Him so they might charge Him with a crime.

According to the law of the day, a person caught in adultery was supposed to be put to death (Lev 20:10) regardless of their gender. The Pharisees brought the adulterous woman to Jesus and reminded Him that under Moses' Law, she was supposed to be put to death by stoning (John 8:5). Jesus knew their hearts, and He also knew the heart of the sinful woman. Jesus ignored the problem at hand for a moment and decided to write on the ground. The people didn't give up and insisted that He do something about this woman. Very wisely Jesus said, "He who is without sin among you, let him be the first to throw a stone at her" (John 8:7b). After He said this, He went back to write on the ground. Little by little they all left the area where they had gathered with Jesus and the adulterous woman. She was left alone with the Savior. Straightening up, Jesus said to her, "Woman, where are they? Did no one condemn you?" (John 8:10). And she said, "No one, Lord." And Jesus said, "Neither do I condemn you; go your way. From now on sin no more." The adulterous woman recognized the divinity of Jesus and called Him Lord! She knew that she was in the presence of God.

In Mathew 7:2–3, Jesus made a powerful statement. He said: "For in the way you judge, you will be judged; and by your standard of measure, it will be measured to you. And why do you look at the speck that is in your brother's eye, but do not notice the log that is in your own eye?" The people in this story who were accusing the adulterous women all fled because there was sin in their lives. They couldn't throw the first stone because instead of specks, there were logs in their eyes! We are usually too fast to judge others for the same sin we commit ourselves. We need to examine our hearts before we can even begin to help a brother in Christ who is in sin.

The people of this story remind me of the nursery rhyme of Humpty Dumpty. "Humpty Dumpty sat on a wall. Humpty Dumpy had a great fall. And all the king's horses and all the king's men couldn't put Humpty together again!" What a story, and what a powerful message. **We are constantly sitting at the edge of the wall of temptation and sometimes we fall and break apart just like Humpty and no one can put us together again**. Only Jesus, who shed His blood on the cross to forgive sin, can help us (Romans 8:34, Mark 16:19). Humpty Dumpty's life depended on the strength of the king's horses and men, and they failed. Ours depends on the strength of the King of kings, Jesus, who is the only one who can put us together again.

The adulterous woman lived a life of dishonor. Her life was consumed with selfish passion, leading or following men into sin. The pleasure of sin makes us slaves to unrighteousness. The Word of God says that when we have intercourse with a person, we become "one flesh" (1 Cor 3:16, 6:19; Gen 3:24; Mark 10:7–9) with that other person. Why would a person be one with just anybody! As Christians, our bodies are the temples of God, and we should treat them as such.

1 Corinthians 6:19-20 tells us, "Or do you not know that your body is a **temple of the Holy Spirit** who is in you, whom you have from God, and that you are not your own? You were bought with a price: therefore glorify God with your body."

Search Your Heart, Thank God, and Pray

Have you ever committed adultery? Did you confess it to your mate? Did you ask God for forgiveness in Jesus' name? Do you judge people all the time? If adultery in an issue in your life, bring it to the throne of grace and ask God to forgive you in Jesus' name. According to Solomon, nothing is new under the sun. Sin is a way of life in the lives of many, but just like Christ forgave the adulterous woman, He can forgive you if you need forgiveness when you truly repent. Read 1 Cor 3:16, 6:19; Gen 3:24; Mark 10:7–9.

Day 13

The Samaritan Woman She Was Asked to Receive the Living Water of Eternal Life from the Lord Jesus' Lips

John 4:7–42

The Samaritan is well known in the Christian community because Jesus took notice of her. She is a great example of how anyone can receive the great gift of salvation regardless of race. Jesus' love for the world as a whole is so encompassing that He never shows favoritism. In the process of showing us His love, Jesus never embarrasses or forces anybody to love him or accept Him. With this woman, He was careful but honest as he pointed out her need for forgiveness. He made her an example, not a victim. The Bible never describes her appearance. We don't know how long her hair was or what color it was, how tall she was, or the color of her eyes. In fact, we don't even know her name! She was a sinner like any one of us and had the privilege of having the Lord Jesus ask her in person to receive His gift of salvation. This woman is a great example of the truth of John 3:16.

Jesus was traveling from one place to the other preaching the good news of Himself. "He left Judea, and departed again into Galilee. And He had to pass through Samaria" (John 4:2–3). He stopped in one of the cities of Samaria called "Sychar, near the parcel of ground that Jacob gave to his son, Joseph; and Jacob's well was there" (John 4:5–6). It is at this well that the Lord Jesus found the Samaritan woman, and He asked her, "Give me a drink." She was surprised because Jews were not supposed to speak to Samaritans or deal with them in any way. Samaritans were considered unclean and a mixed race not accepted by the Jews. These people ". . . sprung originally from an intermixture of the twelve tribes with gentiles nations."[1] Jesus disregarded others' prejudice and greeted her! Even the Samaritan woman was surprised when He asked her for water (v. 9) because she was fully aware of the Jewish prejudices towards her people.

She went to the well of Jacob to get water for her body, and she found water for her soul. Jesus told her that the water in the well was always going to have her coming back for more water. He said, "Everyone who drinks of this water will thirst again; but whoever drinks of the water that I shall give him shall never thirst; but the water that I shall give him shall become in him a well of water springing up to eternal life" (vv. 13–14). She understood Jesus' words. The Samaritans were also waiting for the Messiah. He offered her a new life, and she accepted it (John 4:15), but she still needed to change her ways! Jesus knew she lived a life of sin. To follow Him, we need to change our way of life. Our new life in Christ can't shine through us unless we change our sinful lifestyle. He asked her, "Go, call your husband, and come here." The woman answered, "I have no husband." Jesus said to her, "You have well said, I have no husband, for you have had five husbands, and the one whom you now have is not your husband; this you have said truly" (John 4:16–18). He told her things that only she knew about herself. Jesus helped her to recognize her sin.

The Samaritan woman went out to do what most Christians should go out and do after accepting Jesus as Lord and Savior: she went out to tell others about Jesus! Pastor Eloy, a pastor I heard once made an interesting observation about this woman. He said that Jesus had a three year ministry and He took a whole day and dedicated it to this woman! He also said, "Here is a woman with a bad reputation with men and she went out and said to other men, "A man told me!" Who would believer her!" She took a chance and others believed. She was so happy to actually see the Messiah, and accept Him as Lord, that she forgot the water and the pot she was carrying and went out to testify!" (John 4:28).

The Bible says that she went and told the men and they came to see for themselves what she told them about Jesus. The power of the Word of God! "And from that city many of the Samaritans believed in Him because of the woman who testified, 'He told me all the things I have done'" (John 4:39). The people asked Jesus to stay with them, and He did. The results were wonderful! Many believed because of what they heard Jesus preach. "And they were saying to the woman, 'it is no longer because of what you said that we believe, for we have heard for ourselves and know that this One is indeed the Savior of the world'" (John 4:42). She helped to evangelize the lost by bringing them to Jesus.

The testimony of one person can change a life, a town, or a country! Jesus was able to dwell in the lives of many because one woman decided to be bold and share His gift of eternal life with others.

The Samaritan woman was a tool Jesus used to bring others to Him. He didn't shame her but helped her to start a new life. He kept her sins to Himself. He just made her aware of the life of sin she was living—a life that could not continue after she accepted Him as Lord and Savior.

Search Your Heart, Thank God, and Pray

Have you ever gone out of your comfort zone to share the gospel with people who do not know Jesus? Do you bring unsaved people to your church so they can hear the gospel? Ask the Lord to give you boldness. When you allow the Lord to use you, others are always blessed. Read Luke 12:12; 2 Corinthian 5:17; Proverbs 3:1-7.

1 Logos International, *International Bible Dictionary (*Plainfield: Logos International, 1977),

Day 14

The Widow of Nain The Lord Jesus Raised Her Son from the Dead

Luke 7:11–17

As I researched what a widow was in the days when the widow of Nain lived, it made me understand even more why the Lord Jesus took notice of widows in the way He did. Who was a widow back then?

> Together with the fatherless and the sojourners, widows were members of a disadvantaged class in ancient Hebrew society. To help counter their fight, the Mosaic laws contained a number of very specific provisions to protect and provide materially for the often needy widow.[1]

People who provided for widows were blessed by God (Deuteronomy 14:29 and 16:10–11). According to 1Timothy 5:3-16, there were three kinds of widows:

- The first kind of widow was the one who had children and could be taken care of by them. The widow of Nain is an example of this kind of widow because she had one son (Luke 7:12), and he was grown and able to take care of her. Sadly, when her son died there was no one left to support her financially.

- The second kind of widow was the young widow who could be married according to the Levitical law in Deuteronomy 25:5–10, which says that she had to marry her husband's brother and dedicate their firstborn child in memory of her deceased husband.
- The third was called the "real widow." This widow is described in 1 Timothy 5:5 like this: "The widow who is really in need and left all alone puts her hope in God and continues night and day to pray and to ask God for help" (NIV). In other words, this kind of widow dedicated her life to God and continuously depended on Him for her everyday survival needs. This type of widow also had to qualify to be put on the church list to receive help (1 Tim 5:9-10).

The story of the widow of Nain is short but full of the love of Jesus.

> Soon afterward, Jesus went to a town called Nain, and his disciples and a large crowd went along with him. As he approached the town gate, a dead person was being carried out—the only son of his mother, and she was a widow. And a large crowd from the town was with her. When the Lord saw her, his heart went out to her and he said, "Don't cry." Then he went up and touched the bier [coffin] they were carrying him on, and the bearers stood still. He said, "Young man, I say to you, get up!" The dead man sat up and began to talk, and Jesus gave him back to his mother. (Luke 7:11–15 NIV)

The widow of Nain did not go and rush to Him to tell Him about her suffering. He knew her pain and the reason for her pain and He did something about her pain. He instantly took away her pain by giving her son back to her alive and well. The Bible says, "Jesus gave him to his mother." What a gift that was! What a solution Jesus had for her pain! His compassion for her was unique, and so is the compassion He had for every individual. Jesus restored the peace she lost by taking away her sorrow. Jesus was right on time! He got to the town exactly at the time of the burial.

The Bible only records Jesus raising three people from the dead during His ministry, and this widow's son was one of them (the others were Lazarus in John 11:1-44 and Jairus's daughter in Mark 5:53-42). Jesus was concerned about widows in general, and sometimes He used them as examples to others in order to teach (the giving widow, Mark 12:41-44).

I'm sure Jesus looked at her heart and understood the reason it was so troubled. He probably looked at her eyes and saw the pain that was coming from her troubled heart. The compassion He showed her and the comfort He gave her could only come from Him. The end result of this widow's story is best explained with the following thought given by a member of my Sunday school class, Brother Arévalo. He said that there were two processions that day: a parade of death and of sadness at the beginning and a parade of celebration for life at the end!

Jesus' profound compassion for this widow gave her back her son. When we know Jesus personally, we can experience some of the compassion and love He feels for us, especially when we sin. He is always there to pick us up when we repent. Keep yourself alert so you can hear it in your heart when He says to you, "Do not weep."

Search Your Heart, Thank God, and Pray

Have you ever felt so much pain that you forget who God is? Are you a content widow? Did you find encouragement when you read about the widow of Nain? God has not stopped doing miracles yet! He is still in the business of restoration. Read Jeremiah 33:3, Isaiah 41:10

1 Allen C. Myers, The *Eerdmans Bible Dictionary (*Grand Rapids: WM. B. Eerdmans Publishing CO, 1987), 1

Day 15

Jairus's Daughter The Lord Jesus Raised Her from the Dead

Mark 5:21–43; Luke 8:41–56; Matthew 9:18–25

Jairus was a man of faith, a synagogue official who reached out to Jesus to save the life of his twelve-year-old daughter. Before he asked Jesus to cure his daughter, he "bowed down before Him" (Matt 9:1), begged, showed reverence and respect. He said to Jesus, "My little daughter is at the point of death; please come and lay Your hands on her, that she may get well and live" (Mark 5:23). He had faith and he also knew of the things Jesus was capable of doing and the power that Jesus had; otherwise, he would not have asked Him for such a miracle. He knew Jesus could cure his daughter just by putting His hands on her!

Jesus decided to honor Jairus's humble request. On the way to Jairus's house, Jesus encountered a woman he cured of a long-time hemorrhage. It seems that taking care of her kept Him from getting to Jairus's house on time, and consequently, Jairus's little girl died. The Word of God says, "While He [Jesus] was still speaking, they came from the house of the synagogue official saying, 'Your daughter has died, why trouble the Teacher anymore'" (Mark 5:35). Jairus was devastated. "But Jesus, overhearing what was being spoken, said to the synagogue official, 'Do not be afraid any longer, only believe'" (Mark 5:36). Jesus then decided to go to Jairus' house regardless of the fact that everyone already knew that the child was dead! "And He allowed no one to follow with Him, except Peter and James and John the brother of James" (Mark 5:37). Jairus's house was full of people crying and mourning. "And when Jesus came into the official's house, and saw the flute-players and the crowd in noisy disorder, He began to say, 'Depart; for the girl has not died, but is asleep'" (Matt. 9:23).

The people who were present in the house started to laugh at Jesus because they knew the little girl was dead. The people laughing didn't get to see Jesus' miracle because Jesus made the matter private. He only allowed the disciples He took with Him and the girls' parents to see the miracle (Mark 5:40). "And taking the child by the hand, He said to her, 'Talitha Kum!' which translated means, 'Little girl, I say to you arise'" (Mark 5:41). Luke 8:55 says, "And her spirit returned, and she rose immediately; and He gave orders for something to be given her to eat. And her parents were amazed."

Jesus' request to her parents was to keep the miracle they just had seen to themselves which was a very difficult thing to do because everyone knew that she was dead! This is a beautiful example of the fact that our spirit leaves our bodies when we die, and only God can put it back again. She was the only child that appears in the Bible that Jesus raised from the dead. I was very touched by the love of Jairus for his daughter. The faith and courage Jairus exercised when he forged through the middle of a crowd and asked Jesus to cure his daughter is inspiring.

Jairus's love for his daughter reminds me of Mr. Jenkins, a Christian man who served as a policeman. He came to the school where I worked with preschoolers during the week when the children were learning about community helpers. He talked to them about what a policeman does and why. He told the children about the use of each piece of equipment he carried. When he got to his bulletproof vest, he told the children that the vest protected his heart from incoming bullets and that he always wears it.

His last piece of protection was the most important one. It really touched my heart to the point of tears. Beneath the bulletproof vest, he wore a bulletproof plate that also covered his heart. On the plate, he had written the name of his little girl, Katy. He loves his little Katy so much that he carried her name close to his heart. Every time he puts on his equipment to go on patrol, his plate reminds him who he's working for and why he should protect himself. He took extra measures to protect himself so he could increase his chances of survival because he loved his little Katy and his family.

Jesus gave Jairus's little girl the gift of a new life because Jairus loved her and put his faith in Jesus. Jairus and the apostles were able to see for themselves Jesus' power over death. The people who were laughing at Jesus missed out on the blessing of seeing Him raise someone from the dead.

Search Your Heart, Thank God, and Pray

Can you come to Jesus with a request as big as Jairus's? Is your heart ready for such a request? Like Mr. Jenkins carries Katy's name by his heart, do you love Jesus enough to carry Him in your heart? Pray for a faith in Jesus like Jairus's and to genuinely love someone, like Mr. Jenkins. Read Ephesians 2:8.

Day 16

Martha Sister of Lazarus and Mary of Bethany and follower of the Lord Jesus

Luke 10:38–42; John 11:1–44, 12:2

Martha is very well known for welcoming Jesus to her house and forgetting the purpose of his visit. No one will forget the fact that she was busy being a servant, cooking for Jesus, trying to impress the King of Kings and Lord of Lords with a wonderful meal. She was obviously a woman of hospitality and dedicated to excellent service. As we read about Martha, it is easy to discern that her priorities, even though they were good, were not in the right order.

As soon as Martha welcomed Jesus into her home she immediately decided to get cooking! All of a sudden, she realized that she was working all by herself and decided to go and complain to Jesus about it. Back then, she did not have Paul to remind her to "Do everything without complaining or arguing" (Phil 2:14 NIV). The Word of God tells us, "But Martha was distracted with all her preparations; and she came up to Him, and said, 'Lord, do You not care that my sister has left me to do all the serving alone? Then tell her to help me'" (Luke 11:40). At this point Mary had decided to listen to Jesus instead of helping her sister. "But the Lord answered and said to her, 'Martha, Martha, you are worried and bothered about so many things; but only a few things are necessary, really only one, for Mary has chosen the good part, which shall be not be taken away from her'" (Luke 10:41–42).

"Now Jesus loved Martha and her sister Mary, and Lazarus" (John 11:5). Martha got distracted cooking an elaborate meal when only a simple meal would have been just fine for Jesus. She missed out on the blessing of listening to Jesus. There is always time for another meal, but the times with Jesus are special and Mary knew that. What Mary learned from Jesus would not be taken away from her because it stayed with her for the rest of her life. Sometimes we get so busy serving Jesus that we forget to listen to Him, just like Martha did. We find ourselves too busy to go to church, too busy to read God's Word, too busy to gather with other Christians for fellowship, and too busy to listen to God in prayer.

When Lazarus died and Martha found out Jesus was coming, she went to meet Him. Martha said to Jesus, "'Lord, if You had been here, my brother would not have died. Even now I know that whatever You ask of God, God will give You.' Jesus said to her, 'your brother shall rise again'" (John 11:21–23). Martha thought that Lazarus would rise from the dead in the resurrection with everyone else, but she still had hope that Jesus would bring her brother back from the dead and she said to Jesus, "Even now I know that whatever You ask of God, God will give You," she was very bold and was actually requesting Lazarus's resurrection!

Jesus taught Martha to stop trying to frantically serve Him, and to listen to Him instead. He gave her assurance that her brother would rise again, and that He had the power to give Lazarus eternal life.

He said to her, "I am the resurrection and the life; he who believes in Me shall live even if he dies, and everyone who lives and believes in Me shall never die. Do you believe this?" (John 11:25–26). Martha received assurance of salvation in Jesus. Jesus did answer her previous question/request/suggestion (John 11:21–23) in this way, He proved to her that God would do anything Jesus asked of Him, including raising someone from the dead. Most Christians always focus on the fact that Martha was busy cooking, serving and complaining, while completely missing out on the fact that Martha needed to understand that only Jesus could grant eternal life.

When Martha answered Jesus' question with a yes and moved on with the rest of her life, she was not aware that her faith and words were going to be put to the test! Jesus went by Lazarus' tomb and said, "Remove the stone." Martha, the sister of the deceased, said to Him, "Lord, by this time there will be a stench, for he has been dead four days. Jesus said to her, 'Did I not say to you, if you believe, you will see the glory of God?'" (John 11:39–40). Jesus was still working on Martha's faith when he raised Lazarus from the dead. Martha got to see the power of Christ against physical death. Only Jesus has the power to raise someone from the dead! Martha could no longer doubt it. Talk about one to one evangelism!

Martha loved to serve—it was her gift. Even though she had a listening and complaining problem, she gave Jesus and others what she knew she could do best, and that was cooking and serving! You can find her doing the same thing again in John 12:2. In this passage, she was serving right before her sister Mary anointed Jesus with a very costly perfume. In this scene, again, her sister chose to honor Jesus by anointing Him instead of cooking and serving. Martha learned the importance of listening to Jesus. She also learned that Jesus is who He said He is. Jesus received bread for His body from Martha, and Martha received the bread of eternal life from Him.

Search Your Heart, Thank God, and Pray

There was something about Martha that Jesus was needed to addresses. Do you have doubts about your salvation? Do you think that Martha was jealous of her sister? Martha had a great gift, hospitality; do you know your gift to serve in the body of Christ? Read John 12:1-10 and mediate on what Mary did that Martha missed and what Martha did that Mary missed. (Read the last chapter of this book for assurance of salvation).

Day 17

Salome
The Mother of the Disciple the Lord Jesus Loved, John

Matthew 20:20–24, 27:56; Mark 15:40-41, 16:1–8; Mark 10:35-40

There are two women named Salome in the Bible. The first Salome was the woman responsible for the beheading of John the Baptist on the advice from her mother Herodias (Matt 14:3–11). The second Salome is the mother of two of Jesus' chosen disciples, James and John. John is the writer of the gospel of John and the disciple Jesus loved (John 21:20, 24). This Salome was the wife of Zebedee, who was a fisherman. He owned a fishing business with his sons and with Simon (Luke 5:10). Zebedee was obviously successful in his fishing business because he also had hired servants (Mark 1:20). His financial status was probably the reason why it was easy for Salome to go and minister to Jesus as he traveled throughout Galilee (Mark 15:40–41, Matt. 27:55–56).

Salome was one of the women who witnessed the crucifixion of Christ (Matt. 27:55–56) and one of the women who went out to the tomb to anoint Jesus (Mark 16:1–8). To her and the other women's surprise, He was not in the tomb because He had risen from the dead. This Salome is also believed to be the sister of Mary, Jesus' mother (John 19:25). This would make her the aunt of our Lord Jesus, which would also explain her devotion to Him. Jesus chose her two sons to follow Him (Matt. 4:21,

Luke 5:10, Mark 1:19). He called them "Boanerges, which means, sons of Thunder" (Mark 3:17) in Aramaic. These boys were not shy to speak their minds (Luke 9:54) and were very protective of the Lord Jesus (Mark 9:38-41).

Salome along with her sons had a big request of Jesus. Even though they were already blessed because James and John became apostles of Jesus, she wanted more. Mothers always want the best for their children but Salome crossed the line. She was a bold woman!

> Then the mother of the sons of Zebedee came to Him with her sons, bowing down, and making a request of Him. And He said to her, "What do you wish?" She said to Him, "Command that in Your kingdom these two sons of mine may sit, one on your right and one on Your left." But Jesus answered and said, "You do not know what you are asking for. Are you able to drink the cup that I am about to drink? They said to Him, "we are able." He said to them, "My cup you shall drink; but to sit on My right and on My left, this is not Mine to give, but it's for those for whom it has been prepared by My Father." (Matt 20:20–23).

They were able to "drink the cup" and die for Christ. In fact, James was the first to be martyred for the sake of the gospel Jesus preached (Acts 12:2), but they had their priorities all wrong! I don't blame the other apostles when they were angry with these two brothers and their mother. Jesus loved her sons in a special way. Perhaps they were responsible, loyal and godly. Jesus chose the two brothers to go and pray with Him and Peter (Matt 26:36-46). Maybe they were more teachable than the other apostles, but that doesn't mean they were more special than the others to deserve such as high rank next to Jesus. John, Salome's son, turned out to be the disciple that Jesus loved.

When I read their story in the Bible, I asked myself, "How did John and James agree to do this with their mother? Whose idea was it?" Her sons also made the same request of Jesus (Mark 10:35). I'll never know why the whole thing started, but one thing I know is that Jesus used it to teach the apostles a lesson about service and set them straight about their priorities.

> But Jesus called them to Himself, and said, "You know that the rulers of the Gentiles lord it over them, and their great men exercise authority over them. It is not so among you, but whoever wishes to become great among you shall be your servant. And whoever wishes to be first among you shall be your slave; just as the Son of Man did not come to be served, but to serve, and give His life a ransom for many" (Matt 20:25–28).

"It was evidently the intention of this ambitious mother to have positions of the greatest honor for her two sons. The right hand is usually considered the post of the highest honor."[1] There is no room for power-hungry people in the kingdom of God. To humble ourselves like Jesus did has more value in heaven for the Father than the power we might acquire by sitting at the right and left hand of Jesus. Jesus himself could not give them that power they were seeking. They were not sinless, did not deserve it, were not part of the Trinity, and Jesus was about to die for them. The sinless Jesus was going to die to go and sit at the right hand of the Father to intercede for us (Romans 8:34, Matt 26:64, Mark 16:19).

Search Your Heart, Thank God, and Pray

Do you think you have a better standing with God because you serve Him more than another brother or sister in the Lord? The Lord wants us to be servants just like He was. Read Exodus 23:25; Colossians 3:23-25.

1 M. James Freeman, *Manners and Customs of the Bible* (New Kensington: Whitaker House, 1996), 358.

Day 18

The Hemorrhage Sufferer She Trusted in the Power of the Lord Jesus' Healing

Matthew 9:20–22; Mark 5:25–34; Luke 8:43–48

When Jesus was on His way to the house of Jairus, a synagogue official in Capernaum, to see Jairus's twelve-year-old daughter who was very sick and was dying, a very special woman approached Jesus. This nameless woman had the power of faith as her name. Her example of faith was so great that three of the four gospels record her story (Matthew, Mark, and Luke).

> And a woman who had had a hemorrhage for twelve years, and had endured much at the hands of many physicians, and had spent all that she had and was not helped at all, but rather had grown worse, after hearing about Jesus, came up in the crowd behind Him, and touched His cloak. For she thought, If I just touch His garments, I shall get well (Mark 5:25–28).

Jesus was her last resort. She couldn't do anything else but trust Him. At this point in her life, everything had failed her. She put her faith in Him who is able, and the Word of God says, "And immediately the flow of her blood was dried up; and she felt in her body that she was healed of her affliction" (Mark 5:29).

The Lord Jesus knew someone very special had touched Him in the middle of a crowd of people seeking His attention, and He asked, "Who touched My garments?" I love the human reaction of Jesus' disciples! "And His disciples said to Him, 'You see the multitude pressing in on You, and You say, "Who Touched Me? (Mark 5:31). The disciples probably figured it would be impossible to find out who touched Him, but Jesus knew who did it! The Bible says, "And immediately Jesus, perceiving in Himself that the power proceeding from Him had gone forth, turned around in the crowd and said, 'Who touched Me?'"(Mark 5:30). Jesus started looking around for the person who touched Him, and I'm sure that just His looking into her eyes gave her the courage to speak. She couldn't keep it to herself anymore, and she came forward. "But the woman fearing and trembling, aware of what had happened to her, came and fell down before Him, and told Him the whole truth" (Mark 5:33). And lovingly with great compassion towards her, He addressed her. "And He said to her, 'Daughter, your faith has made you well; go in peace, and be healed of your affliction'" (Mark 5:34). She received special attention from Jesus in the middle of a crowd!

I can imagine the new life this woman started to have when she finally was cured. From a woman's point of view, having a constant blood flow is a very uncomfortable, unclean, and bothersome kind of situation. I say unclean because in those days, according to the Levitical law, she was considered ceremonially unclean due to the blood that was flowing out of her (Lev 15:25-30). It is enough having to have a menstrual flow every month; I can't begin to imagine having it for twelve years! What a relief it must have been!

I started to think about the faith of this woman. She could have asked for direct attention from Jesus. Instead she didn't even want to be noticed. But He noticed her. Jesus commended her for her faith, and I believe her great faith is the reason we know of her today. Sometimes God asks us to take a step of faith and we procrastinate. In the case of this woman, she took the step of faith without being asked. The Word of God says that, "…without faith it is impossible to please God" (Heb 11:6). Her faith is also a great example of Hebrews 11:1: “Now faith is the assurance of things hoped for, the conviction of things not seen.”

Search Your Heart, Thank God, and Pray

When was the last time you took a step of faith? Do you pray for healing? May the Lord give you the strength to trust Him enough to take a step of faith when you need to take it! Read Hebrews chapter 11.

Day 19

The Weeping Sinner She also Anointed the Lord Jesus with Perfume

Luke 7:36–50

This woman is usually confused with Mary of Bethany because she worshiped Jesus in the same way Mary of Bethany did. After meditating on her story and reading commentaries, I came to the conclusion that the two episodes were completely separate from each other. I call her the Weeping Sinner, Edith Dean called her "Sinful Woman," and Herbert Lockyer called her the "Woman Who Was a Sinner." Since she remained nameless in the Bible, no matter what name we give her, she is a great example of the love someone can receive from Jesus. This woman did not hide her sin. She was known in the city for being a sinner. In the opinion of many, she was most likely a prostitute. What kind of sinner was she? Nobody really knows! The only thing we know is that Jesus thought that her sins were many (Luke 7:47).

> And behold, there was a woman in the city who was a sinner; and when she learned that He was reclining at the table in the Pharisee's house, she brought an alabaster vial of perfume, and standing behind Him at his feet, weeping, she began to wet His feet with her tears, and kept wiping them with her hair of her head, and kissing

> His feet, and anointing them with her perfume (Luke 7:37–38).

This woman humbled herself, asking Jesus for forgiveness for her sins without using one word. In her case, her actions expressed her thoughts.

The action of this woman offended the Pharisee who had invited Jesus into His house. The Pharisee said to himself, "If this man were a prophet He would know who and what sort of person this woman is who is touching Him, that she is a sinner" (Luke 7:39a). Jesus knew who she was, and He knew what was in her heart. He also knew what was in the heart of the Pharisee. Jesus called the Pharisee, whose name was Simon, and Jesus said to him, "A certain moneylender had two debtors: one owed five hundred denarii, and the other fifty. When they were unable to repay, he graciously forgave them both. Which of them therefore will love him more?" (Luke 7:41–42). And Simon said, "I suppose the one whom he forgave more." And He said to him, "You have judged correctly."
Jesus took the opportunity to teach Simon a lesson. Jesus said to Simon:

> "Do you see this woman? I entered your house; you gave Me no water for my feet, but she has wiped My feet with her tears, and wiped them with her hair. You gave Me no kiss; but she, since the time I came in, has not ceased to kiss My feet. You did not anoint My head with oil, but she anointed My feet with perfume. For this reason I say to you, her sins, which are many have been forgiven, for she loved much; but he who is forgiven little, loves little." And He said to her, "*Your sins have been forgiven.*" (Luke 7:44–48) Jesus reassured her and said to her, "Your faith has saved you; go in peace" (Luke 7:50).

Simon was judging without looking at his own sins first! All the things Simon forgot to do to honor Jesus, this woman did them all at once. She did them using her faith, her perfume, her tears, her hair, and her love with repentance.

This woman anointed, kissed and cleaned Jesus' dirty feet! What a great honor! I think about my feet. By choice when I was a young girl, I used to love to walk around without shoes. I walked without shoes on my grandfather's farm, around the house, and while playing outside. Only my feet know what I made them step on! In the time Jesus walked the earth, I'm sure a lot of dirt accumulated in His sandals and on His feet during a simple walk! Simon was supposed to clean Jesus' dirty feet before He entered his house, but he didn't! But this sinner did. She proved to me that the more sins we have, the more we need Jesus' forgiveness. This woman, like the debtor who owed more in Jesus' story, showed that she loved Him more. Her soul was lost, and Jesus saved it, "For the Son of Man has come to seek and to save that which was lost" (Luke 19:10).

Search Your Heart, Thank God, and Pray

Have you asked Jesus' forgiveness for your sins lately? Is your heart focused on someone else's sins? Ask the Lord to allow you to see your own sin. Read Matthew 7:3; Matthew 6:22-23.

Day 20

The Canaanite Woman The Lord Jesus Healed Her Daughter

Matthew 15:22–28, Mark 7:24–30

The Canaanite woman (Matt 15:22), also known as the Syrophoenician woman (Mark 7:26), was a gentile (Mark 7:26) who was blessed by Jesus because of her great faith. "By culture and language this woman was a Greek, by religion a pagan, [and] by position in her community a nobody".[1] Even though she was not a Jew, somewhere along the way she learned about Jesus and started to believe in Him. Her story is very short, and in it her life is not displayed for us to study. The only thing we know about her is where she came from and the fact that she believed.

> And behold, a Canaanite woman came out from that region, and began to cry out, saying, "Have mercy on me, O Lord, Son of David; my daughter is cruelly demon-possessed. But He did not answer her a word. And His disciples came to Him and kept asking Him, saying, "Send her away, for she is shouting out after us." But He answered and said, "I was sent only to the lost sheep of the house of Israel." But she came and began to bow down before Him, saying, "Lord, help me!" And He answered and said, "It is not good to take the children's bread and

> throw it to the dogs." But she said, "Yes, Lord; but even the dogs feed on the crumbs which fall from their master's table." Then Jesus answered and said to her, O woman, your faith is great; be it done for you as you wish." And her daughter was healed at once (Matt 15:22–28). And going back to her home, she found the child lying on the bed, the demon having departed (Mark 7:30).

Jesus did this woman a favor. She was willing to humiliate herself in order to free her daughter from demon slavery. The love of a mother was able to break the reaction of Jesus towards her. She asked Jesus to give her some of the crumbs that fell from His table because even though she didn't deserve it, she was willing to eat from her Master's crumbs.

She was rewarded for her faith. Jesus did a miracle by removing the demons from inside her daughter. Since He is all knowing, He took care of the matter from a distance. At first she came for help to Jesus and He rejected her. She is the only woman who came to the Lord Jesus for help and He didn't want to give her help. We will never know why Jesus reacted towards this woman the way He did but, her faith was great and He honored it. There was a reason for Jesus' rejection of this woman's request. In his book *The Purpose Driven Church*, Rick Warren used this woman to make a point when he was writing about a targeted ministry. According to Warren, Jesus didn't want to help her because He was targeting a specific group of people for evangelism and she was not part of it. He wrote:

> The practice of targeting specific kinds of people for evangelism is a biblical principle for ministry. It's as old as the New Testament. Jesus targeted his ministry. When a Canaanite woman asked Jesus to minister to her demon-possessed daughter, he publicly stated that the Father had told him to focus on "the lost sheep of Israel" (see Matt. 15:22–28). Although Jesus went ahead and healed the Canaanite woman's daughter because of her faith, he publicly identified his ministry target as the Jews. Was Jesus being unfair or prejudiced? Certainly not!

> Jesus targeted his ministry in order to be effective, not to be exclusive.

The beauty of her story is that even though she knew she didn't belong to the group Jesus was focusing on at the time, she persisted. I thought of three reasons why she probably pressed Jesus. First, she had to know through testimonies of those healed by Jesus of what He was capable of doing, and she had faith He could do it for her daughter as well. Secondly, her pain as a mother suffering for her daughter must have been tremendous. Finally, she was aware of Jesus' true identity because she called Him "Lord" and "Son of David" when she asked for mercy. She reminds me of the verse that says, "Ask, and it shall be given to you; seek and you shall find; knock and it shall be opened to you. For everyone who asks receives, and he who seeks finds, and to him who knocks it shall be opened" (Matt 7:7–8).

Search Your Heart, Thank God, and Pray

When you ask of Jesus in prayer for a miracle, are you willing to keep on asking? Jesus cured the Canaanite woman's daughter from a distance and today He is in heaven and is only a prayer away. If trust in Him is what you need, pray for Him to allow you to see His miracles in the lives of others. It is a wonderful experience to see Him work personally in your life. Read Psalm 31:24; Psalm 27:8.

1 Edith Deen, *All the Women of the Bible* (New York: HarperCollins, 1983), 189.

2 Rick Warren, The Purpose Driven Church (Grand Rapids: Zondervan Publishing House, 1995), 158.

Day 21

Pilate's Wife The Lord Jesus' Situation Affected her Sleep

Matthew 27:19

Married women, godly or ungodly, are usually trying to do what's best for their husbands, their families, and themselves. Pilate's wife was one of these women: she was concerned about her husband's future. It seems as if she wanted to stop Pilate from making a mistake. Pilate was the governor of Judea (Luke 3:1) appointed by the emperor Tiberius Caesar in AD 26. His main job was to keep the peace in Judea. Pilate wanted to please everybody so he could gain more power from the people and from the emperor. He had the power to put people to death by making capital punishment decisions. He also had the power to control the army for military operations, and appointed the high priest.

Pilate's wife's words were very few but very powerful. "And while he was sitting on the judgment seat, his wife sent him a message saying, 'Have nothing to do with that righteous Man; for last night I suffered greatly in a dream because of Him'" (Matt 27:19). She knew Jesus was righteous! How did she know that? Why? Who knows! The one thing we know is that she blamed Jesus for her nightmares! Her nightmare must have been very scary for her to send a message like that to her husband. Here was Pilate judging Jesus, pressured by his people and the government, the Jews, and finally his wife. The pressure was on!

Pilate was afraid of the Jews who were questioning his loyalty to the Caesar (John 19:12), and He had to follow Jewish laws because he needed to be able to control the people (John 19:7–8). Pilate was even afraid of Jesus' power. To be certain, he asked Jesus if He was the King of the Jews (John 18:33) to double check that Jesus was not going to be a political threat to him. He knew Jesus was innocent (John 18:38, 19:6), and tried to free Him (Luke 23:15–25). In order to look good, he left it all up to the people and delivered Jesus into the hands of those who would kill Him.

Pilate's wife received what she wanted. She asked her husband to make sure he was not responsible for Jesus' death, and that's exactly what Pilate ended up doing! He gave in to the Jews' demands while all the time carefully balancing his political responsibilities. He washed his hands and said, "I am innocent of this Man's blood; see to that yourselves" (Matt 27:24). His innocence was signaled by the washing of his hands.

Regardless of whether or not Pilate's wife had any more nightmares or if Pilates cleared himself of killing Jesus, Jesus had to die to redeem men from sin. If Jesus would not have died on the cross, Satan would have reigned and obtained the souls of humanity. By dying on the cross, Jesus prevented Satan from continuing to enslave men to sin and experiencing eternal separation from God. Jesus dying on the cross has given the world a chance for spiritual healing particularly those individuals who receive Him as Savior. Pilate's wife could have received this gift, and maybe she did!

Search Your Heart, Thank God, and Pray

Have you ever tried to stop someone from doing something that you felt was wrong? If you have ever persuaded someone to make a wrong decision intentionally or accidentally, ask that person for forgiveness and then ask God for wisdom for the next time you need to help someone make a decision. Read Proverb 4:7-9; Proverbs 8:13.

Day 22

Susanna and Joanna They Helped the Lord Jesus' Ministry

Susanna—Luke 8:1–3
Joanna—Luke 8:1–3, 23:55, 24:10

Susanna and Joanna were women who appear to have supported Jesus' ministry financially, and they are listed among the women Jesus healed from evil spirits and sicknesses in (Luke 8:1-3). It seems that they both contributed to Jesus' ministry from their own personal funds. They are named together with the disciples as part of the group that went out proclaiming the gospel with Jesus from city to city and village to village. It is encouraging to know that women were also walking with Jesus while He was teaching and preaching.

Susanna is only mentioned in Luke 8:3, and God made sure you and I know at least her name and what she did. We know she was healed by Jesus, but of what? It could have been from something spiritual, physical, or demonic. Nobody really knows!

Joanna, on the other hand is made more known to us from God's Word. Joanna is said to be the "wife of Chuza, Herod's steward" (Luke 8:3). Chuza had a very high position because he handled Herod's finances. He was in charge of the financial affairs of a very large estate, which indicates that he had to be educated to be able to have such a job. Even though he had such an important job as Herod's steward, he had to be aware of his wife's beliefs. There are no indications that Chuza was a Christian. We can only assume that he was because his wife was a part of Jesus' ministry. In those days, she had to have permission from her husband in order to go about serving with Christ. If he was not saved while he was working for Herod, his wife probably prayed for him every day. Joanna was one of the women who discovered the empty tomb! She was named in the group of the women who went to speak to the disciples about Jesus' resurrection. She was spoken to by the angel who reminded them of Jesus' words, "Saying that the Son of Man must be delivered into the hands of sinful men, and be crucified, and the third day rise again" (Luke 24:1–10). We know the disciples did not believe her or the other women, but they were faithful to go and tell what they had discovered and knew.

Susanna and Joanna knew who they followed and why they followed: they were proclaiming the name of Jesus (Luke 8:1–3). They took a chance to come out and demonstrate their faith in Christ at a time when Jesus was a controversial figure.

These two women had the privilege to be healed by Jesus personally from that which caused them to suffer. They walked with Jesus, talked to Jesus, served Jesus, and witnessed to others about Jesus. Yet, they are not famous. Not many girls are named after Joanna which is a variation of Joan, and you will hardly find a girl named Susanna. In fact the name Susanna doesn't even appear in the 100,000+ Baby Names book![1] But Jesus knew their names just like He knows yours and mine.

Search Your Heart, Thank God, and Pray

Like Joanna and Susanna, do you need spiritual, physical, or mental healing? Are you serving the body of Christ, the church? These women were not famous but God made sure we would know them today because of their love and service to Christ. How will people remember you when you die? Read Matthew 11:28-29; Romans 12:10-18.

1 Bruce Lansky, 100,000+ *Baby Names (*Minnetonka: Meadowbrook Press, 2006).

Day 23

The Woman and Her Coin —A Woman in One of Jesus' Parables

Luke 15:8–10

Jesus was speaking in parables about His love for sinners, and He used the example of a woman who lost a coin to illustrate a powerful message. He said:

> Or what woman, if she has ten silver coins and loses one coin, does not light a lamp and sweep the house and search carefully until she finds it? And when she has found it, she calls together her friends and neighbors, saying, "Rejoice with me, for I have found the coin which I had lost!" In the same way, I tell you, there is joy in the presence of the angels of God over one sinner who repents (Luke 15:8–10).

Jesus used brief stories with powerful meanings. Let's look at this one a little closer:

- *The use of a woman by Jesus in this parable:* Jesus probably used the woman in this parable to relate to all the women who followed Him while He was preaching.

- *The silver coins*: These were Greek coins called drachmas, and they had the same value as Roman denarii, which represented the wage for a day's work.
- *House sweeping*: In those days, most of the floors were made out of dirt. Dirt floors get very dry and dusty, and they had to be swept every day, to make them look nice and even. My grandfather's farmhouse had dirt floors, and we had to sprinkle water on them to control the dust they created and also to be able to sweep it and make it look nice! It is very hard, if not impossible, to find small objects on dirt floors. The woman in this parable had to work hard to find this coin.
- *The lamp*: The woman in this parable had to go through the trouble of using her lamp to find the coin. She was very determined. It was costly to light her lamp if she had an oil lamp because oil was a precious commodity. It could also have been a candle that she lit; we don't know. All we know is that she was determined to find that coin!
- *Rejoicing to find her coin:* She was happy to find what had much value. Jesus values us and wants us to take advantage of the sacrifice He made for us. There is joy in heaven when one of us repents of our sins and decides to have Jesus control us. When a person accepts Christ as Lord and Savior, they gain eternal life! If you are a Christian that has allowed sin to dominate your life, remember that **you are like a precious lost coin that Jesus treasures and is looking to restore to Himself**.
- *She told everyone:* I love to be around new Christians because they are so genuine in sharing Christ, especially when they pray. They pray simply and humbly. The woman who told everybody about the precious coin she found reminds me of new believers in Christ who are full of joy when they find Christ and make Him Lord of their life. Just as the woman from this story went out and shared the good news with her friends, Christians need to do the same and share the good news of the gospel with others.

There is healing available in knowing that Jesus died so we can have the joy of salvation. The woman in this parable was determined to find that lost coin and used all her means to do it. Christ is available for all but we need to ask Him to be Lord of our lives. The woman in the parable lost something important and desired it, but she had to do her part to find it!

Search Your Heart, Thank God, and Pray

If you are a Christian, are you willing to do all you can to help others find Jesus? If you are not a Christian and you want healing for your soul, read the last chapter of this book. Ask God to give you wisdom in finding a church that will minister to your needs. Read Matthew 28:16-20; Acts 2:21.

Day 24

The Persistent Widow/ A Woman from Jesus' Parables

Luke 18:1–8

Jesus used a woman in this parable to show His disciples the importance of consistency in prayer and also to point out to them that they ". . . ought to pray and not to lose heart" (Luke 18:1). The part of the parable where he used the woman says:

> In a certain city there was a judge who did not fear God and did not respect man. There was a widow in that city, and she kept coming to him, saying, "Give me legal protection from my opponent." And for a while he was unwilling, but afterward he said to himself, "Even though I do not fear God nor respect man, yet because this widow bothers me, I will give her legal protection, otherwise by continually coming she will wear me out" (Luke 18:2–5).

This widow was persistent because she had a big need. She needed legal protection from an opponent. What was her fear? We do not know. All we know is that she knew where to go for help! Widows did not have rights. They were disadvantaged, but there were Mosaic Laws to give them some kind of protection and to provide for their needs (Deut 14:28–29, 16:10–11; Lev 22:13). Anyone could have taken advantage of widows. Widows were poor and depended on other people to provide for their needs. Ruth was one of these poor women who received help. Boaz made sure to leave extra food in the fields for her to collect so she could provide for herself and for her widowed mother in-law Naomi (Ruth 2:8–17). The widow in this parable knew the laws that would protect her, so she went to ask for help from the strongest available source: a judge. She was persistent to the point of nagging! Sometimes we want our needs met right away, but we need to go to the right source to get it just as the widow did. In the case of believers in Christ, we can go to God in prayer in Jesus' name and ask. Prayer is a time to praise God, acknowledge who He is, and intercede for others. The answers to our prayers may not come right away, and we can get discouraged. We need to be persistent and not lose heart because God will keep His promise to answer our prayers. There are three answers that we should expect when we pray:

- **No!** God knows what is best for us, and even when He says *no,* we need to trust Him because He is our Father in heaven (Luke 11:9–13).
- **Yes!** He will bless us right away. Jesus told us to ask in His name (Matt 7:7, John 16:23–24). He also promised to provide for our needs, not necessarily our wants, and all according to His riches in glory (Phil 4:19).
- **Wait!** The hardest thing to do for most people is to wait! Sometimes He will give you what you request, but for your own good He makes you wait. Yet, He is never late. He knows what you need before you even think about it because God is all knowing. He wants us to trust Him. Wait! "Be anxious for nothing but in everything by prayer and supplication with thanksgiving let your request be made known to God. And the peace of God which surpasses all comprehension, will guard your heart and your minds in Christ Jesus" (Phil 4:6–7). He will answer in due time, in His time, the best time.

The widow was persistent and Christ followers should also be persistent. I want to challenge you today to ask God in prayer for your needs, the needs of others around you, and the will of God for you. Exalt His name as you pray just like Jesus did (Matt 6:5-15). "An exalted view of God brings a clear view of sin and a realistic view of self. A diminished view of God brings a reduced concern for sin and an inflated view of self."[1]

Search Your Heart, Thank God, and Pray

When you pray, do you pray for God's will for your life? Are you persistent in prayer? Before you pray, always confess any sin that might hinder your prayer. Read Matthew 6:5-15; Psalm 51:10.

1 Henry Blackaby, Blackaby, Richard, *Experiencing God Day by Day* (Nashville: B&H Publishing Group, 2006), 3.

Day 25

The Ten Virgins from the Lord Jesus' Parable Jesus Used Them as a Warning for His Return

Matthew 25:1–13

The Bible uses the word *virgin* to describe a woman who has not experienced sexual intercourse. A virgin is a symbol of purity. Virginity was and is considered a virtue. Virginity was serious business during the times of the Patriarchs. There were Mosaic Laws protecting virgins and also protecting a male who could be lied to about obtaining a virgin. If a virgin was dishonored (Deut 22:13-20)—had sex before marriage—the male had to pay her father a dowry and marry her (Ex 22:16–17). If a virgin got married and was found not to be a virgin, her husband had the choice of demanding from her father "a token of virginity." There were special tokens that could be submitted as proof of virginity, for example, "a sheet or garment stained with the blood of the consummation from the wedding night."[1] And if the father of the bride did not produce this token, the husband had the right to have her stoned for harlotry. In other words, the bride had to make sure she secured proof of her virginity and gave it to her father so if she was accused of not being a virgin, her father would have undisputable proof that she was. Jesus used the cultural norms about virginity to engage the Jews on the topic of heaven.

This parable shows how five of the ten virgins were prepared for the bridegroom and the other five were not, so they missed out. Jesus started the parable by saying that the ten virgins went out to meet the groom, "And of them five were foolish, and five were prudent. For when the foolish took their lamps, they took no oil with them, but the prudent took oil in flasks along with their lamps" (Matt 25:-24). The groom was late to the party and the virgins fell asleep. When the groom was on his way someone shouted that he was coming and the virgins lit their lamps. The foolish virgins didn't have enough oil to make it to the groom's house so they asked for oil from the prudent, but the prudent virgins answered, "No, there will not be enough for us and you too, go instead to the dealers and buy some for yourselves" (Matt 25:9). The foolish virgins were not prepared and went to buy oil. They missed the bridegroom and they were shut out! When they came back, they tried to have the groom open the door, and the groom said, "Truly I say to you, I do not know you."

Be ready! The ten virgins in this parable remind us of the need that we have to be ready when Jesus returns to earth by knowing Him as Savior. In His second coming He will take us, His bride, and His church to heaven with Him. We need to be prepared to receive Jesus as our Bridegroom. If we do not know Him as our Lord and Savior, He will not know us as children of God either. Jesus tells us, "Be on the alert then, for you do not know the day or the hour" (Matt 25:13). We need to be spiritually prepared for when He returns. Jesus said many would come to Him, like false prophets, and many will call Him Lord, wanting to prove to Him that they are His followers. He will have to tell them, "I never knew you" (Matt 7:23). In which of the two groups of virgins would you find yourself in today: the ones who were ready for the bridegroom or the foolish ones who were not? To be ready all we need is Jesus as Lord. Because of Jesus' sacrifice, the Holy Spirit lives in us and that is sufficient!

Search Your Heart, Thank God, and Pray

If Jesus came today, would you be ready to receive Him? In order for us not to miss the Bridegroom, Jesus, we need to repent of our sins and accept Him as Lord. Have you ever done that? If you have, thank Him for His enormous sacrifice for you, and if you have not, accept Him by faith as

Lord and Savior. Jesus said in John 14:6, "... I am the way, the truth, and the life; no one comes to the Father but through Me". He is the only way to heaven. Read John 14:1-31.

1 Allen C. Myers, The *Eerdmans Bible Dictionary (*Grand Rapids: WM. B. Eerdmans Publishing Co, 1987), 1039.

Day 26

The Widow and Elijah, Remembered by Jesus

Luke 4:26–27; 1 Kings 17:8–24

Jesus started His ministry and decided to go to His hometown, Nazareth, to teach in the synagogues. There was confusion in Nazareth about who He really was because of the way He spoke to them. They knew Him as the son of Joseph! He addressed them and said, "Truly I say to you, no prophet is welcome in his home town" (Luke 4:24). He gave the example of how Elijah was sent by God to a widow in another land, Zarephath in Sidon, to provide for her and for him. He ended up helping this widow instead of helping the many widows who were suffering in Israel (Luke 4:25; 1 King 17:1). Israel had a drought for three years and six months (Luke 4:25, 1 Kings 17:1), there was a famine, and God protected Elijah from that famine. God said to Elijah, "Arise, go to Zarephath, which belongs to Sidon, and stay there; behold, I have commanded a widow there to provide for you" (1 Kings 17:8). God used this widow to provide for Elijah and Elijah to provide for the widow, and He used them both to teach us lessons about faith, trust, and hope.

Elijah went to her house and asked her, "Please get me a little water in a jar, that I can drink" (1 Kings 17:10) and "Please bring me a piece of bread in your hand" (1 Kings 17:11). The famine had reached her household too, and she was humble enough to tell Elijah, "As the Lord your God lives, I have no bread, only a handful of flour in the bowl and a little oil in the jar;

and behold, I am gathering a few sticks that I may go in and prepared for me and my son, that we may eat it and die" (1 Kings 17:12). This widow feared God because she used God's name to make sure Elijah knew she was telling the truth. She had just about run out of food to feed herself and her son, and now she had another person who was in need of the little she had to eat.

Elijah told her not to be scared and asked her to make him a small bread cake for him, one for her, and one for her son. He gave her a promise, "For thus say the Lord God of Israel, 'The bowl of flour shall not be exhausted, nor shall the jar of oil be empty, until the day that the Lord sends rain on the face of the earth'" (1 Kings 17:14). The widow obeyed Elijah and, sure enough, the promise was kept and she had enough food for her family for a long time.

God provided for Elijah and also for the widow's family, but there was more work to be done in the life of this widow. She had one more tragedy to go through, and that was the death of her son. The widow's son got sick and died, and the widow blamed Elijah's presence in her house for his death (1 Kings 17:18). Elijah recognized that what she said was true and went to God for help (1 Kings 17:20-21). Elijah took her son and carried him to the child's own room and started to pray to God. Elijah knew the death was God's doing, so he stretched himself three times upon the child and asked God to return life into the child's body, and God did as Elijah requested (1 Kings 17:17–23). Then Elijah took the child to his mother and told her, "See your son lives." "Then the woman said to Elijah, 'Now I know that you are a man of God, and that the word of the LORD in your mouth is truth'" (1 Kings 17:24). She received the ultimate proof of God's power, the life of her son. Even though God had used Elijah to miraculously provide food (1 Kings 17:11-16), this widow needed to see God's glory to **deepen her trust in God and truly believe** that Elijah was a man of God.

Sometimes it takes two miracles for someone to believe. Sometimes it takes deep hurt for us to understand what God is trying to tell us. It is easier to do as Jesus said to Thomas: "Blessed are they who did not see, and yet believed" (John 20:29a).

This widow was ready to prepare her last meal so she and her son could die. She had no hope, but God gave her a new life by using Elijah. God gave her revival. God caused her to have faith in Him and He also showed her that He can be trusted. If you believe, you will also trust in God, and if you have trust in God, hope will be present in your life.

Search Your Heart, Thank God, and Pray

At one time, this widow found herself alone with no husband and a dead son in her arms. God restored what she valued the most, the life of her son. She was helpless! Are you helpless today? How is your trust in God today? How is your hope? Do you need proof to believe that God is who He says He is? Read Romans 5:5; John 20:19-26; Isaiah 66:2;

Day 27

A Voice in the Crowd Corrected by the Lord Jesus

Luke 11:27

As Jesus was preaching and healing, and casting out demons, some of the people thought of Him as the ruler of demons because He had power over them. Others demanded a sign from heaven to verify that He was who He said He was (Luke 11:14–16). Jesus started to answer them when a woman diverted the people's attention by addressing Jesus. Luke 11:27–28 says:

> While Jesus was saying these things, one of the women in the crowd raised her voice and said to Him, "Blessed is the womb that bore You and the breasts at which You nursed." But He said, "On the contrary, blessed are those who hear the word of God and observe it."

This woman in the crowd was so excited about Jesus and about what He was doing that she interrupted Jesus' important defense of the kingdom of God and blessed his mother instead! Jesus had to direct the people's attention to what was important: the Father and His words. Perhaps she was a tool of Satan to divert people to the path of idolatry towards His mother.

Jesus' focus was the word of God! Hebrews 4:12 says, "For the Word of God is living and active and sharper than any two-edged sword, and piercing as far as the division of the soul and spirit, of both joints and marrow, and able to judge the thoughts and intentions of the heart."

According to this verse, the Word of God is real, powerful, and active. God offers us a lot of freebies, and sometimes we take them for granted. We can have free eternal life because Jesus paid the cost. He gave us His Word, the Bible, for free. We did not have to pay God for it! God gave us free will because He made us individuals and unique. We can even decide where we want our souls to live eternally!

The Word of God has many purposes. In Psalm 119:105 the psalmist said, "Your word is a lamp to my feet and a light to my path." In Matthew 4:4, Jesus said, "It is written, 'Man shall not live on bread alone, but on every word that proceeds out of the mouth of God.'" The Bible is God's Word. Meditate on God's word (Joshua 1:8) and the Holy Spirit will reveal Himself to you while you read it. In John 8:31–32 Jesus said, "If you abide in My word, then you are truly disciples of Mine; and you will know the truth, and the truth will make you free." Freedom in God gives us peace and a purpose to go on with our daily lives.

There is a blessing for those who hear the Word of God and do what it says! The powerful Word of God is revealed to the believer by the Holy Spirit. The Bible contains God's message to us (His love letter to us) to shows us how to live, how to please Him by doing His will, how to honor Him, and how to be saved from sin and have eternal life. Jesus is also known as the Word of God. In John 1:1, John referred to Jesus as "the Word" during the time of creation. John also wrote, "In the beginning was the Word, and the Word was with God, and the Word was God." Later on John assures us that the "Word became flesh" (John 1:14). Jesus calls us to listen to the Word of God [Himself] and do what He says!

The woman in this story was concerned about blessing the woman who gave birth to such a wonderful man instead of paying attention to the man

Himself, and Jesus corrected her. Jesus' mother is to be respected and she is blessed indeed, but she is not the main source of our salvation, Jesus is.

Search Your Heart, Thank God, and Pray
Do you know how to live as a child of God? Who do you adore today? Read 1 John 5:1-13; Philippians 2:10.

Day 28

She Was Healed on the Sabbath by the Lord Jesus

Luke 13:10–17

In Luke 13:10–17 we find a woman who was very sick spiritually because she was bound by Satan with a bad spirit for eighteen years (Luke 13:16) and Jesus healed her on the Sabbath. The synagogue officials were not happy because a person could not work on the Sabbath, and healing for them was considered work. Jesus was teaching in a synagogue on the Sabbath. The story goes as follow:

> As He was teaching in one of the synagogues on the Sabbath, a woman was there who had been disabled by a spirit for over 18 years. She was bent over and could not straighten up at all. When Jesus saw her, He called out to her, "Woman, you are free of your disability." Then He laid His hands on her, and instantly she was restored and began to glorify God. But the leader of the synagogue, indignant because Jesus had healed on the Sabbath, responded by telling the crowd, "There are six days when work should be done; therefore come on those days and be healed and not on the Sabbath day." But the Lord answered him and said, "Hypocrites! Doesn't each one of you untie his ox or donkey from the feeding trough on the Sabbath and lead it to water? Satan has bound this

> woman, a daughter of Abraham, for 18 years—shouldn't she be untied from this bondage on the Sabbath day?" When He had said these things, all His adversaries were humiliated, but the whole crowd was rejoicing over all the glorious things He was doing. (Luke 10:11–13HCSB)

Here is a woman who had been miraculously freed from lifelong physical bondage. Yet, instead of praising God, the religious leaders criticized Jesus for performing the miracle on the Sabbath, their day of rest. This woman received physical healing and spiritual rest on the Sabbath. God's day! The Sabbath was a day created by God so we could worship Him (Ex 8–11) and not our selves. God required the Sabbath and He made as it part of the Ten Commandments. The Jews made the Sabbath part of their Mosaic Laws but they added tasks that were not meant to be there. Jesus celebrated the Sabbath and the Sabbath is still celebrated every seven days by both Jews and Christians today but not in the same manner.

The synagogue officials learned a lesson from Jesus. They felt humiliated because of their own hypocrisy. They, of course, complained to Jesus about working on the Sabbath because they did not recognize the Healer. Many of us do not recognize the Healer, Jesus, and many do not experience a relationship with Him because their minds are focused on the wrong things. These officials were willing to bend the rules for the animals because it was to their benefit. However, this woman meant nothing to them, and could not benefit them in any way. After all she was only a woman, and women were second class citizens to them. Women are important to Jesus! Even though she was not important to the others, Jesus demonstrated His love and compassion for this woman by giving her physical freedom. Jesus was not concerned about what others thought about Him. It was more important to Him to do His Father's work and honor the Father with His actions than to care about people's opinions.

Suffering has many faces, and each person's response to suffering is different, but our Lord Jesus has compassion and knows what causes us to suffer. The woman in this true story could not heal herself at all. Can you imagine yourself looking at your feet for eighteen years not being able to look at anyone else's face? You do not have to wait until the Sabbath! Healing from Jesus can come to you at any day, at any time, and anywhere. *God is not concerned about holidays and He doesn't take vacation.* He is constantly watching after us 24/7.

The healing of this woman was not important to the synagogue officials, but it was important to Jesus, and so are you! Jesus knew that this woman was bound for eighteen, years-a lifetime for many. Jesus decided to rescue her from her physical and spiritual pain on His day!

Search Your Heart, Thank God, and Pray

Blinded by sin, the synagogue officials, in Jesus' time, did not recognize the Healer. How about you? The woman in this story suffered for eighteen years. How long have you been suffering and why? Are you more concerned about doing God's will or listening to people's opinions? Jesus can heal you from the inside out! He died and rose again to rescue your soul. Read 2 Corinthians 4:16-18.

Day 29

Peter's Mother-in-Law—Healed by Jesus

Matthew 8:14–17; Mark 1:29–34; Luke 4:38–41

There are very few people who Jesus physically touched in order to heal them, and Peter's mother-in-law is one of them. The Word of God tells us that Jesus "touched her and her fever left her" (Matt 8:15). The only reason we know that Peter was married is because his mother-in-law is mentioned in scripture. In 1 Corinthian 9:5, Paul makes a statement that indicates some of the apostles were married, but he does not name any of them or their wives.

Once Peter's mother-in-law was healed by Jesus, He helped her get up and she started to serve Him! This was a perfect response, to serve the King of Kings. Peter's mother-in-law did not throw herself a party or call everyone to show what Jesus had done for her. Instead she served Him immediately. Mark 1:31 says Jesus helped her to get up holding her by the hands, and that is when the fever left her. Luke tells us that her fever was high so her healing should have been a motive for celebration. Instead it was a moment of gratitude shown by service. The news was not kept quiet because after she was healed many came to request healing and freedom from demonic bondage (Mark 1:32).

Peter's mother-in-law was blessed with physical healing and perhaps spiritual healing as well. What about you? Jesus healed fevers; gave sight to the blind; blessed those who were crippled with the ability to walk; cleansed and liberated the demon possessed; He encouraged the poor in heart (Matt 5:1–12); and He brought healing to the world by giving His life for it (John 3:16). He purchased spiritual freedom for us with His blood. You can also receive healing today by placing your trust in Him and accepting Him as Lord and Savior. There is no formula; you just need to believe by faith that Jesus came to die for you, was crucified, buried, and rose again on the third day to give us eternal life. It is that simple!

The healing of Peter's mother-in-law gives us an idea of Jesus' love for the disciples and their families. Jesus restored families! Consider the following: Jesus restored Jairus' family by giving him his daughter back; to Martha and Mary he restored their family by raising their brother Lazarus from the dead; and he gave back a suffering widow her only son. But He did much more. He gave Himself to restore families all over the world.

Search Your Heart, Thank God, and Pray

Besides giving you eternal life and healing your soul, Jesus can also heal your emotional and physical pain. Jesus can give you a new life so that you can also become part of His family. Read Roman 3:23, 1 John 1:9 Ephesians 2:8-9.

Paul

"As he neared Damascus on his journey, suddenly a light from heaven flashed around him. He fell to the ground and heard a voice say to him, "Saul, Saul, why do you persecute me? Who are you, Lord?" Saul asked. "I am Jesus, whom you are persecuting," he replied. "Now get up and go into the city, and you will be told what you must do ..." But the Lord said to Ananias, "Go! This man is my chosen instrument to proclaim my name to the Gentiles and their kings and to the people of Israel. 16 I will show him how much he must suffer for my name" (Acts 9:3-6, 15-16, NIV).

Day 1

Eunice
Mother of Timothy, a Disciple of Paul

Acts 16:1; 2 Timothy 1:5

Eunice was the mother of Timothy, one of the men chosen by the apostle Paul as a companion to go out and share the gospel with others. Timothy is described as "the son of a Jewish woman who was a believer, but his father was a Greek" (Acts 16:1). Eunice is mostly known for teaching her son the Word of God. She did not teach Timothy religion; she taught him the salvation found in the love of Jesus. When Paul got a hold of Timothy, Eunice had already prepared her son for the battle of evangelism, making Timothy's upbringing a plus to Paul's ministry. Eunice transferred her faith to her son through her example and teaching; even his name has God as the center. The name Timothy means, "Honoring God." Herbert Locker wrote, "The important feature we glean from the record of Timothy is that of the value of a positive Christian training in the home."[1] In one of Paul's letters to Timothy he wrote, "From childhood you have known the sacred writings which are able to give you the wisdom that leads to salvation through faith which is in Christ Jesus" (2 Tim 3:15). Paul knew very well where Timothy acquired his godly training, and in his writing, Paul made Timothy's mother unforgettable by sharing with us Eunice's influence in Timothy's childhood training.

Paul loved Timothy as a son (2 Tim 1:2–5), and he was so proud of him that he even sent Timothy to represent him and teach the Corinthians. Paul was writing to them about how he, Paul, became their "father through the gospel," and now he was sending Timothy to them. "For this reason I have sent to you Timothy, who is my beloved and faithful child in the Lord, and he will remind you of my ways which are in Christ just as I teach everywhere in every church" (1 Cor 4:17). Paul also wrote to the Philippians when he sent Timothy to them as his substitute. "But you know of his proven worth that he served with me in the furtherance of the gospel like a child serving his father" (Phil 2:22). Timothy's godly walk was, and is, worthy of repeating.

The legacy of Timothy's mother Eunice lived on in the life of Timothy, and Paul's ministry was blessed by it. "Eunice and Lois seem to step right out from the pages of the Bible and tells us that nothing is more important in a mother's life that the early training of her child" [2] Eunice is a great example of Proverbs 11:30: "The fruit of the righteous is a tree of life, and he who is wise wins souls." Eunice was a righteous woman whose fruit was Timothy and was a woman who did a good job of putting the Word of God into practice: "Train up a child in the way he should go, even when he is old he will not depart from it" (Prov 22:6).

Eunice had a problem: it seems that her husband was not a believer; he was Greek: "Paul came also to Derbe and to Lystra. And a disciple was there, named Timothy, the son of a Jewish woman who was a believer, <u>but</u> his father was a Greek" (Acts 16:1). Because Timothy's father was a Greek, Paul had Timothy circumcised (Acts 16:2-4). Eunice is an encouragement to Christian women who have children and are married to unbelieving husbands. Even though her husband was Greek, Eunice managed to teach her son the Word of God. No excuses. The wisdom God gave Eunice to teach her child God's Word, while living among two cultures, is amazing. Paul recognized Eunice's work with her son, and God made sure that you and I would know about it today as well. Not only did Eunice raise a Christian man, but she raised a godly man. Her legacy can live on. . .

Search Your Heart, Thank God, and Pray

What is keeping, or will keep you, from teaching your children God's Word and praying for their salvation? Are you taking advantage of the free training available to you at church? Are you married to a non-believer? Read 1 Peter 3:1-2

1 Herbert Lockyer, All *the Women of the Bible (*Grand Rapids: Zondervan Publishing House, 1995), 54

2 Edith Deen, *All the Women of the Bible* (New York: HarperCollins, 1983), 239.

Day 2

Lois
Grandmother of Timothy, A Disciple of Paul

2 Timothy 1:5
Day 2

Lois is one of the most famous grandmothers in the Bible of which we know absolutely nothing about beside the fact that she helped her daughter, Eunice, to teach God's Word to Timothy who was a follower of Christ and the Apostle Paul's apprentice. She was Eunice's mother and Timothy's Grandmother. Her name only appears once in the Bible, but her godly example as a mother to Eunice can be seen in her grandson Timothy's life. The legacy of wisdom and healing came to Timothy from his mother and grandmother Lois. How? This training in faith served Timothy well all the days of his life.

The apostle Paul used Timothy's faith and heritage to help Timothy get focused on the ministry instead of on fear. Paul used what Timothy learned from his mother and grandmother to give him confidence to keep on doing God's work and to trust God. Paul wrote, "For I am mindful of the sincere faith within you, which first dwelt in your grandmother *Lois*, and your mother Eunice, and I am sure that it is in you as well" (2 Tim 1:5). This verse indicates that Paul knew both of these women, and used their faithful examples to encourage Timothy in his spiritual life saying, "For God has not given us a spirit of timidity, but of power and love and discipline" (2 Tim 1:7). Paul again reminds Timothy to continue walking in the way he learned to walk with God by following what he learned from his mother and grandmother. Lois and Eunice's teachings helped Timothy to resist being influenced by false teachers (2 Tim. 3:13). Paul wrote to Timothy, "You, however, continue in the things you have learned and become convinced of, knowing from whom you have learned them" (2 Tim 3:14). From where did he learn them? He learned them from his mother and grandmother and reinforced by the apostle Paul. Paul again used Timothy's heritage to help him serve the Lord wholeheartedly. Paul simply came along and reaped what these women sowed into Timothy for the glory of God.

Lois was an obviously a woman of faith whose wisdom helped her daughter to guide her son, Timothy. As a mother, work hard daily and teach your children God's Word because you do not know how the Lord is going to use them someday. Someone will come along and reap what you sowed in your children's hearts for the glory of God. As a mother, you too can teach your children by just reading the Word of God and trusting that the Holy Spirit of God will do the rest. Five minutes per day of reading God's Word will reap eternal rewards and will give your children the opportunity to get to know their Maker. The legacy you pass on to your children depends on you.

If you are a grandmother, reach out to your grandchildren. Volunteer to babysit for the toddlers and teach them God's Word. You can take the teenagers on outings of their choice and pray that God will give you the opportunity to share His Word. You can use technology to communicate with your college-age grandchildren. Share a verse per day or become a member in one of the social media sites where they are members. You will become the cool grandma! Whatever it takes for you to reach your grandchildren for Christ, you are to do it. "Grandchildren are the crown of old men" (Prov 17:6a). These sweet blessings will grow up one day, and you must be the one to sow into them a godly heritage. Who else will do it? Lois passed God's Word to her daughter and to her grandson, are you passing it to anyone today?

Search Your Heart, Thank God, and Pray

What legacy are you passing on to your grandchildren? Do you *pray* for your family or with your children every day? Read Hebrews 4:14

Day 3

Lydia
Paul Touched Her Heart for Christ

Acts 16:14–15, 40

Lydia was a woman from Thyatira, "a city in the ancient region of Lydia," [1] who moved to Philippi. "Thyatira was re-founded in the early third century B.C. by Seleucus I on the site of an earlier settlement and became a city of commerce and industry, famous for its purple dye industry and metalworking and other trades."[2] This was an important city because the church in Thyatira is also the focus of one of the letters of John to the seven churches in Revelation 2:18–29. According to Acts 16:12, Philippi was "a leading city of the district of Macedonia, a Roman colony." In Philippi, Lydia, with her knowledge in sales, became part of the city and its commerce. This is the city Paul references when he wrote his famous letter to the Philippians, which is part of our Bible today. This famous church was started in Lydia's home because she was one of the first to believe in Christ in that city.

Lydia's conversion is described as follows in Acts 16:14–15: "And a certain woman named Lydia, from the city of Thyatira, a seller of purple fabrics, a worshiper of God, was listening; and the Lord opened her heart to respond to the things spoken by Paul." Lydia already had faith in God, and her search for Him on the Sabbath (Act 16:13) led her to meet the

Son of God through Paul's words guided by the Holy Spirit that day. Now besides being a smart businesswoman, who experienced financial success, she became she became a child of God, spiritual success!

Lydia was blessed that day, and she also helped to bless her family. Acts 16:15 says, "And when she and her household had been baptized, she urged us, saying, 'If you have judged me to be faithful to the Lord come into my house and stay.' And she prevailed upon us." Lydia somehow influenced her household to receive Jesus as Lord and Savior. Maybe she did some evangelism herself. After all, she was a salesperson, so she would not be afraid to talk to people. She probably brought the people in her household to the same source from which she received the blessing of salvation, the Holy Spirit in Paul. She didn't keep Jesus to herself! After she proved her faithfulness to Paul and his companion, she opened her house to them for ministry.

After Paul and Silas were released from prison, they went to Lydia's house. When they arrived, they encouraged the new church. "And they went out of the prison and entered the house of Lydia, and when they saw the brethren, they encouraged them and departed" (Acts 16:40). There is always a place to go when we need to be in a godly environment, and Lydia's house was for Paul and Silas.

Lydia was the first convert in Europe and she supported the work of Christ with her home (Acts 16:40), her family and her finances. When you receive the Lord, your heart is inclined to give generously to Kingdom work. Even though we don't know how Lydia's life started or ended, we will never forget her because she left us a legacy of evangelism, service and hospitality.

Search Your Heart, Thank God, and Pray
Why do you think we remember Lydia centuries after she died? Lydia had the ability to open her house to God's service. Are you opening your house to do the same? Read Galatians 5:13.

1 *The Ryrie Study Bible* (Chicago: The Moody Institute of Chicago, 1978)

2 Allen C. Myers, The *Eerdmans Bible Dictionary (*Grand Rapids: WM. B. Eerdmans Publishing Co, 1987), 1

Day 4

Demon-Possessed Slave-Girl Paul Gave Her Freedom

Acts 16:16–40

This nameless girl had a big impact in Paul's life. Because Paul cast a demonic spirit of divination out of her, he ended up beaten and thrown in prison, a prison where God manifested Himself. Luke wrote in Acts 16:16-18:

> And it happened that as we were going to the place of prayer, a certain slave-girl having a spirit of divination met us, who was bringing her masters much profit by fortune telling. Following after Paul and us, she kept crying out, saying, "These men are bond-servants of the Most High God, who are proclaiming to you the way of salvation" She continued doing this for many days. But Paul was greatly annoyed, and turned and said to the spirit, 'I command you in the name of Jesus Christ to come out of her!' And it came out at that very moment."

The girl's masters were very angry with Paul because he had destroyed their business. No demon, no money! They took revenge on Paul and Silas by taking them to the authorities and charging them by saying, "'These men are throwing our city into confusion, being Jews, and are proclaiming customs which are not lawful for us to accept or to observe, being Romans.'

After this, Paul and Silas where beaten with rods and put in prison" (Acts 16:20–21). The story didn't stop there. The life of the jailer who was put in charge of Paul and Silas changed.

> But about midnight Paul and Silas were praying and singing hymns of praise to God, and the prisoners were listening to them; and suddenly there came a great earthquake, so that the foundations of the prison house were shaken; and immediately all the doors were opened, and everyone's chains unfastened (Acts 16:25–26).

When the jailer, who was sleeping, finally realized what had happened, with his own sword he was about to kill himself because of the disgrace it would be for him to have all his prisoners escape. "But Paul cried out with a low voice saying; Do yourself no harm, for we are all here!" The jailer "trembling with fear, he fell down before Paul and Silas" (Acts 16:28-29). The jailer couldn't believe that the prisoners had a chance to escape and didn't. Paul probably preached to the prisoners while the jailer was sleeping. Witnessing the conversion of so many prisoners because of Paul's preaching, the jailer said to them, "Sirs, what must I do to be saved?' And they said, "Believe in the Lord Jesus, and you shall be saved, you and your household'" (Acts 16:30–31). The jailer then took care of Paul and Silas by cleaning their wounds, caused by the beatings, and probably the earthquake, and removing the chains that bound their feet. "And he brought them into his house and set food before them, and rejoiced greatly, having believed in God with his whole household" (Act 16:34).

Because Paul released a slave girl from her spiritual bondage, all the prisoners received Jesus as Lord and Savior. Philippi lost a demon but gained more believers to continue the work that Paul started there. Paul left Philippi, but he did not forget to write to them. "Only conduct yourselves in a matter worthy of the gospel of Christ; so that whether I come and see you or remain absent, I may hear of you that you are standing firm in one spirit, with one mind striving together for the faith of the gospel" (Phil 1:27).

Someone can see Christ in you just like the jailer saw Christ in Paul. God will use anything and everything a Christian person goes through for His kingdom, just like He used Paul's imprisonment, Paul's freedom, and Paul's sufferings. The question remains: Are we willing to let Him use us to the point Paul allowed Him to use him? We need to let the Spirit of God control our souls so we can serve Him with all of our might. Proverbs 20:27 says, "The spirit of man is the lamp of the Lord, searching all the innermost parts of his being." Allow the Spirit of God to control your spirit so that when He searches your soul, He can find a flame of everlasting desire to serve Him.

Search Your Heart, Thank God, and Pray

A demon possessed slave girl was freed from her oppression because God used a man who served Him, with the help of the Holy Spirit, to heal her. Are you letting the Spirit of God control your spirit? Are you standing together with your brothers in Christ to proclaim the gospel? Ask the Lord to give you a spirit of determination to share His Word with others. Read Acts 16:16-40.

Day 5

Euodia and Syntyche Paul's Concern at Philippi

Philippians 4:2–4

Euodia and Syntyche were two members of the church in Philippi. The only reason we know about them today is simply because they were causing problems within the church there. Their behavior was affecting others around them. Both of these women maintained their position in the church. Neither one of them solved the dispute they were having, and neither one of them pulled away from the church to allow the work of God to continue without them.

It is believed that the apostle Paul was in prison when he wrote the letter to the Philippians, and in the fourth chapter he became a mediator to try to solve the problem these women where having. Paul wrote:

> I urge Euodia and urge Syntyche to live in harmony in the Lord. Indeed, true companion, I ask you also to help these women who have shared my struggle in the cause of the gospel, together with Clement also, and the rest of my fellow workers, whose names are in the book of life (Phil 4:2–3).

Paul asked the person to whom he sent this letter, for the benefit of the Philippians church, to please help these women resolve their differences so they would be able to keep serving and living in harmony. The problem between these two women was affecting the ministry, and Paul needed for them to be humble and end their dispute. Paul said in Philippians 2:2–4 when he was encouraging the Philippians to be humble:

> Make my joy complete by being of the same mind, maintaining the same love, united in spirit, intent on one purpose. Do nothing from selfishness or empty conceit, but with humility of mind let each of you regard one another as more important than himself; do not merely look out for your own personal interests, but also for the interest of others.

Maybe these were the things Paul was calling Euodia and Syntyche to follow. Paul told the Philippians to take life as God gives it to them and to "do all things without grumbling and disputing [arguing]" (Phil 2:14).

Paul's letter to the Philippians has one of the best verses on the peace of God for good living. In Philippians 4:8 Paul wrote, "Finally, brethren, whatever is true, whatever is honorable, whatever is right, whatever is lovely, whatever is of good repute, if there is any excellence and if anything worthy of praise, let your mind dwell on these things." These verses alone are convicting enough for anyone to examine their soul and focus on God.

In the hearts of believers, where the real focus is Christ, there is no room for personal quarrels. When there is no peace between brothers in Christ in the church, Jesus can't be honored or served until the matter is solved. Jesus Himself said in Matthew 5:23–24, "If therefore you are presenting your offering at the altar, and there you remember that your brother has something against you, leave your offering there before the altar, and go your way; first be reconciled to your brother, and then come and present your offering." If you follow the guidelines of biblical confrontation and you have the peace that you tried to solve the problem and there was no cooperation from the other person, you can say what David said in Psalm 101:2b: "I will walk within my house in the integrity of my heart." We can also do what Paul suggested in Romans 13:21: "Do not be overcome with evil, but overcome evil with good.

If as a Christian, you go to your church worship service every Sunday, and there is a person who you are in conflict with, you must take the first step to reconciliation. Try to encourage anyone who has a similar problem to the one Euodia and Syntyche had, to do something about it before it becomes a cancer that will eat your heart out one day at a time. This cancer can spread to the church, and most important of all, it will contaminate your walk with God. Personality conflicts are going to come your way because we can't get along with everybody! Sometimes it is better to pull away and allow God to use you somewhere else.

Search Your Heart, Thank God, and Pray

Are you a Euodia or a Syntyche in your church? Is there someone you need to reconcile with at your church, home or place of work? Are you taking the necessary steps to do what you know is the right thing to do? Read Matthew 5:20-26, Proverbs 3:1-7

Day 6

Damaris Saved Through Paul's Ministry in Athens

Acts 17:34

Damaris lived in Athens, Greece, and her conversion is a result of Paul's passion to reach the city of Athens with the gospel. Paul had been driven out of Thessalonica, also a city in Greece, because he preached the Word of God to the Jews there. He ended up in the city of Athens, where he was waiting for Timothy and Silas to meet him. Acts 17:16 says, "While Paul was waiting for them in Athens, his spirit was being provoked within him as he was beholding the city full of idols." These people had a god for everything; they even had an altar for a god they didn't know just in case they missed one. Paul took advantage of this fact and said, to the Athenians, "Men of Athens, I observe that you are very religious in all respects. For while I was passing through and examining the objects of your worship, I also found an altar with this inscription, 'TO AN UNKNOWN GOD' Therefore what you worship in ignorance, this I proclaim to you (Acts 17:22-23). Paul decided to preach, and "to reach out and touch someone," and Damaris was touched.

Paul started to preach the Word of God to anybody who would listen, from Jews to gentiles to philosophers or commoners. He didn't care who they were as long as they listened. "Now all the Athenians and the strangers visiting there used to spend their time in nothing other than telling or hearing something new" (Acts 17:21). This was a very good opportunity for Paul because their curiosity led him to share the gospel with them. Paul became a source of curiosity to this people. Acts 17:19 says that "they took him and brought him to the Areopagus, saying, 'may we know what this new teaching is which you are proclaiming?'" According to theologian Ryrie, the Areopagus was, "The venerable council that had charge of religious and educational matters in Athens. It met on the Hill of Ares west of the Acropolis, the hill also being known as the Areopagus." [1]

Some of the men, and women, who heard the gospel presented by Paul that day believed, the Bible says, "But some men joined him and believed, among whom also was Dionysius the Areopagite and a woman named Damaris and others with them" (Acts 17:34). Paul presented the Gospel to all! And that is why Damaris was won for the Lord and brought Paul such great joy. Her conversion had to be special for Paul to take the time and tell us that she got saved, and maybe she was the only woman to receive the Lord that day!

Damaris doesn't have a church attributed to her in Greece and she did not leave a well known legacy of ministry. She is not mentioned as the wife or mother of anybody, but there are many women who carry her name! She was probably a woman of knowledge or maybe she was a simple woman who was at the right place at the right time! The one thing we know is that she was saved by the blood of Jesus, and God is allowing us to at least know of her existence.

Damaris' salvation is a great example of how much God loves us all no matter what country or family He chooses to give to us. "For there is no distinction between Jew and Greek; for the same Lord is Lord of all, abounding in riches for all who call upon His name; for WHOEVER WILL CALL UPON THE NAME OF THE LORD WILL BE SAVED" (Rom 10:12–13).

Search Your Heart, Thank God, and Pray

Why do you think Paul mentioned Damaris in his writing? Have you ever experienced the joy of having someone receive Jesus as Lord? Read Act 17:16-34 and Luke 12:12.

[1] *The Ryrie Study Bible* (Chicago: The Moody Institute of Chicago, 1976), 1679.

Day 7

Pricilla (Prisca) Wife of Aquila and Follower of Paul's Ministry

Acts 18:2, 18, 26; Romans 16:3–4; 1 Corinthians 16:19; 2 Timothy 4:19

Priscilla is a great example of a wife working together with her husband for the sake of the Gospel of Jesus Christ. She was a woman who followed her husband wherever he went. They left their city because of political reasons, and later on they went together to Syria to minister with Paul. They ended up in Ephesus, the city where Paul left them to minister. How did Paul meet this couple? After Paul left Athens and went to Corinth, "He found a certain Jew named Aquila, native of Pontus, having recently come from Italy with his wife Priscilla, because Claudius had commanded all the Jews to leave Rome" (Acts 18:1–2). Priscilla and Aquila were tent-makers, and they kept Paul in their home while Paul went to preach the gospel. Paul worked with them because he was also a tent maker (Acts 18:3).

Priscilla worked together as a team with her husband and one of the best places to see them in action was at Ephesus, where they made a difference in the life of Apollos. Apollos was preaching about the coming of the Lord Jesus, but he was preaching according to John the Baptist. Apollos was not aware that Jesus had come and left and was coming back! The Bible says in Acts 18:26 that Apollos "began to speak out boldly in the synagogues. But when Priscilla and Aquila heard him, they took him aside and explained to him the way of God more accurately." The boldness of this couple gave Apollos a new start in his walk with God. He was able to continue boldly preaching but with the right information.

Paul loved this couple very much because of their commitment to Christ and their love towards him. In Romans 16:3–4 Paul sent greetings to them and said: "Greet Prisca and Aquila my fellow workers in Christ Jesus, who for my life risked their own necks, to whom not only do I give thanks, but also all the churches of the Gentiles." Paul never exactly tells us what they did to save his life, but it must have been a big deal because even the churches knew about it!

There is no evidence of Priscilla having children, and there is no background on her to elaborate. All we know is that she loved God, loved her husband, and loved Jesus. She dedicated her life to Christ and even had a church in her house (1 Cor 16:19). Priscilla and her husband are an example of a faithful couple working together for Jesus and achieving great results. They are always named together in the Bible, which shows unity. This couple is a great example of Ephesians 2:10: "For we are his workmanship, created in Christ Jesus for good works, which God prepared beforehand, that we should walk in them."

I want to encourage you today to allow God to work in your life, especially if you have a mate. God can do great things with you. "Now God is able to do exceeding abundantly beyond all that we ask or think, according to the power that works within us [The Holy Spirit]" (Eph 3:20). May the Lord give you a heart to want to follow Him, and may the Holy Spirit minister to you while you serve Him.

Search Your Heart, Thank God, and Pray

If a preacher makes a biblical mistake, are you bold enough to privately bring it to their attention? If you are married, are you ministering with your husband? Are you ready to do the work the Lord has prepared for you? Not all couples serve God from the heart, read Acts 5:1-11

Day 8

Drusilla Wife of Felix—Witnessed to by Paul

Acts 24:24

Drusilla was "The third and youngest daughter of Herod Agrippa I and the sister of Herod Agrippa II . . . [she was] supposed to marry "Epiphanes of Commagene in Asia Minor."[1] This guy supposedly proposed to her when she was six years old and then didn't agree with being circumcised or becoming a Jew, so the wedding was off. Then her brother ". . . arranged a marriage for her with Azizus, king of Émesa in Syria." [2] After she was married for a year, she was asked by "Antonius Felix the Roman prosecutor to divorce her husband and marry him." [3] Drusilla accepted the challenge and married Felix. Some say that she was not divorced when she married Felix. They had a son which they also named Agrippa.

While Paul was already in prison in Caesarea, more unjust charges were brought against him. "Ananias came down with some elders, with a certain attorney named Tertullus; and they brought charges to the governor against Paul" (Acts 24:1). The governor's name at that time was Felix. Felix listening very carefully, considered the situation, ". . . and gave orders to the centurion for him to be kept in custody and yet have some freedom and not to prevent any of his friends from ministering to him" (Acts 24:23). "But some days later, Felix arrived with Drusilla, his wife who was a Jewess, and sent for Paul, and heard him speak about faith in Christ Jesus" (Acts 24:24). This is how Drusilla met the apostle Paul. The Bible says that when Paul started to talk to them about "righteousness, self-control and the judgment to come, Felix became frightened and said 'Go away for the present, and when I find time, I will summon you'" (Acts 24:25).

Felix had other things on his mind. He wanted to call on Paul whenever he felt like it, but he was hoping Paul would bribe him (Acts 24:26). Felix was also corrupt, but perhaps the Lord used that so Paul was able to minister to Felix. Drusilla and Felix probably didn't have access to Paul again after their two years of conversation with him, because, "Felix was succeeded by Porcius Festus; and wishing to do the Jews a favor, Felix left Paul imprisoned" (Acts 24:27).

We will never know for sure what happened to Drusilla but there are some pieces of history that can give us a clue:

> In respect to Drusilla, Josephus the historian, who lived about the same time, relates that about 20 years after Paul's transfer from Felix to Festus, the terrible eruption of Vesuvius occurred when prosperous Pompeii and Herculaneum were buried under the burning lava. Many fled to escape the catastrophe but Drusilla, endeavoring to escape with her child, Agrippa, was too late to evade disaster. Underestimating her danger, she left the retreat too late, and with her son was buried beneath the lava. [4]

Drusilla had multiple chances to listen to the apostle Paul preach. Perhaps, due to her behavior at the time, the deep truths of the gospel probably did not penetrate her heart. When the heart is not ready, no truth can enter!

Search Your Heart, Thank God, and Pray

Are you encouraged by Paul's example? If you shared the gospel with someone and that person didn't respond, keep on praying for him or her. You plant the seed and let the Holy Spirit of God do the rest. Read John 5:24

1 Allen C. Myers, The *Eerdmans Bible Dictionary (*Grand Rapids: WM. B. Eerdmans Publishing Co, 1987), 295.

2 Ibid

3 Ibid

4 Herbert Lockyer, All *the Women of the Bible (*Grand Rapids: Zondervan Publishing House, 1995), 49.

Day 9

Bernice Concubine and Sister of King Agrippa II—Listened to Paul at Caesarea

Acts 25:13, 23, 26:30

Bernice's name stands together with the sin of incest. She is a woman with a history of many husbands but one who listened to Paul's Gospel presentation.

> "She was the oldest daughter of King Herod Agrippa I (AD 37–44) and sister of Drusilla. After her first husband, Marcus, died, she married his brother and uncle, Herod Chalcis. When he died, she remained with her brother Herod Agrippa II in an incestuous relationship". The incestuous relationship between Agrippa and the twenty-year-old widow proved scandalous, and Bernice persuaded King Polemo of Cicilia to undergo circumcision and marry her. This marriage lasted but a short time and Bernice returned to the unmarried Agrippa, with whom she appeared as queen on official occasions. She later won the favor of Vespasian's son Titus when he was in Palestine in connection with the Jewish war and became his mistress, but her hope of marrying him and becoming

> empress of Rome were unrealized because of the Roman hatred of the Jews. [1]

The book *The Jewish War* by Josephus states that when Herod Agrippa I died, “He left 3 daughters born to him by Cyprus, Bernice, Mariamme, and Drusilla, and one son by the same wife, Agrippa. The order of appearance of the 4 children indicates that Agrippa II was the youngest of all 4 children. So Bernice, the oldest, was the lover of her youngest sibling, her little brother.”[2] While Bernice was with her brother and lover, Agrippa II, appearing in one of their official functions, they met Paul.

Festus, who succeeded Governor Felix, brought Paul before Agrippa II on Agrippa II’s request (Acts 25:22). Even though Paul had already appealed to the Caesar, Agrippa wanted to hear him. Agrippa II listened with attention while Festus laid Paul’s case before him. Festus said the people who brought charges against Paul “simply had some points of disagreement with him about their own religion and about a certain dead man, Jesus, whom Paul asserted to be alive” (Acts 25:19). Like Felix, Festus didn’t know what to do with Paul because he didn’t understand the charges brought before him either (Acts 25:25–17).

When Paul was brought to King Agrippa II, Bernice was with him. Acts 25:23 says, “When Agrippa had come together with Bernice, amid great pomp, and had entered the auditorium accompanied by the commanders and the prominent men of the city, at the command of Festus, Paul was brought in.” This was a big entrance to have an audience with a prisoner, don’t you think? Paul was able to preach to all of these officials.

Paul shared his testimony with the king and everybody else, including Bernice. After Paul finished talking, King Agrippa II said to Paul, “In a short time you will persuade me to become a Christian” (Acts 26:28). Paul’s testimony was so strong that the king was almost convicted to follow Christ. Maybe he was! But after “the king arose and the governor and Bernice, and those who were sitting with them, and when they had drawn aside, they began talking to one another, saying, ‘This man is not doing anything worthy of death or imprisonment.’ And Agrippa II said to Festus, 'This man might have been set free if he had not appealed to Caesar'" (Acts 26:30–32).

Bernice and her sister both had the privilege to hear Paul speak, because God gave both of these women the chance to be saved, but their sinful life was so deeply rooted in their hearts that they probably missed out! Bernice's opportunity to walk the streets of gold in heaven was opened to her and she missed it because she preferred to walk the luxurious streets of the sinful world she lived in.

Search Your Heart, Thank God, and Pray

Has anybody shared the good news of Christ with you recently or long ago? Have you let the opportunity pass you by to go to heaven someday, just like Bernice probably did? A simple prayer of repentance and acceptance of Jesus as Lord is all you need to do. Read Romans 3:23, 6:23, and 8:1

1 Allen C. Myers, The *Eerdmans Bible Dictionary (*Grand Rapids: WM. B. Eerdmans Publishing Co, 1987), 138.

2 Josephus, G.A. Williams, *The Jewish War* (Baltimore: Penguin Books, 1959), 131.

Day 10

Phoebe
Served Paul's Ministry and Many Other Believers

Romans 16:1–2

"I commend to you our sister Phoebe, who is a servant of the church which is at Cenchrea; that you receive her in the Lord in a manner worthy of the saints, and that you help her in whatever matter she may have need of you; for she herself has also been a helper of many, and of myself as well" (Rom 16:1–2).

Cenchrea was a city at an eastern port of Corinth. Phoebe was considered to be a deaconess of the church in Cenchrea because the word *servant* used by Paul in the above verse is *diakonos*, and according to the Vine's Dictionary, is translates from the Greek as "deacon," someone who is "the servant of Christ in the work of preaching and teaching" and of "those who serve in the churches." As we all know, women didn't have major roles in the early church as leaders of any kind, and here we see Phoebe as such. Just like we do today, women served other women. Phoebe served in a special way and because of it, Paul had to be specific about asking the Romans to receive her and take care of her as a good Christians would do.

When Paul referred to the saints in Rome, he was referring to all of those who accepted Jesus as Lord and Savior. He made sure to remind them that they needed to receive her "in a manner worthy of the saints." He also went on to tell them that she had served others as well as him. When Paul wrote the letter to the Romans, he was in Corinth, and Phoebe is believed to be the person who delivered the letter from Paul to Rome. Learning that Phoebe was a deaconess made me go and research what the requirements for deacons were back then. In Acts 6:1–3 we find some of the things required to be a deacon, such as having good reputation and being full of the Spirit and of wisdom. We also find some more requirements in 1Timothy 3:8–13. Here the requirements are also very specific. They needed to have "dignity, not double-tongued, or addicted to much wine"; they were also called to be faithful to their mates and be good managers of their homes and families.

There is no proof that Phoebe was married, had children or was leading men. Perhaps she was probably leading women. If she was a deaconess, being single probably made life much easier for her in relation to ministry. Deaconess or not, she was a servant who was endorsed by the apostle Paul. She must have shown that she could handle the responsibility she had; otherwise she would not have had it. She had the honor of being the first woman to be called deaconess in the Bible, and in the early church.

All women should be proud of Phoebe today because Phoebe, under the authority of Paul, was able to break barriers that existed in those days in order to serve our beloved Lord. She did it by helping spread the gospel of Jesus Christ and proclaiming the word of God with love and determination. Perhaps, she is an example of a single woman who dedicated her life to Christ; she left women a legacy of courage and love for the Lord Jesus.

Search Your Heart, Thank God, and Pray

Do you admire Phoebe? Why? Did you find encouragement reading about her? Pray for boldness and determination to go out and reach the lost. Read about other women who also served God. Read Judges 4:1-24, 5:1-31

Day 11

Julia
Remembered by Paul

Romans 16:15

Julia's name only appears once in the Bible. She is found in Romans 16:15. When Paul wrote the letter to the Romans, with the help of Tertius, Paul's stenographer (Rom 16:22), he asked the receiver to please say hello for him to many people, and in this list of people is where we find Julia. "Greet Philologus and Julia, Nereus and his sister, and Olympas, and all the saints who are with them" (Rom 16:15). There are a lot of people listed in Romans 16:3–16 who Paul wanted to greet in his letter! There are twenty-five people mentioned by name, out of which only three are names of women (Priscilla, also known as Prisca, Mary, and Julia).

Because Julia is named after Philologus, some people feel that she was probably his wife because they are paired up, just like Paul paired up Priscilla and Aquila in verse three of the same chapter. The only thing that can be said about Julia is that she was a woman who walked with God because Paul includes her in the list of people Paul considered as saints in the faith. By the list she appears in, it looks like she kept a good company of believers around her.

That fact that there is nothing to document about the life of Julia and that her name is on a special list, made me think of how important it is for us to feel like we belong to something, someone, or somewhere. There is a list of names which, because of Jesus, we all want our names to appear on when we die: The Book of Life! This is not a list of the most popular and famous people in the world; it is not a list of the richest people in the world; and it is not a list of people who served the most! It is a list of those who accepted Jesus as Lord and Savior and lived for Him! There is no better list in the world. Julia is part of it! Are you? There is a book owned by God in heaven that has the names of all those who have believed in Christ and accepted Him as Lord and Savior. This Book of Life is real and permanent (Rev 3:5. 13:8, 17:8, *20:12, 15*, 21:27; Heb 12:23; Luke 20:10; Phil 4:3). The moment that you accept Jesus as Lord of your life, your name gets written in His book.

John, having the tremendous and exclusive experience of seeing into the future of Christ's revelation, said that when Jesus comes back, sinners are going to be judged by God. John said he saw this inspection being done after the Second Coming of Christ. He said that the books were opened "and if anyone's name was not found in the book of life, he was thrown into the lake of fire" (Rev 20:15).

God included Julia in His Word via Paul and we are grateful. Perhaps He placed her there so that we can appreciate that He recognizes us when we work for Him and that there is no need for everyone to know everything we do for Him. We work and live for the audience of One.

Search Your Heart, Thank God, and Pray

What is more important for you right now, your fame or your silent work for God? If you never thought about having your name in the Book of Life, make sure it is! Jesus is the One and Only that can get you on the list. Read Revelations 3:5. 13:8, 17:8, *20:12, 15*, 21:27; Hebrews 12:23; Luke 20:10; Philippians 4:3

Day 12

Claudia
She did not desert Paul

2 Timothy 4:21

Claudia, like many of the women around the ministry of the apostle Paul, only appears once in the Bible. Like many others, she is mentioned in a list of people sending salutations in a letter of Paul to Timothy. At the end of Paul's letter to Timothy he said, "Make every effort to come before winter. Eubulus greets you, also Pudens and Linus and Claudia and all the brethren" (2 Tim 4:21). By this verse we can see a lot about Claudia. First she is a Christian working with Paul. Second, her love for Timothy or Timothy's love for her must have been great as a sister in the Lord because Paul makes sure that Timothy knows that she sends him greetings. Thirdly, it shows us that she knew of the growth of the church and was part of it. Paul loved Timothy and if Claudia was comfortable asking Paul to greet Timothy and Paul did it that shows Paul respected her.

There are many traditions/legends about Claudia. Herbert Lockyer had these things to say about Claudia in his book *All the Women of the Bible*:

> Tradition has more to say about this Roman Christian than the Bible. She can be included among the chief and honorable women of Gentile origin who heard and believed the Gospel. Doubtless she was a member of one of the great old houses in Rome. Several scholars suggest

> that Claudia was the wife of Pudens, with whom she is mentioned, and that Linus, who became bishop of Rome, was their son. … There is an interesting legend that affirms Claudia, as a British lady of high birth -the daughter of the British king, Cogidubnus. She was put under the patronage of Pomponia, wife of Aulus Plautius, conqueror of Britain and this Christian learned the truth of the Gospel. Tacitus the Roman historian speaks of an inscription found in Chichester, England, declaring Claudia to be of British Stock. [1]

Again these concepts are legends, and they may not be true. We can only assume, then, that she probably used her power to help the ministry in Rome even though Paul was in prison most of the time. Just like many women around the ministry of Paul and other women involved in the business of serving God, we will never know more about them than what the Bible says.

I usually look up to the women God placed in the Bible to find guidance, encouragement and a better way to live the Christian life. I look for a better way to serve, a better way to know God, a better way to understand other women, and a better way to focus on loving the individuality of each person. With Claudia, I realized that she was one of the four people Paul could count on in Rome. If you read 2 Timothy 4:8–11, you can see that a lot of believers deserted Paul but she was not one of them. Her name is listed in association with a great company of believers Paul was able to depend on. David said in Psalm 133:1, "Behold, how good and how pleasant it is for brothers to dwell together in unity!"

Search Your Heart, Thank, and Pray

Do you find encouragement in the little things in life? Are you faithful to your church, and its pastor, to help reach the lost? Pray for the Lord to give you wisdom to serve Him better. Read 2 Timothy 4:8–11, Proverbs 17:17

1 Herbert Lockyer, All *the Women of the Bible (*Grand Rapids: Zondervan Publishing House, 1995), 38.

Day 13

Apphia
Sister in Christ of Paul and Wife of Philemon

Philemon1:2

Paul usually included the name of women in his greetings at the end of his letters, but in the case of Apphia, she is mentioned in the beginning of the letter to Philemon. Apphia is believed to be the wife of Philemon because she is part of the three to whom the letter is addressed. He started his letter this way. "Paul a prisoner of Christ Jesus, and Timothy our brother, to Philemon our beloved brother and fellow worker, and to Apphia our sister, and to Archippus our fellow soldier, and to the church in your house: Grace to you and peace from God our Father and the Lord Jesus Christ" (Philemon 1: 1–3). In these verses Paul tells us that he and Timothy loved Philemon; so we know there is a bond of trust between them. Paul also tells us that he and Timothy love Apphia as a sister in the Lord. And finally, he tells us that Archippus was a good soldier of Jesus Christ because he calls him a "fellow soldier." They are all followers of Christ and working with Paul for Christ in the war with sin.

Paul's big request of them was to receive back Onesimus, Philemon's and Apphia's slave, because he was now a new creature. "I appeal to you for my child, whom I have begotten in my imprisonment, Onesimus, who formerly was useless to you, but now is useful both to you and to me"

(Philemon 1:10–11). Paul really loved Onesimus because he wrote, "I have sent him back to you, in person, that is, sending my very heart." This slave had changed his life to such an extent that Paul didn't want him to leave, but he knew that he had to do the right thing by sending Onesimus back to his master.

Paul even said to Philemon, "But if he has wronged you in any way, or owes you anything, charge that to my account" (Philemon 1: 18). Paul had a line of spiritual credit with Philemon based on trust, and integrity. Paul's immeasurable love and trust for Onesimus' new life made me think of the importance of credit. I looked up the word *credit* in the dictionary, and it says that credit means: "Belief or confidence in the truth of something; trust, 2. A reputation for sound character or quality."[1] Onesimus developed a credit line of trust with Paul by his behavior and new reputation. The second definition of this word is the most appropriate because it really explains Paul's feelings for Onesimus's new life.

One of the best explanations of credit I know came from a fifth-grade teacher I once worked with. She gave a great definition of credit while she was addressing the school staff during devotional time. She said, "To have credit means you are worth the risk; you are trusted to pay the debt, there is belief in your name, and your name is honorable." Then she said something that will always stay with me: "We have a great line of credit built up with God— pre-approved even. There is no annual fee, no introductory interest rate or maximum credit line. God gave His Son to pay the debt of sin so we can have a perfect credit with God the father". When Paul wrote to Philemon and Apphia, he was also claiming the credit line he had with them. Paul was trustworthy to them, and Onesimus was trustworthy to Paul. Both parties had established a credit line of love and trust because of Jesus. Onesimus needed to forget the past and have a new start and Paul was requesting that he have it. "Let the past sleep, but let it sleep on the bosom of Christ" [2]. Apphia was asked by Paul to trust him based on a spiritual line of credit and trust.

Search Your Heart, Thank God, and Pray

Are you sure you have a line of credit with God because of Jesus' sacrifice for you? Did you know that just like Paul desired to pay for Onesimus' debts, Jesus already paid our sin debt? Read 3:1-16

[1] Houghton Mifflin Company, "credit," in *The American Heritage Dictionary*, 2nd ed.

[2] Oswald Chambers, *My Utmost for His Highest,* (New York: Dodd, Mead & Company, 1963), 366.

Day 14

Mary, a Christian Woman in Rome A Servant in Jesus' Kingdom—Praised by Paul

Romans 16:6

This Mary I call the "unknown Mary" because there is no history about her in the Bible. She only appears in one verse because the apostle Paul mentions her in his letter to the Romans as part of his greetings, "Greet Mary, who has worked hard for you" (Rom 16:6). We know that she was a servant of the Lord Jesus through her ministry at Rome. How she served is not indicated. The important thing is that she served. Paul appreciated it, and because of her hard work, she is included in the Bible. Mary was obviously doing a good job because Paul said that she "worked hard." The Romans to whom Paul was writing clearly knew which Mary he was writing about in this letter.

The fact that this Mary served is a challenge to get deeper into the meaning of service. Jesus served and He made sure, in a humble way, we all knew why he did it. He said, "For even the Son of Man did not come to be served, but to serve, and to give His life a ransom for many" (Mark 10:45). He did it to honor the Father (John 12:26). Maybe there is an opportunity for service at your local church, your kid's school, or even with your neighbor next door. Right now you might be wasting an opportunity to serve. You don't need an invitation. Do you know that you can serve just by praying for someone? It doesn't have to be something physical, even though many times it is. Remember that Jesus is the best example of service that we have. He came to serve, and He served so much, that He gave His life as a living sacrifice to God to give us eternal life.

Why should we serve? We serve because Jesus was the first example of service (Mark 10:45), because of reverence to God (John 12:26; Hebrews 12:28), and because of love for the Lord (Galatians 5:13). Why do we serve? We serve for the edification of the body of Christ the church (Ephesians 4:12), to make God exclusive (Matt 6:24). Is it costly to serve? Sometimes it is because it takes you dying to self (Romans 12:1). Service does not have limits, and no service is too small when we serve to honor God.

In his book, *The Master Plan of Evangelism*, Robert E. Coleman makes reference to Jesus' example of service to His apostles. He states: "As they watched Him minister to the sick, comfort the sorrowing, and preach the gospel to the poor, it was clear that the Master considered no service too small, nor sacrifice too great when it was rendered for the glory of God".[1] So I'm encouraging you today to serve. "Therefore, since we receive a kingdom which cannot be shaken, let us show gratitude, by which we may offer to God an acceptable service with reverence and awe" (Heb 12:28).

Search Your Heart, Thank God, and Pray

Have you ever done something for the sake of the gospel that only God knows? Are you holding back on serving God because you think you are not good enough? Is there something holding you back that does not allow you to serve the body of Christ, His church? Read Exodus 23:25, Joshua 24:15, Read John 12:26

1 Robert E. Coleman, *The Master Plan of Evangelism*, (Grand Rapids: Fleming H. Revell, 1993)

Day 15

Paul's Sister—Her Son Warned Paul of Potential Harm

Acts 23:16

Paul's family is never mentioned in the Bible except for this one time. As a result no one knows about his family. For some reason, the Lord wanted us to know that there was someone in his family who cared enough about him to go and warn him about possible danger. Paul was arrested by the Jews (Acts 21:27–40, 22:1–29), and was brought before the officials. He claimed his Roman citizenship (Acts 22:22–29), and his life was saved for the moment. His nephew found out that the Jews were planning to kill him. This event allows us to see that God uses anyone, including family members, to help us in time of need. It does not matter whether it is physical, spiritual, or emotional. God used Paul's sister to produce a son who would risk his life to save Paul's.

Paul received love from Christ and from a family member during a tough time in his life. The Lord Himself gives Paul courage and reassurance, "But on the night immediately following, the Lord stood at his side and said, 'Take courage; for as you have solemnly witnessed to my cause at Jerusalem, so you must witness at Rome also'" (Acts 23:11b). Paul was assured that he was going to continue the ministry that God placed in his hands.

After Paul was placed in custody, the Sanhedrin was still determined to kill him. "When it was day, the Jews formed a conspiracy and bound themselves under an oath, saying that they would neither eat nor drink until they had killed Paul. There were more than forty who formed this plot" (Acts 23:12–13). But God was faithful to Paul. Paul's nephew risked it all to go and inform Paul of the danger that he was in at that time (Acts 23:16). Paul sent his nephew to the commander to tell him what the Jews were planning (Acts 23:16–22). By God's grace Paul's nephew received an audience with the commander of the guards and Paul's life was saved. Paul, a Christian Jew, was a perfect target for the Sanhedrin.

Because God is good all the time, Paul ended up escorted and protected by a mini-army of two hundred soldiers and two hundred spearmen, who were sent at night to the governor with a letter from the commander (Acts 23:23–35). The action taken by the commander placed Paul in safer hands, because it placed him in the care of the governor.

Paul was saved by the help of a family member but most important of all, he was a sheep and part of Jesus' pastures. The words of David in Psalm 23: 4a became a reality for Paul, "Even though I walk through the valley of the shadow of death, I fear no evil, for You are with me." God did not abandon Paul and He will never abandon those who place their faith in Jesus Christ as Lord and Savior!

Search Your Heart, Thank God, and Pray

God was always in charge of Paul's life (Romans 8:28-29). Paul listened to the Lord's voice and focused on the hope given to him. Do you listen to God's voice? Jesus tells us in John 10:27–29, "My sheep hear My voice, and I know them, and they follow Me; and I give eternal life to them, and they will **never perish**; and no one will snatch them out of My hand. My Father, who has given *them* to Me, is greater than all; **and no one is able to snatch *them* out** of the Father's hand." A sheep is a symbol of those who are saved. Are you saved? Read the next chapter to learn how to become a Christian and a sheep in His pasture.

Receiving Jesus as Savior

"I am the way, the truth, and the life; no one comes to the Father except through me" (John 14:6).

"My sheep hear My voice, and I know them, and they follow Me; and I give eternal life to them, and they will never perish; and no one will snatch them out of My hand. My Father, who has given them to Me, is greater than all; and no one is able to snatch them out of the Father's hand" (John 10:27-29).

If you are reading this book and do not know if you are a Christian, please read the information below so that you can understand what it means to be saved. The following are the steps someone should take to receive Christ as Lord and Savior.

1. **Understand God's love for you**. God demonstrated His love for us. John 3:16 tells us, "For God so loved the world, that *He* gave His only begotten Son, that whoever believes in Him shall not perish, but have eternal life." God loves all of us sinners. He hates sin but loves the sinner and gave His Son as a sacrifice for the forgiveness of the sins of the whole world. This is the ultimate sacrifice He had to make to show His love. Without Jesus, there is no forgiveness of sin.
2. **Recognize that you are a sinner** because we are all born sinners. The Word of God tells us, "For all have sinned and fall short of the glory of God" (Rom. 3:23). The sin in the Garden of Eden (Gen. 3:1–24) separated us from God, and we became lost sheep looking for restoration. Today we still suffer as a result of that original sin, but the difference is God's love: "All of like sheep have gone astray, each of us has turned to his own way, but the LORD has caused the iniquity of us all to fall on Him" (Isa. 53:6). How? By the sacrifice of Jesus at the cross.
3. **Understand that Christ is the only way to Heaven:** Christ said in John 14:6, "I am the way, the truth, and the life; no one comes to the father except through me." Jesus is the only way to heaven, and His sacrifice is sufficient for us all. It cost Him His life, and salvation will cost you absolutely nothing other than receiving Him as Lord and Savior. *Your soul and mine were purchased with the blood of Jesus.*
4. **Confess your sins:** "If we confess our sins, He is faithful and righteous to forgive us our sins and to cleanse us from all unrighteousness" (1 John 1:9). This is a promise you can only claim in Jesus' name, but if Jesus is not your Lord and Savior, the promise does not apply to you! "But if we confess with our mouth Jesus as Lord, and believe in your heart that God raised Him from the dead, you will be saved" (Rom. 10:9). Confessing is usually the forgotten condition. Without confession of sins,

repentance of sins, and acceptance of Christ by faith as Lord and Savior, there is no salvation. When we confess, there has to be a commitment to change. Repentance means that you are sorry for the sins you committed and you are intending to stay away from those sins. There is no true repentance without real change. When you confess a sin, you need plan to stay away from committing that sin again! Solomon explained it very plainly in Proverbs 26:11, "Like a dog that returns to its vomit is a fool who repeats his folly." *Sin is a choice!* You need to walk closely with God and apply His Word to your life, imitate Christ, and seek the guidance of the Holy Spirit. You must seek out Christians and find a good church where the preacher teaches the Word of God so you can have victory against repeated sin.

5. **Accept Jesus as Lord by faith:** "For by grace you have been saved through faith; and not of yourselves, it is a gift of God; not as a result of works, so that no one may boast" (Eph. 2:8–9). We are reminded in this verse that a person can never earn salvation because it is a free gift! The grace of God is so great that it provided salvation. Your faith will determine where you go after you die! There is nothing you can do to earn salvation. It is a free gift and it is all by the grace of God.
6. **Receive Christ as Lord and Savior, pray, and receive the Holy Spirit of God:** After you understand that Jesus is the Christ (Savior) and that there is nothing you can do to earn salvation, pray to Jesus a simple prayer. You need to pray from your heart and with sincerity. Try to include the following thoughts in your prayer: Confess your sins, repent, and ask God to help you change your life. Accept the free gift of eternal life by faith in Jesus, understand that He is the only way to heaven, and ask Him to save your soul. Thank Him for His sacrifice, and praise God for the gift of eternal life.
7. **Enjoy your new life in Christ:** By accepting Jesus as Lord (your God who leads you) and Savior, you are starting a new life in Christ. You are a new creature born again into the kingdom of God and the family of God. You have a heavenly Father who loves you. "Therefore if anyone is in Christ, he is a new creature; the old things

passed away behold, new things have come" (2 Cor. 5:17). Enjoy the new life God has given you. When we accept Jesus as our Lord and Savior, sin can no longer rule over us because we have a new life in Christ. Romans 6:12–14 gives us encouragement to fight sin when it says: "Therefore do not let sin reign in your mortal body so that you obey its lusts, and do not go on presenting the members of your body to sin as instruments of unrighteousness; but present yourselves to God as those alive from the dead, and your members as instruments of righteousness to God. For sin shall not be master over you, for you are not under law but under grace."

8. **Never doubt! Once you accept Christ, you are God's and God's alone.** No one can take you out of His kingdom. You are His forever, even if you sin. If you sin, God will not listen to your prayers until you make it right by confessing them to Him in Jesus' name, but you will not lose your salvation. *When you receive Christ as Lord and Savior, you are sealed with the Holy Spirit* (Eph. 1:13–14) of God, and no one can take that away. First Peter 3:18 tells us, "For Christ also died for sins once for all, the just for the unjust, so that He might bring us to God, having been put to death in the flesh, but made alive in the spirit."

We can't commit any sin that was not paid for by Jesus' sacrifice. He died for all sins—those already committed and those that are going to be committed. That is why a murderer in jail can claim Jesus as Lord, and even though he may die in prison, he will be forgiven if he accepts Jesus as Lord and Savior. *That, by the way, does not give you the right to commit sins on purpose.* Sins can separate you from having a daily growing relationship with God. That is why David confessed his sin to God in Psalm 51—because he needed his relationship with God restored, and his sin was in the way. (Read all the following verses to help with doubts about your salvation: 1 John 5:11–12, John 20:31, Romans 5:8, Ephesians 2:8–9, 1 Peter 3:18, John 1:12, John 5:24, 2 Corinthians 5:17.) I also recommend that you study your Bible, get baptized (Acts 2:41, 8:12–13) and join a Bible believing church to become part of the big family of God.

May God bless you as you seek Him and walk with Him!

Printed in the United States of America

Printed in the United States
By Bookmasters